Contents

Editorial Note

The articles presented here are a selection of the papers given at two symposia held in 1984 to coincide with the Arts Council exhibition at the Hayward Gallery, 'English Romanesque Art 1066–1200' (5th April–8th July 1984). The Society of Antiquaries held a one-day seminar on 6th April entitled 'Romanesque Art', the seventh in a series of such events devoted to a variety of topics; and the Victoria and Albert Museum's two-day symposium, 'Patronage of the Arts in England in 1066–1200', took place on 25th–26th February. However, it was not thought appropriate to publish the full proceedings of both symposia, partly for reasons of cost and partly because the subject-matter of some of the papers overlapped with that of the exhibition *Catalogue* or with other publications generated by it.

We are most grateful to all those who took part in the Society's seminar, and in particular to Professor Christopher Brooke, F.S.A., who took the chair and kindly contributed an introduction to the present volume. We are also very grateful to Dr Margaret Gibson, F.S.A., who made the suggestion that some of the papers from the Victoria and Albert symposium might be included in this publication and advised on their selection.

S.M.
F.H.T.

Art and Patronage
in the
English Romanesque

Edited by Sarah Macready and F. H. Thompson

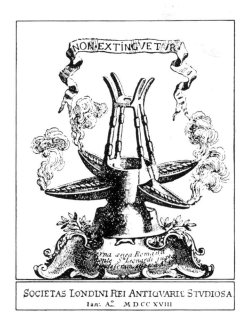

NON EXTINGVETVR

Vrna ænea Romana ante S. Leonardi...

SOCIETAS LONDINI REI ANTIQVARIÆ STVDIOSA
Ian: A.° M DCC XVIII

Occasional Paper (New Series) VIII

**THE SOCIETY OF ANTIQUARIES
OF LONDON**

Burlington House, Piccadilly, London W1V 0HS
1986

Distributed by Thames and Hudson Ltd

© 1986 The Society of Antiquaries
ISBN 0 500 99043 3

TYPESET AND PRINTED IN GREAT BRITAIN
BY THE BATH PRESS, AVON

Illustrations

v

Abbreviations

Antiq. J.	*Antiquaries Journal*
Arch. Ael.	*Archaeologia Aeliana*
Arch. Camb.	*Archaeologia Cambrensis*
Arch. Cant.	*Archaeologia Cantiana*
Arch. J.	*Archaeological Journal*
BAA	British Archaeological Association
BAR	British Archaeological Reports
BL	British Library
BM	British Museum
BN	Bibliothèque Nationale
Burl. Mag.	*Burlington Magazine*
Catalogue	*English Romanesque Art 1066–1200*, catalogue of the exhibition held at the Hayward Gallery, London, 5th April–8th July 1984 (Arts Council of Great Britain in association with Weidenfeld and Nicolson, 1984)
CCSL	*Corpus Christianorum Series Latina*
CNRS	Centre National de la Recherche Scientifique
DNB	*Dictionary of National Biography*
JBAA	*Journal of the British Archaeological Association*
JWCI	*Journal of the Warburg and Courtauld Institutes*
Med. Arch.	*Medieval Archaeology*
MTB	*Materials for the History of Thomas Becket, Archbishop of Canterbury*, vols. i-vii, ed. J. C. Robertson (i-vi) and J. B. Sheppard (vii), PRO, Rolls Series 67 (London, 1875–85)
NMT	Nelson's Medieval Texts
OMT	Oxford Medieval Texts
PIMS	Pontifical Institute of Medieval Studies (Toronto)
PL	*Patrologiae cursus completus. Series Latina*, ed. J. P. Migne (Paris, 1844–55)
PRO	Public Record Office
PSA	*Proceedings of the Society of Antiquaries*
PSAS	*Proceedings of the Society of Antiquaries of Scotland*
RAL	*The Registrum Antiquissimum of the Cathedral Church of Lincoln*, 8 vols., ed. C. W. Foster, Lincoln Record Society (1931–)
RCHM	The Royal Commission on Historical Monuments
Survey	*A Survey of Manuscripts Illuminated in the British Isles*, ed. J. J. G. Alexander (London, 1975–)
VCH	The Victoria County History

Introduction

Christopher Brooke, F.S.A., *Chairman*

ENGLAND AND ROMANESQUE

Half in jest, half in self-rebuke, the humanist John of Salisbury summarized
the disturbances of a scholar's life as he drew to the close of the *Metalogicon*
in 1159. 'I have been distracted by other tasks, not different merely but inimical
to study, so that I could scarcely snatch an hour here and there, and then furtively,
to play philosopher. Ten times I have crossed the chain of the Alps since I
left England first; twice I have travelled through Apulia; I have done business
often in the Roman court on behalf of my superiors and friends; and on a variety
of counts I have traversed England, and France too, many times.'[1] His furtive
hours somehow produced the *Metalogicon*, a substantial study of contemporary
schools of logic and the like, and the *Policraticus*, a massive treatise on political
ideas and much else; but John was truthful in listing his many travels and in
attributing them in part to his work as an envoy to the Roman Curia; he paid
many visits to it as the archbishop of Canterbury's expert on Roman affairs
and appeals. In the twelfth century the love of travel enormously stimulated
communication across the cultural frontiers of the known world; it generated
commerce and the passage of wealth; it made possible the brutal wars we call
crusades; it stimulated pilgrimage to Compostela and Rome and Jerusalem; it
helps to explain the frequent recourse to Rome by litigants and others which
created the papal monarchy of the late Middle Ages. Without it, the cosmopolitan
exchanges, the flow of influences, which we can see vividly revealed in what
survives of the art and architecture of the Romanesque world, would be unthink-
able.

   Over twenty years ago, in a celebrated paper, Sir Richard Southern explored
'The place of England in the twelfth-century Renaissance'.[2] Many of us think
he rather understated the English presence in this great movement of the human
spirit; but he drew attention to a fascinating problem in a manner as fresh and
relevant as when it was written. The title is evidently ambiguous, for it tends
to concentrate our minds on the literary and artistic modes—in the writing of
history and biography and fiction, in book illumination, ivory carving, and sculpture in stone—where a specifically English contribution may be seen and isolated;

and these local styles were a vital part of the culture of the age. But John's career reminds us that the English role had a much wider and deeper meaning. His later letters, written when he was in exile for his support of Thomas Becket in the 1160s, reveal a depth of feeling for England and his English friends which combined in a very confusing way with a strong current both of the French world in which he had lived for many years as student and the cosmopolitan Latin culture of his day. The combination of practical task and philosophy in his summary of his life in the 1150s reflects another kind of link between widely differing regions of experience. It was because there were men like John, born in this remote island, educated mainly in France, travelling ceaselessly over the Alps and into Italy—and combining professional labours with delicious opportunities to meet other scholars and browse in distant libraries—in a world in which travel seems to us infinitely slow and tiresome, that close communication over great distances was possible. John was one among many such travellers; and a little reflection on the message of the Romanesque Exhibition of 1984 and the contents of this book shows us—in a fragmentary manner, yet vivid too, and profoundly interesting—some of the ways in which we should answer the question: what did England and the English give and receive in the age of Romanesque?

'It is not always appreciated that the English contribution to Romanesque art was enormous', wrote George Zarnecki with the characteristic scholarly fervour which set the events of 1984 in train;[3] but if we look back from 1985, perhaps his words seem already dated—for he and his colleagues have compelled us to realize it, by the vivid experience of the Exhibition itself, by the mixture of scholarship and enthusiasm which marked the Catalogue, and by the research it stimulated. Of this research the result was particularly visible in the two symposia—at the Victoria and Albert Museum and the Society of Antiquaries—whose *acta* form the basis for this book. The Exhibition roused a deep and timely interest in a much wider audience than the scholars who have studied Romanesque in recent generations can normally hope to touch. It bred a new attitude among owners; and it was a delightful experience at the private view to wander among owners confessing, with pleasure and bewilderment nicely mingled, that Professor Zarnecki had uncovered possessions they hardly knew they had. This revival of interest, and the skilled conservation work which was a part of the Exhibition's mounting, would alone make it a turning point in the survival and appreciation of an important part of the medieval heritage. It also affected owners less absent-minded. The Victoria and Albert have created what amounts to a new department of Romanesque art and remounted and added to their treasures. The Society of Antiquaries has brought Stothard's magnificent reproduction of the Bayeux Tapestry out of its cupboard and thus revealed its interest and importance—for it represents the Tapestry before most of the restorations of the nineteenth century had been undertaken. Above all, the Exhibition sharpened the wits of scholars to face the problems which are our theme.

This book is a set of variations on the basic theme: the links and connexions which recent scholarship, brought to a head in the Exhibition, has revealed to us. One delightful element in the Exhibition was the collection of antiquarian paintings, drawings and other material, showing how Romanesque scholarship was born; and from this world Thomas Cocke conjures the 'old conventual church' at Ely. The Ely infirmary, with its twelfth-century arches and its aisles converted into ample residences, is a pleasant reminder of the history of the close, of the continuity which has led from the great hall and chapel for the sick monks to the private apartments of the late medieval priory, and through them to the larger quarters of the canons. Cocke shows how an intelligent guess in the eighteenth century led first to an entirely false trail—to identify the infirmary as the Anglo-Saxon cathedral—and yet by inspiring others to correct the error led in its turn to a truer appreciation of Norman architecture. It is startling to find how recent are the vital discoveries on which our knowledge of Norman Romanesque is based.

The growth of literacy in the eleventh and twelfth centuries has been intensely studied by historians and philologists in recent years; and of this the much enhanced use of seals is an ironical witness: ironical, because the large seals of the period were designed precisely to impress illiterate beholders with the authority of their owners—the signature, long used in Italy and brought to England for a brief space by the Lombard Archbishop Lanfranc, made little headway in this age. Alexander Heslop's paper shows how the art historian has added a dimension to the many studies of the sigillographer by making the seal matrix tell him some of the secrets of metalwork—of all the great crafts of the Romanesque world the one most plundered and damaged by posterity.

Yet the abiding impression of these studies for a historian is the flood of light they throw on the travels of influences, of craftsmen and of patrons. George Zarnecki argues that the stone sculpture of the Canterbury crypt shows a clear German influence, that a Bury capital and some other of the pieces he collected show the impact of Italian, and specifically Lombard sculpture, and that the evidence is sufficient to make probable the presence of Italian craftsmen in this country. He maintains that a greater element of native tradition is visible in the Ely tympana, the remnants of the Reading cloister, and the works of Roger of Salisbury—and above all in the delectable sculpture of the Herefordshire churches he himself put on the map over thirty years ago.[4] But in Ely he sees Anglo-Scandinavian as well as Anglo-Saxon motifs, in Herefordshire the hand of Aquitaine. In a closely argued technical discussion on niello Neil Stratford penetrates the relationship of England and Lower Saxony and reopens the question: where did the craft first flourish?—who helped whom? He ends by setting German craftsmen in eleventh- and twelfth-century England beside Zarnecki's Italians. It has long been known that a rich variety of Continental links could be found in Anglo-Norman buildings, though some of them have remained controversial. But few would doubt that the vaults over the nave of Durham cathedral are a vital document in the history of building technology and style—quite simply, a stage in a technological and artistic development which is a part of the history of north-western Europe at large: Durham was not on the periphery but in the centre of Romanesque history. More precise, and especially satisfying to the scholar since for once literary and art-historical evidence are in perfect accord, is Richard Gem's demonstration of the way in which Robert of Lorraine, bishop of Hereford, a noted figure in the intellectual history of the late eleventh century, based his bishop's chapel at Hereford on the octagon at Aachen—just as William of Malmesbury said he did—and yet employed an Anglo-Norman craftsman to make his design.

It has long been known that the St Albans Psalter of the 1120s or so betrayed deep influence from Ottonian Germany and contemporary Byzantium; and the Winchester Psalter has two leaves directly attributed to Byzantine artists, presumably from Sicily. Brian Golding, building on the recent, comprehensive studies of Rodney Thomson, and his own deep knowledge of the literary sources for St Albans, sets us thinking—why St Albans? Why did this wealth of craftsmanship flourish in a centre not conspicuously rich? How was the great tradition of monastic patronage formed and sustained? Michael Kauffmann sets the stage for future enquiry into this and many other aspects of book illumination by a bibliographical survey, including a sustained appreciative criticism of Thomson on St Albans, and a fascinating insight into the current dispute about the place of Eadwine and his portrait in the Eadwine Psalter in Trinity College, Cambridge. To this precise topic Margaret Gibson contributes a study penetrating deeply into the region where the historian and art historian meet, and revealing the Psalter as a splendid example from the autumn of monastic dominance in such crafts, before the professional secular makers of books took over in the late twelfth century—a moment's reflection on Matthew Paris and thirteenth-century St Albans will remind us of the many exceptions to such a generalization or serve to prove the rule. Whatever the truth about Eadwine's picture, his Psalter has a secure place in the history of the cloister and the scriptorium as well as of the art of book illumination.

It is evident that a volume of this character cannot embrace every aspect of the art and culture of twelfth-century England: in its emphasis, art predominates over architecture and Latin and vernacular literature are wholly absent. But a paper on music is a useful reminder of the missing arts—in this case a major art which has mainly gone away on the air. Ursula Nilgen's paper on Becket sketches the tastes and activities of a courtier and patron—chancellor and archbishop—of exceptional panache; what conspicuous display could mean in dress, vestments, plate, goblets and jewels, in beautiful objects and learned books, is unusually well documented in Becket, since a few objects and books survive and his murder inspired over a dozen biographers, including two at least of the best of the century, to record the ostentation which was so striking a feature of Becket the chancellor. The Bestiary is a piquant example of a kind of book which brought learned and lay, writer and artist, into a single compass; and Xenia Muratova discusses in depth the world of art, ideas and patronage which we can find encapsulated in Pierpont Morgan MS 81, given by Philip Apostolorum, canon of Lincoln, to Worksop Priory in 1187, as he recorded in an elaborate note of gift, with a mighty curse on anyone who should separate it from the priory; and the full extent of his gift—'a very fine book of Psalms, glossed, in one most elegant volume, a glossed Genesis, the Meditations of St Anselm, archbishop of Canterbury, a Bestiary and a Mappa Mundi'—shows an intriguing cross-section of the interests of Philip and his circle.

Among all the patrons, outstanding and obscure, of the Romanesque world, few can compare with and none eclipse Henry of Blois, favourite nephew of King Henry I, brother of King Stephen, monk of Cluny, abbot of Glastonbury, bishop of Winchester. George Zarnecki invokes the help of David Knowles, who dedicated some of his most eloquent pages to a surprisingly sympathetic appreciation of a man whom Dom David could see at a glance was not a monk after his own stamp. 'The commander who erected half a dozen fortresses in his diocese and burnt out his episcopal city, together with a great monastery and nunnery, was also the man who rebuilt Glastonbury on a grand scale, who re-established Cluny, who founded the hospital of St Cross, and who decorated his cathedral with the most precious and varied works of art, from the fonts which still remain to illuminations and enamels and masterpieces of the goldsmith's art which have almost entirely disappeared.'[5] More has survived than this might seem to say, and Zarnecki explores with intricate and loving care the objects which remain and the wide scatter of Henry's interests which are recorded. John of Salisbury, writing in the mid 1160s, still remembered Henry as the dangerous rival to his master Archbishop Theobald for control of the English church, and poked fun at him for buying old statutes when disappointed in his appeals in Rome.[6] But only a few years later he was rejoicing both that Henry was generous in his support of the persecuted church of Canterbury and a leader in protest against some of Henry II's measures—the aged prince-bishop could afford to resist his young cousin the king to his face, and so add John, most eminent of English scholars of his age, to the long list of monks and scribes and artists and craftsmen and masons who were beholden to the wealth and generous patronage of this notable monk, who paid so little attention to his vow of poverty, and yet died universally admired just over ten years before the birth of St Francis.

Among the men of the twelfth century Henry of Blois must be the hero of this book; and by the same token it does honour to George Zarnecki among our own contemporaries. His zeal and scholarship inspired the Exhibition, his tireless work—the ceaseless efforts of a great expert on sculpture to leave no stone unturned—ensured its success. The affection he inspires in friends and colleagues and pupils made it impossible for any of us not to join in his enterprise; the scholarship of which he is master sets him on a peak among the many collaborators needed to make the exhibition and the symposia a success. He stands among the scholars like Henry among the patrons of the Romanesque; and the earnestness and moral force of his persuasions not only inspired the Arts Council and the many bodies which aided it, but the owners of all but a handful of the mobile survivals of Romanesque art to generous support and ready loans of their treasures. Many a day will pass before the impression fades of the splendours of the Romanesque world deployed on the quaint stairways and in the grottoes of the Hayward Gallery; and the books which record its beauties and the scholarly work it inspired will remain as a perpetual monument to George Zarnecki.

NOTES

[1] *Metalogicon*, ed. C. C. J. Webb (Oxford, 1929), iii, prol., p. 117, translated in *Letters of John of Salisbury*, i, ed. W. J. Millor, H. E. Butler and C. N. L. Brooke, NMT (Edinburgh, 1955), xxiv. On John, see now esp. *The World of John of Salisbury*, ed. M. Wilks (Oxford, 1984).

[2] *History*, xlv (1960), 201–16, reprinted (revised) in Southern, *Medieval Humanism and other Studies* (Oxford, 1970), ch. 9.

[3] *Catalogue*, 15.

[4] *Later English Romanesque Sculpture* (London, 1953), ch. 2.
[5] D. Knowles, *The Monastic Order in England* (Cambridge, 1940; 2nd edn., 1963), 289.
[6] John of Salisbury, *Historia Pontificalis*, ed. M. Chibnall, NMT (Edinburgh, 1956), 79. For what follows, John of Salisbury, *Letters*, ii, OMT (Oxford, 1979), nos. 260, 296, pp. 524–9, 682–5.

Sculpture in Stone in the English Romanesque Art Exhibition

George Zarnecki, F.S.A.

Almost all the major English Romanesque manuscripts, ivories, metalwork, textiles, seals, coins and pottery which have survived and have been identified as English were shown in the *English Romanesque Art* exhibition, provided their physical condition permitted their transport to the Hayward Gallery.[1] By contrast, many of the monumental sculptures were not, since they form integral parts of the buildings which they decorate and obviously could not have been included. Moreover, some of the sculpture which, at least in theory, was available was too heavy to be moved without risk of damage. Consequently, the sculpture shown in the exhibition was to a great extent what was available and movable. This being so, the sculpture was not as representative of the surviving artistic output from the Romanesque period in England in this medium as works in other fields. Inevitably, therefore, some aspects of English Romanesque sculpture were better illustrated than others, with some totally unrepresented.

Nevertheless, the sculpture in the exhibition was universally acclaimed. 'La diversité, l'originalité et la beauté de la sculpture romane anglaise sont sans doute la principale révélation de cette exposition' wrote Elisabeth Taburet,[2] while Willibald Sauerländer, after discussing the manuscripts in the exhibition, continued: 'But the pre-eminence of England in this field was, after all, well known. The great surprise came with the richness and the originality of English Romanesque sculpture as it has been revealed by discoveries and studies during the last thirty years . . .'[3]

The introductory room of the exhibition contained three English and three Norman objects. Two of the English sculptures were selected for their stylistic contrast, one (no. 96), the *Harrowing of Hell* from Bristol,[4] illustrating the Winchester School style, of which there were splendid examples in other media in this room, the other (no. 95), the tombstone from Old St Paul's, London, the Scandinavian Ringerike. Both were important sources for English Romanesque sculpture, but unfortunately, except for the early twelfth-century capitals from Hereford Cathedral (nos. 109a–f), which, to a limited extent, are indebted to the Winchester School,[5] the continuation of that important style in Romanesque sculpture was not illustrated in the exhibition at all. To do this, we would have had to show, for instance, the Majesty tympanum of the Prior's Doorway at Ely or the Water Stratford tympanum, but both these are, happily, still *in situ*.[6]

On the other hand, the influence of the Scandinavian Ringerike and of the later Urnes styles was very well demonstrated in the exhibition by the two reliefs from Ipswich (nos. 121 and 122), the Southwell (no. 123) and the St Bees (no. 124) lintels and, above all, by the Norwich capital (no. 126) which compares so closely with the Urnes brooch found in Pitney in Somerset (no. 225). Incidentally, the removal of the Southwell lintel for repair before it was exhibited at the Hayward Gallery has revealed in full the carving on the soffit (pl. I*a*), which was partly obscured when it was reused in the nineteenth century.

The third relief in the introductory gallery (no. 97) was intended to stimulate discussion. Is it from the reign of King Cnut or is it Romanesque? The archaelogical evidence points to the former, but the style to the latter.[7]

The three capitals from Normandy which were shown fall into two categories. The two block-shaped capitals from Jumièges Abbey (nos. 98a and b) 'are among the first examples of an important trend of architectural sculpture in England, Normandy and northern France, where carved ornamentation in low relief on the whole surface of the block is closely related to manuscript illumination and ivory carvings'.[8] In this case the manuscripts are those in the Winchester School style. The ivory head of a tau-shaped crosier found at Jumièges (no. 181), which was exhibited close by, displays a style so similar to some of the Jumièges capitals,[9] that their common authorship can hardly be doubted.

The Jumièges capitals, in their shape and decoration, belong to pre-Romanesque traditions. By contrast, the capital from Rouen (no. 99) is of a type common in Normandy between 1050 and 1080, consisting of a carved mask between prominent volutes and a row of schematic leaves above the necking. Based on the Corinthian type, such capitals point to the future development in which the shape of the capital serves to unite the supporting column with the rectangular springing of the vaulting, while the decoration enhances the structure and function of the capital.

In the next gallery of the exhibition, devoted to the reigns of the two Williams, it was planned to show sculpture in the geometric style which was so characteristic of Normandy at the time of the Conquest and was transmitted to England after 1066, gaining great popularity and lasting throughout the Romanesque period.[10] Unfortunately, the loans from Caen and Evreux had to be abandoned for financial reasons and it was too late to find substitutes in England.

In this gallery there were two capitals related to the one from Rouen, both sharing with it prominent volutes at the corners and a human head between them. The closest to the Norman prototypes is the capital from Durham (no. 100). The huge York Minster capital (no. 101), with its more classical rendering of the acanthus, is related to the type of capital popular in the Loire valley around the middle of the eleventh century. Such capitals were occasionally employed in Normandy, for instance in Bayeux Cathedral, and it is likely that the model for the York capital existed there.[11] It should be remembered that the first Romanesque cathedral at York was built by Thomas of Bayeux, the archbishop of York between 1070 and 1100.[12] The small capital from St Mary's Abbey, York, shown nearby (no. 102), seems to be a slightly later local simplification of this type, the head being placed at the angle. The capital from St Mary's Church at Campsall in Yorkshire, which was exhibited beside these two, provides a striking contrast to them, for it is cushion-shaped, or cubic, as it is sometimes called, and its decoration is in exceedingly flat relief, while the style is largely Anglo-Danish.[13] The cushion capital originated in Byzantium and, through Italy, was introduced into Germany, where it was firmly established by the early eleventh century.[14] Such capitals were at first decorated with paint rather than sculpture, but in the second half of the eleventh century foliage, and then figural, motifs were frequently carved on them. As far as I am aware, carved cushion capitals in Germany pre-date the Italian, those of St Emmeram, Regensburg (1060s) being earlier than those at S. Abondio, Como, and S. Maria d'Aurona in Milan (pl. I*b*), but this may be due to the accident of their survival.[15] In view of the close artistic relations between Germany and Italy at that time, it is difficult to determine, especially in architectural sculpture, what originated in Germany and what in Italy. The mass migration of Italian masons and sculptors across the Alps makes such judgements particularly difficult.

In addition to a cushion capital from a rural Yorkshire church, we would have liked to show, for instance, one of the three eastermost crypt capitals from Canterbury Cathedral, had they been available. They are carved with motifs derived from at least two different sources. The foliage on two capitals is clearly the Anglo-Saxon acanthus, based on manuscripts of the Winchester School style, while the lion with two bodies and the foliage below, on the third, are closely related to contemporary Canterbury illuminations.[16] On the other hand, the figural motifs on the capital in St Innocent's chapel (pl. II*a*) show intriguing similarities to the capitals in S. Abondio, Como (pl. II*b*), and the capitals at the entrance to the chapter house of Hersfeld Abbey in Hesse (pl. III*a*).[17] The characteristic imposts of these last seem to have inspired the decoration of the chapter house of Rochester and this suggests a German affiliation in these two centres in Kent. This would seem to agree with the architectural sources behind the vast Canterbury crypt, which, it is generally recognized, were German. But the matter is complicated by the fact that imposts such as at Hersfeld and Rochester are also found at St Peter's, Northampton (pl. III*b*), decorated by a sculptor who was very familiar with what was the fashion in northern Italy at that time.[18]

Cushion capitals in England were sometimes partly disguised by their decoration, as at Reading Abbey and Durham Cathedral.[19] In the cloister arcade at Reading, carved capitals resting on round colonnettes alternated with trefoil capitals on octagonal supports. These trefoil capitals, an English elaboration of the cushion form, seek a compromise with the Corinthian type by using upright leaves at the angles, a device first found on the cushion capitals of S. Abondio, Como (pl. II*b*).[20]

There can be no doubt that as a result of the Norman Conquest England had formed many more links with the Continent than ever before. The artistic influence of the Empire on Romanesque art in England is now generally acknowledged and involves not only metalwork, ivories and manuscripts related to the St Albans Psalter, but is also found in the field of sculpture, for example the Chichester reliefs and such important fragments in the exhibition as the South Cerneywood crucifix (no. 115) and the Old Sarum stone head of Christ (no. 114).[21]

Another foreign link in English sculpture, that with Italy, has been discussed in two articles, one by Joselita Raspi Serra,[22] the other by Henry Maguire.[23] Most recently Jill Meredith went over the same ground in greater detail in an unpublished doctoral thesis for Yale University.[24] Maguire deals specifically with one regional school of sculpture, of which the tombstone from St Peter's, Northampton, shown in the exhibition (no. 142), is a typical example. Meredith concentrates on the portals of Ely Cathedral, but also discusses sculptures which she considers to have been carved under Italian influence.[25] Raspi Serra's cavalier treatment of previous studies of English Romanesque sculpture does not endear her work to me, but of course I recognize that there is considerable Italian influence on English sculpture, though the problem is far more complex than she realizes, since not all Italian elements in English sculpture are derived directly from Italy.

Ever since the fundamental studies by Adolph Goldschmidt,[26] Rudold Kautzsch[27] and Géza de Francovich,[28] it has been recognized that Italian, and especially Lombard, art exercised a profound influence outside Italy. This influence on English Romanesque sculpture took different forms, depending on the way in which it was transmitted. For instance, an English patron or sculptor could have seen Italian decoration and tried to imitate it at home. There may have been cases of Italian sculptors working in England. Then again, Italian-inspired decoration may have been transmitted to England second-hand, by way of Germany, France or other countries, and such decoration could have been diluted by local elements.

In the exhibition there was the capital with the dragon-slayer from Bury St Edmunds Abbey (no. 117) (pl. IV*a*), recently acquired by the British Museum, which I described in the catalogue as 'unmistakably of northern Italian inspiration'. I would like to go a little further and suggest that this capital, as well as the little head excavated at Bury (no. 118), are both related to another Italian-inspired work in this part of the world, the Prior's Doorway at Ely. The enormously long arm of the dragon-slayer is somewhat like the disproportionately long arms of the angels at Ely (pl. IV*b*), while the dragon has several close parallels on the doorway. Similarly, the little head from Bury (pl. V*a*) shares common features with the figures in roundels on the jambs of the Ely doorway (pl. V*b*).[29] They are clearly products of the same workshop, to which I would add the much weathered, but still lively, sculptures from Crowland Abbey, now in the City and County Museum, Lincoln.[30] It is unlikely that the sculptor of those works was Italian, as the design of the three Ely doorways includes motifs of Anglo-Saxon and even of Anglo-Scandinavian origin. One of them is the acrobatic lion which frequently embellishes the portals of stave churches in Norway (pl. V*c*) and which, sitting as it does on its own back, is a distinctive feature not found anywhere outside Norway, except at Ely (pl. V*d*).[31]

That Italian sculptors found employment in England, as they did in Germany, Hungary, Bohemia, Poland and the Scandinavian countries, there can be no doubt.[32] The works of Lombard sculptors outside Italy are often of high quality,

PLATE I

Photograph: Courtauld Institute of Art

a. Soffit of the lintel in Southwell Minster

b. Capital from S. Maria d'Aurona, Milan, now in Castello Sforzesco, Milan, no. 472

PLATE II

a. Capital in crypt of Canterbury Cathedral

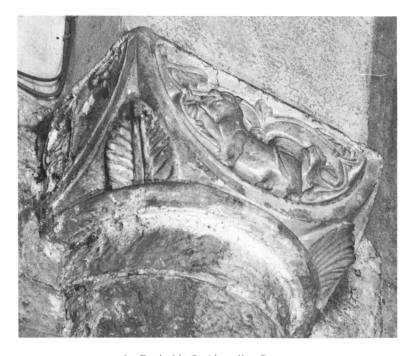

b. Capital in S. Abondio, Como

PLATE III

Photograph: Jutta Brüdern, Institut für Kunstgeschichte, TU Braunschweig

a. Capital of chapter house, Hersfeld Abbey, Hesse

b. Capital in St Peter's, Northampton

PLATE IV

b. Detail of tympanum of Prior's Doorway, Ely Cathedral

Photograph: Courtauld Institute of Art

a. Dragon-slayer on capital from Bury St Edmunds, now in the British Museum

PLATE V

a. Head from Bury St Edmunds Abbey, now in Bury Museum

b. Roundel on Prior's Doorway, Ely Cathedral

c. Detail of west doorway, Ål church, Norway

d. Detail of Prior's Doorway, Ely Cathedral

c–d. Drawn by Lady Eva Wilson

PLATE VI

a. Angel carrying Habakkuk on doorway of S. Fedele, Como

b. Pulpit in S. Giulio, Lake Orta

PLATE VII

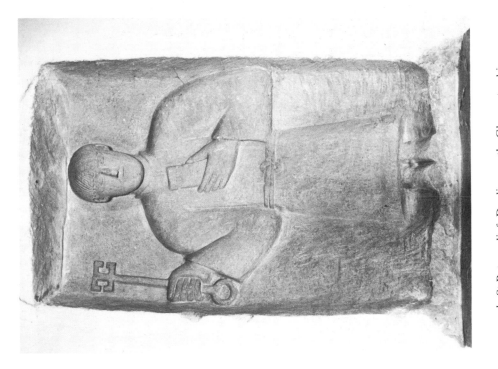

b. St Peter relief, Daglingworth, Gloucestershire

a. Detail of font from Alsleben, now in St Cyriakus, Gernrode

PLATE VIII

Photograph: RCHM (England)

a. Lintel in Tarrant Rushton, Dorset

b. Font in Castle Frome, Herefordshire

PLATE IX

b. South doorway of St-Pierre, Aulnay-de-Saintonge

a. A doorway formerly in Shobdon Priory, now in Shobdon Park

PLATE X

b. Lavabo from Much Wenlock Priory, Shropshire

Photographs: Courtauld Institute of Art

a. Voussoirs from a doorway, Yorkshire Museum

PLATE XI

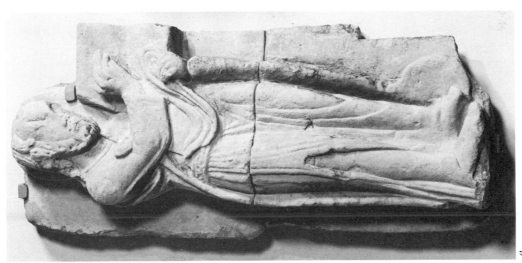

a. Figure of St Paul from Ivychurch, Wilts., now in the Victoria and Albert Museum
b. Voussoirs from St Mary's Abbey, York

Photographs: Courtauld Institute of Art

b

a

as at Quedlinburg, Mainz and Lund. But there were also many masons who migrated north in search of work and who did some surprisingly indifferent carving. They obviously much admired the portal of S. Fedele at Como (pl. VI*a*), knew the pulpit in S. Abondio (now in the Museo Civico) at Como, and some might even have known that masterpiece, the pulpit on Isola di S. Giulio on Lake Orta (pl. VI*b*).[33] The smooth, short and massive figures on a plain background were easy to imitate, though in the process what was impressively monumental and solemn often became doll-like and expressionless. The early twelfth-century font from Alsleben, now in St Cyriakus Abbey, Gernrode (pl. VII*a*),[34] is a good example of this kind of work, and especially significant in betraying the Italian workmanship are two angels with characteristically narrow wings at the base, just as at Como and S. Giulio. In France, reliefs in a similar style and clearly carved by itinerant Lombards are found at Rosiers, Côtes d'Aurec (Hte-Loire)[35] and at Marcilhac in Quercy.[36] These last were recently described as Carolingian, no doubt because they look so archaic. In England, I know works in two churches which are in this style and must have been executed by Lombard sculptors: the reliefs at Daglingworth in Gloucestershire (pl. VII*b*), generally considered Anglo-Saxon,[37] and the mutilated gabled lintel at Tarrant Rushton in Dorset (pl. VIII*a*).[38]

The sculpture from Reading Abbey was represented in the exhibition by many, some may think too many, pieces. But because Reading was a royal foundation of Henry I and was lavishly decorated, it was clearly very influential. Most, if not all, of the surviving sculpture is from the cloister, which consisted, as far as one can tell from the preserved material, of alternating carved and trefoil capitals, crowned by carved springers, supporting carved and embossed arches which seem to have alternated with arches consisting of beak-heads. There were also some arches decorated with the chevron ornament.[39]

Both Raspi Serra and Meredith consider the Reading sculpture to be deeply indebted to Lombardy. In his review of the exhibition, Willibald Sauerländer wrote "... it remained for the long series of decorative capitals from Reading and Hyde Abbey to evoke the original splendour and richness of Romanesque sculpture in the English monasteries. Nobody would here speak of Continental influence. The flowers, griffins, dragons and masks, which are familiar from the initials of English manuscripts, turn up again on the faces of these capitals—often as fantastic and as exuberant.'[40] I had already drawn attention to the remarkable similarities between manuscript initials, especially those from St Albans, and the Reading capitals, so I have no reason to disagree with these views.[41] Yet there is also some truth in the claim that there are certain common features between the sculpture from Reading and Lombardy, and I believe that this should be explained not by a direct link but by way of western France. That the art of Aquitaine was deeply influenced by northern Italy is common knowledge.[42] However, the radiating voussoirs, so lavishly used at Reading (nos. 127o–r), were invented in western France. They were taken up at Reading soon after 1125 and spread with great rapidity to all parts of England. They also became very popular in Spain, but are unknown in northern Italy.

One of the most common forms of radiating voussoir in England was the beak-head. In the exhibition beak-heads from three sites were shown: from Reading Abbey (no. 129), where they first appeared in England, from Old Sarum

Cathedral (no. 130), and from Sherborne Castle (no. 131). These last two were due to King Henry I's Chancellor, Roger, Bishop of Salisbury, who, in artistic matters, seems to have emulated his master. The double beak-heads from Sherborne Castle are, as I have argued in the catalogue, derivatives of Reading. Roger Stalley was undoubtedly right in connecting the Sherborne beak-heads with those still *in situ* at Avington[43] and, in fact, the capital in the form of a fierce head from Sherborne[44] is a near relative of that supporting the arch with the double beak-heads at Avington. Not even the most ardent believer in the Italian derivation of English Romanesque sculpture would claim that the beak-head is of Italian origin; the only example of this form of decoration in Italy is in the extreme south, in the former cathedral at Anglona in Lucania, and is demonstrably the work of a foreign sculptor.[45]

The very distinctive style of sculpture which flourished in the second quarter of the twelfth century in Herefordshire and the adjoining counties was represented in the exhibition by two tympana (nos. 137 and 138) and one font (no. 139), especially restored for the exhibition (pl. VIII*b*). I am particularly attached to the sculpture of this group since it formed part of my doctoral thesis.[46] But that was a very long time ago and since then our knowledge of the period has vastly increased, and so it is natural that my views have been modified. This part of my thesis was based on the documented pilgrimage to Santiago de Compostela of the founder of the earliest church of the school, Shobdon, which became the first English priory of the Order of St Victor in Paris. I argued that a sculptor from England was taken on this pilgrimage and that the Shobdon, Kilpeck, and a long list of other monuments in the region include elements of sculpture observed on this pilgrimage, among which those from Aquitaine predominate. By isolating individual motifs in Herefordshire and comparing them with those in Lombardy, Raspi Serra and others try to link this school of sculpture with Italy.[47] I accept these connections but suggest that most of them are not direct, but rather transmitted by way of Aquitaine. The radiating voussoir, that tell-tale element of an arch, which characterizes Shobdon (pl. IX*a*), Kilpeck and Brinsop, is an Aquitainian feature (pl. IX*b*), while the capital frieze, an undoubted Lombard invention, which is found at Leominster and Rock, came to Herefordshire not from Milan or Pavia, but from Saintes or Fontevrault.

The tombstone from St Peter's, Northampton (no. 142), on the other hand, as suggested long ago by Henry Maguire,[48] has a direct stylistic connection with the exuberant sculpture of Lombardy. It is one of many works in Northamptonshire in which such connections can be detected.

A different source of inspiration, namely Burgundy, has been suggested by Christopher Wilson[49] for the remnants of a doorway from York (no. 141 (pl. X*a*)), a characteristic product of the local regional school which flourished in the second and third quarters of the twelfth century. Although foreign elements undoubtedly exist in this prolific school of sculpture, its roots are to be sought in the early twelfth-century sculpture of the south of England, and it seems to me that there are fairly close connections between the York archivolts and the cloister arcades from Reading Abbey (compare no. 141 with nos. 127o–r).

In the last gallery of the exhibition, there were some pieces of sculpture which, I hope, pleasantly surprised even those who knew them. The two unpublished Ivychurch figures (pl. XI*a*) extracted from a Wiltshire house (nos. 157a and

b) were repaired and cleaned and, when the exhibition was over, found a new home in the Victoria and Albert Museum. Most of the pieces from the Canterbury screen were shown reunited with the relief which is now in the Royal Museum and Art Gallery, Canterbury (nos. 164a–m). The related mask from Rochester (no. 165) was close by. The Patron of the exhibition, the Archbishop of Canterbury, the Most Reverend and Right Honourable Robert Runcie, has taken a personal interest in those precious pieces and, since the exhibition ended, those which were cracked have been repaired and there is every hope that they will soon be shown at Canterbury in an appropriate setting.

The three unpublished keystones from Keynsham Abbey (nos. 163a–c) attracted a great deal of interest and they certainly deserve a far more detailed study than my brief catalogue entries. I was unfortunately unaware that a very beautiful and expressive head came to light in the excavations of the Keynsham chapter house in 1983; otherwise this would have been included in the exhibition.[50]

The display of the Much Wenlock lavabo (no. 169a–c) was particularly impressive (pl. X*b*). Those who remember the fragments from the cistern stored in a garden shed and the two overgrown panels in danger of disintegrating will, I am sure, welcome this rescue work and partial reconstruction.[51] The future destination of this important work is still uncertain. Happily, the lectern (no. 170) from the same Cluniac priory has now been purchased by the Victoria and Albert Museum. The statues and voussoirs from St Mary's Abbey, York, newly cleaned for the exhibition, at last present a dignified appearance worthy of sculpture of this quality and importance (pl. XI*b*).[52] Traces of colour discovered on them suggest that these statues when new looked exactly like the figures in contemporary manuscripts. Christopher Wilson's reconstruction of the original setting of the statues in the chapter house, the apostles above the prophets, was bound to be questioned, as is also his suggestion that the seven narrative voussoirs (nos. 174a–g) were part of the east window of the same building.[53] It is one of the great benefits of exhibitions such as this that they stimulate discussion and lead to a greater understanding of the art of this distant past.

One of the aspects of English Romanesque sculpture in the exhibition which particularly surprised non-English scholars was the originality and quality of the sculpture from secular buildings. The material was limited to what was movable and thus we could show neither the extraordinary capitals from Durham Castle nor the musicians decorating the great hall of Oakham Castle.[54] But we exhibited the capitals from Westminster Hall (nos. 105a–f), fragments from Wallingford (no. 112) and Sherborne (no. 131) castles, important remnants from the palace of Henry of Blois at Winchester (nos. 147 and 148) and very fine pieces from Clarendon Palace (nos. 155a–f). The Westminster Hall capitals especially, displayed above the Stothard engravings of the Bayeux Tapestry (no. 551), hinted at the existence in England of epic sculpture comparable to the Tapestry and aimed at the same class of patron.

The warm approval of the exhibition by both the general public and the critics was very gratifying to the organizers, but it is too early to estimate what long-term effects such an exhibition will have on our knowledge of English Romanesque sculpture. One can, nevertheless, hope that detailed research will follow, since, despite the fragmentary state of so much of the surviving material, much can still be learned from it.

Acknowledgements

The exhibition was the collective work of many people, scholars, administrators, museum and library staffs, and the clergy. But I would like to single out those who wrote the catalogue, for now that the exhibition has long been over, this is the record of it and the basis for future research. Many pieces of sculpture were cleaned and restored especially for the exhibition and this will benefit them greatly. It is hoped that it will encourage the owners of medieval sculpture to do likewise. There are a number of experts who are extremely competent in this very specialized field of conservation and those acknowledged in the catalogue rendered us valuable service. Finally, the designer of the exhibition, Paul Williams, should be congratulated for the memorable presentation of the objects.

The seminar organized by the Society of Antiquaries at the suggestion of Neil Stratford, at which this paper was read, is one more proof of the concern which the Society is showing in promoting medieval studies, something which, in the past, was the prerogative of the universities.

A number of objects in the exhibition were lent by the Society, including the important Stothard engravings of the Bayeux Tapestry, which were originally commissioned by the Society. I would like to conclude by expressing our warm thanks to the President, the General Secretary, the Librarian and all other Officers for their help with the exhibition and for organizing the seminar.

NOTES

[1] Amongst the important objects requested but refused by the owners were the Durham door-knocker and the enamel plaque in Lyon Museum. Corpus Christi College, Cambridge, allowed the loan of only one volume and thus the Dover Bible was painfully missing. Similarly, the Museo Nazionale del Bargello in Florence refused all but one object, and thus the English ivory and a wooden casket were not shown. The wooden casket was said to be now too fragile to travel, though it was sent not long ago to an exhibition in Stuttgart, where it was wrongly catalogued as German.

[2] 'L'art roman anglais', *Archéologia*, xci (June 1984), 18.

[3] 'English Romanesque at the Hayward', *Burl. Mag.*, August 1984, 511.

[4] References to objects throughout this paper agree with the numbers in the exhibition's *Catalogue*. The relief no. 96 has been fully discussed by M. Q. Smith, 'The Harrowing of Hell relief in Bristol Cathedral', *Bristol & Glos. Arch. Soc. Trans.* xciv (1976), 101–6.

[5] M. Thurlby, 'A note on the Romanesque sculpture at Hereford Cathedral and the Herefordshire School of sculpture', *Burl. Mag.*, April 1984, 233–4.

[6] Both these tympana were brilliantly discussed by T. D. Kendrick, *Late Saxon and Viking Art* (London, 1949), 142–4.

[7] The relief has been fully discussed again by its discoverer, Martin Biddle, in *The Golden Age of Anglo-Saxon Art 966–1066*, ed. J. Backhouse, D. H. Turner and L. Webster (London, 1984), no. 140, 133–5. It has been suggested to me by Jolanta Zaluska that the subject of the relief is likely to be biblical, dogs licking the blood of Naboth, stoned on the order of Jezebel, I Kings, 21. Professor Lech Kalinowski drew my attention to the painting by Bernardino Campi in S. Prospero, Reggio nell'Emilia, showing this rare subject. Yet another interpretation is being propounded by Jonathan Alexander, who I hope will publish it shortly.

[8] Quoted from Maylis Baylé's entry in the *Catalogue*, no. 98, 51.

[9] See in particular the capital still *in situ*: M. Baylé, 'La sculpture du XIe siècle à Jumièges et sa place dans le décor architectural des abbayes normandes', *Aspects du monachisme en Normandie (IVe–XVIIe siècles)* (Paris, 1982), fig. 8.

[10] Except for a useful article on the chevron ornament (A. Borg, 'The development of chevron ornament', *JBAA*, 3rd ser. xxx (1967), 122–40) there is no recent study of the geometric decoration in England.

[11] The York Minster capital is the better preserved of two similar capitals, found in the excavations under the building. For a preliminary report on the recent excavations, see B. Hope-Taylor, *Under York Minster* (York, 1971). For Bayeux Cathedral see L. Musset, *Normandie romane*, i: *La Basse Normandie*, Zodiaque series (1975), 249 ff.

[12] I discussed the York capitals in 'Romanesque sculpture in Normandy and England in the eleventh century', *Proceedings of the Battle Conference on Anglo-Norman Studies*, i (1978), 173–4, pls. 6 and 7.

[13] Compare, for instance, animal reliefs on pre-Conquest stones, chiefly from York, in I. R. Pattison, 'The Nunburnholme Cross and Anglo-Danish sculpture in York', *Archaeologia*, civ (1973), figs. 1 and 2.

[14] E. Licht, *Ottonische und frühromanische Kapitelle in Deutschland* (Marburg, 1935), 75 ff.

[15] For Regensburg, see R. Strobel, *Katalog der ottonischen und romanischen Säulen in Regensburg und Umgebung*, offprint from *Jahrbuch für fränkische Landesforschung*, xxii (1962), 367–8, Taf. 2 and 3. For Milan, see A. K. Porter, *Lombard Architecture*, ii, (New York, 1967) (1st edn. 1917), 528 and pl. 115, fig. 1.

[16] 'Romanesque sculpture in Normandy and England' (see note 12), 184, pls. 27 and 28.

[17] M. Backes, *Hessen* (G. Dehio, *Handbuch der deutschen Kunstdenkmäler*) (Munich and Berlin, 1966), 40.

[18] H. P. Maguire, 'A twelfth-century workshop in Northampton', *Gesta*, ix, 1 (1970), 19.

[19] *Catalogue*, no. 127b and G. Zarnecki, *English Romanesque Sculpture 1066–1140* (London, 1951), pl. 60.

[20] *Catalogue*, 127k (for Reading). For Como, see O. Zastrow, *Scultura carolingia e romanica nel Comasco*, Società Archeologica Comese (n.d.), fig. 88.

[21] For ivories and their connections with Flanders and the Empire proper see *Catalogue*, 211, and P. Lasko, *Two Ivory Kings in the British Museum and the Norman Conquest* (Newcastle upon Tyne, 1983), 15–16. For a specific instance of connections between English and Mosan metalwork, see a recent study by N. Stratford, 'Three English Romanesque enamelled ciboria', *Burl. Mag.*, April 1984, 206 ff. In the same number, devoted to English Romanesque art, other articles also stress the connections between English and German (including Flemish) art.

[22] J. Raspi Serra, 'English decorated sculpture of the early twelfth century and the Como-Pavian tradition', *Art Bull.* li (1969), 352–62.

[23] See note 18.

[24] J. Meredith, 'The Impact of Italy on the Romanesque Architectural Sculpture of England', unpublished Ph.D. thesis, Yale University, 1980.

[25] The view put forward by Dr Meredith (*ibid.*, 108–10) that the Prior's Doorway of Ely Cathedral was originally intended for the position where today the Vestry Doorway is located and that the Prior's Doorway preceded the other two by ten to fifteen years is demonstrably mistaken.

[26] A. Goldschmidt, 'Die Bauornamentik in Sachsen in XII Jahrhundert', *Monatshefte für Kunstwissenschaft*, iii (1910), 299–314.

[27] R. Kautzsch, 'Oberitalien und der Mittelrhein in 12 Jahrhundert', *Atti del X Congresso Internazionale di Storia dell'Arte in Roma: L'Italia e l'arte straniera* (Rome, 1922), 123–30.

[28] G. de Francovich, 'La corrente comasca nella scultura romanica europea', *Rivista del R. Istituto d'Archeologia e Storia dell'Arte*, v (1935–6), 267–305. Part II, 'La diffusione', *ibid.*, vi (1937–8), 47–129.

[29] See esp. pls. 83, 88 and 89 in my *The Early Sculpture of Ely Cathedral* (London, 1958).

[30] They were exhibited beside the sculpture from Norwich Cathedral in the Sainsbury Centre for the Visual Arts, 1980, but were not included in the catalogue.

[31] The following Norwegian examples can be quoted: Ål (Hallingdal), Attra (Telemark) and Tuft, all in Oslo University Museum. The first two are illustrated in P. Anker, *The Art of Scandinavia*, i (London, 1970), pls. 209, 211 and 216, the third in L. Dietrichson, *De Norske Stavkirker*

(Kristiania, Copenhagen, 1892), fig. 253. In the same study is illustrated a portal at Øifjeld on which one lion is in a normal position (fig. 290a), the other (fig. 290b) is the 'acrobatic' type.

[32] The literature on the subject is vast. The earlier studies are conveniently listed by Z. Swiechowski, 'Die Bedeutung Italiens für die romanische Architektur und Bauplastik in Polen', *Acta Historiae Artium*, x (Budapest 1964), 1–55, while the later can be found in Meredith, *op. cit.* (note 24), 349–61.

[33] B. C. Chiovenda, *L'Ambone dell'Isola di San Giulio* (Rome, 1955).

[34] Conveniently reproduced in the *Courtauld Institute Illustration Archives*, ed. P. Lasko, Archive 3, Part 5: *Germany / DDR* (London, 1978), pls. 53–9.

[35] O. Beigbeder, *Forez-Velay roman*, Zodiaque Series (1962), pls. 98–100, 114 and 116.

[36] M. Vidal, J. Maury and J. Porcher, *Quercy roman*, Zodiaque series (1979), pl. 70. In the text (161), the reliefs are said to be some decades earlier than the reliefs of St-Sernin, Toulouse, but in the caption to the illustration the reliefs are described as 'remplois carolingiens'.

[37] Sir Alfred Clapham, 'Some disputed examples of pre-Conquest sculpture', *Antiquity*, c (1951), 194–5, and D. T. Rice, *English Art, 871–1100* (Oxford, 1952), 100. Rice suggests 1050 as the date, Claphan 'before the middle of the eleventh century'.

[38] The best description of this lintel is given by S. Alford, 'Romanesque Sculpture in Dorset: a Selective Catalogue', M. A. report, 1981, Courtauld Institute of Art, University of London, now published as 'Romanesque architectural sculpture in Dorset', *Proc. Dorset Nat. Hist. & Arch. Soc.* cvi (1984), 17–18, pl. 18.

[39] The rich remains of sculpture from Reading Abbey deserve a detailed study. So far they have been discussed only in my doctoral thesis 'Regional Schools of English Sculpture in the Twelfth Century', Courtauld Institute of Art, University of London, 1950, 80–123.

[40] *Burl. Mag.*, August 1984, 515.

[41] 'Regional Schools' (see note 39): for Reading see 80–123, for Hyde Abbey 124–36.

[42] Most recently discussed by A. Tcherikover in her doctoral thesis, 'Saint-Jouin-de-Marnes and the Development of Romanesque Sculpture in Poitou', Courtauld Institute of Art, University of London, 1982.

[43] R. A. Stalley, 'A 12th century patron of architecture: a study of the buildings erected by Roger Bishop of Salisbury', *JBAA*, 3rd ser. xxxiv (1971), 78.

[44] Discussed but not illustrated by Stalley, *ibid.*

[45] The most recent work on this little-known building is by R. Bruno, *Anglona, una città, un vescovado, un santuario* (Matera, 1984). For the beak-heads, see F. Henry and G. Zarnecki, 'Romanesque arches decorated with human and animal heads', *JBAA*, 3rd Ser. xx–xxi (1957–8), reprinted in G. Zarnecki, *Studies in Romanesque Sculpture* (London, 1979), vi, 28, pl. xiv, 4.

[46] See note 39.

[47] Raspi Serra, *op. cit.* (note 22), 356, 357 and 362; Meredith, *op. cit.* (note 24), 335–7.

[48] Maguire, *op. cit.* (note 18), 15 ff.

[49] All sculptures lent to the *English Romanesque Art* exhibition by the Yorkshire Museum, York, were catalogued by Dr Wilson.

[50] I owe this information to Mrs Barbara J. Lowe, who very kindly supplied me with the photograph of the head.

[51] It is sad to think that this important work is now in storage, not accessible to the public.

[52] Two of the statues are now displayed in the Victoria and Albert Museum, on extended loan from the Yorkshire Museum.

[53] Sauerländer, *op. cit.* (note 3), 515.

[54] For Durham Castle see G. Baldwin Brown, 'Saxon and Norman Sculpture in Durham', *Antiquity*, v (1931), 438–40, pls. i–v and Zarnecki, *op. cit.* (note 19), 12 ff. It is just possible that the capital no. 100 came from Durham Castle. For Oakham Hall see R. Emmerson, *Twelfth-Century Sculpture at Oakham Castle*, Leicestershire Museums, Art Galleries and Records Service (1981).

Niello in England in the Twelfth Century

Neil Stratford, F.S.A.

In memory of Hanns Swarzenski[1]

There is still some doubt as to what Romanesque niello is. Members of the British Museum Research Laboratory, and particularly Susan La Niece, are actively engaged on a programme of niello analysis.[2] This has so far shown that 'all Roman niello on silver consists of silver sulphide only but that, at least from the sixth century A.D., mixed silver/copper sulphides were in use'. Unfortunately the Museum's collections include very few twelfth-century nielloed silver objects which prove susceptible of sample analysis. However a Mosan (or north French) crosier of the second quarter of the thirteenth century, related in style to some of the Oignies Treasury pieces, is enriched with nielloed silver plaques, where the niello contains lead, in fact a mixture of copper/silver sulphide and lead sulphide.[3] Recent analysis has discovered no lead, only silver sulphide, in the niello of the ring from the Larkhill hoard (pl. XIII*a*, top left). Nor is there lead sulphide in the niello of the Victoria and Albert Museum's Mosan griffon aquamanile of the mid twelfth century, but this niello may be atypical in that it is inlaid directly into brass, not silver.[4] On the other hand, the silver Durham book-clasps, which I will be discussing in greater detail and dating to *c.* 1170–80 (pl. XIV*c*), are nielloed with a composition which is a mixture of copper, silver and lead sulphides;[5] so far this is the earliest example analysed of a triple sulphide recipe of the type recommended by Theophilus.[6] But we still do not know whether this recipe was in wide general use by the twelfth century. More analyses will be needed before the date of the introduction of lead sulphide niello can be firmly established. It would be of some interest to establish this date, because the new technique was dominant until the end of the Middle Ages and beyond.[7]

Secondly, it is not always easy to distinguish niello from dark enamelled glasses, without the use of a microscope. Thus, I read recently that the inscriptions on the 'Chartres crosier' in Florence are nielloed; I am fairly confident that this is incorrect and that they are filled with dark blue enamel, but I mention the mistake at the outset as an illustration of the inherent difficulty of recognizing niello as opposed to enamel. Other problems of identification are caused by wear and dirt. For instance, the Stockholm laboratory states that the bowl of a drinking-cup from the Dune treasure, which is signed 'Simon Me Fecit' and is probably by an English goldsmith working in the 1180s, does not have niello inlaid into the engraved lines of the figures (pl. XII*a*); yet it is still possible that where dirt now fills the worn lines, there once was a niello inlay.[8]

Some of the English Romanesque niellos imply an unbroken tradition inherited from Anglo-Saxon art, and there are enough minor survivals to suggest that niello inlays on silver were absolutely current in England in the twelfth century, as they had been in the eleventh century and even earlier. The twelfth-century survivals are by no means numerous. That is hardly surprising, when one remembers that precious metal survivals are in themselves so few and far between, and all the surviving niello inlays are on silver. In fact a very high percentage of the small body of silver plate, whether secular or ecclesiastical, is indeed nielloed. The chief exceptions are the plain, part-gilded, later twelfth- or early thirteenth-century chalices of Oman's Group III.[9]

The silver studs on the boss of the Gloucester candlestick (pl. XII*b*) are the first dated post-Conquest examples of the use of niello inlay. They were made between 1107 and 1113.[10] This is not the place to argue in detail the insular origins of the great artist who made the candlestick; Anabell Harris has already fully demonstrated them,[11] and the exhibition will, I believe, have removed any last doubts on the subject, since the Canterbury pen initials so closely related to the candlestick were shown beside it. But what is often forgotten about the candlestick is that it combines wax-casting of the most intricate kind (perhaps in many separate moulds, as at least one of the heads was cast separately) with the use of cold inlay (dark blue glass for the eyes and the bodies of the dragons), niello inlay on silver and fire-gilding. All this implies a highly sophisticated metal-worker, even if his close relationship to contemporary pen drawings in manu-scripts tends to go against the hypothesis that he was exclusively a 'specialist', any more than Master Hugo of Bury St Edmunds was in the second quarter of the twelfth century.[12] The extremely unusual and uneven alloy from which the candlestick is made (it contains as much as 22·5 per cent silver in the base, 12·1 per cent silver in the stem, 5·76 per cent silver in the pan) suggests that it could have been a 'one-off' commission, the goldsmith being supplied with a Late Antique coin hoard of debased 'silver', which looked like copper and was handed over to him for melting down.[13] Nevertheless niello inlay on silver, filling simple floral patterns, was a part of this English artist's repertoire. He too, like his continental European contemporaries, admired the effect produced by the black and silver plaques framed by gilded surfaces.

Filling simple patterns with niello was probably popular and widespread. One of the six silver finger-rings (pl. XIII*a*, top left) found with the hoard at Larkhill, near Worcester, in 1853, has a flattened rectangular bezel decorated with three separate square fields, alternating a single cross with four little crosses reserved against nielloed grounds. The hoard was deposited *c.* 1173–4 and consists over-whelmingly of English coins, with a very few imports.[14] In theory, then, the nielloed ring could also be an import, but this is rather unlikely; it is not the sort of prestige object that one would expect to see widely traded, rather a local simplified version of grander rings: the nielloed crosses of the Larkhill ring occur, for instance, on the 'shoulders' of the magnificent gold and sapphire ring buried with Archbishop Absalon of Lund at Sorø in 1201.[15] The Iona spoon (pl. XIII*b*), one of the other English nielloed silver objects discussed later in this essay, is also decorated with simple cross-patterns. Even if these patterns are so basic that they had international currency (particularly in Germany, where they are a legacy of Ottonian metalwork, e.g. on the Heinrich von Werl portable altar of 1100 and the Bonn Museum lion's head stem[16]), they can still be accounted a *leitmotif* of English Romanesque metalwork. They even occur on some of the English enamels: the lid of the Fitzwilliam casket and the Christ medallion of the Balfour ciborium.[17] Minor and apparently insignificant as such a motif may be, it is nevertheless a reflection of how English metalwork after the Conquest borrows from a common European language for its decorative repertoire.

The Larkhill rings as a group represent part of the accumulated capital of a rich layman. They are not a great man's rings, or so it would seem, since two are set with cheap 'artificial' gems (glass backed with foil; paste). By the reign of Henry II, then, a wide variety of rings was evidently in relatively common usage, among them simple nielloed rings (the twisted ring (pl. XIII*a*, top right) may be at least a century older, being of a late Anglo-Saxon and Viking type). This use of niello inlay on rings continued: among Matthew Paris's drawings of jewellery at St Albans, executed between 1250 and 1259, are four of rings or pendants whose accompanying descriptions make it clear that they were inscribed with nielloed letters for the donor and in one case a nielloed Christ on the cross, on the back of the pendant.[18] The St Albans objects were of gold. Three were made for great churchmen of the day (Stephen Langton, Edmund Rich and prior Roger of St Albans), but the fourth was nielloed with the initials of Richard, known as Animal, who had been given the ring by Queen Eleanor of Aquitaine, with whom he had been taught in his youth. It was therefore presumably made in France and must have been in existence by *c.* 1140, though of course we do not know when the nielloed initials were added. The 'stirrup-shape' of the ring also has English parallels.[19]

Silver spoons are another class of object which may have been commonly inlaid with niello. Of four spoons, dug up beside the south chancel pier of the Nunnery church on Iona, one (pl. XIII*b*) has the nielloed cross-patterns on the handle.[20] The Pevensey spoon (pl. XV*b*) was also inlaid with niello, and it is not impossible that two of the other Iona spoons (pl. XIII*c*) originally had niello on the polygonal bosses half-way down their handles. In their case, they are certainly English, for the flowers engraved in their bowls are closely comparable to initials in the Winchcombe manuscripts of *c.* 1130–40.[21] As the Iona spoons are of the same form as the Pevensey spoon and the Taunton spoon, both dug up on secular sites,[22] there is no reason to assume anything but a secular function for the Iona spoons. Once again, here are simple nielloed patterns on silver objects made for everyday usage.

Not so with the exquisite little silver nielloed bottle at St-Maurice d'Agaune (pl. XIV*a–b*).[23] It is an outstanding work of art, perhaps made to be slung as a container for perfume or some other elixir from a belt; although the present conical top of plain silver with its suspension loop is probably not original, there is on the side of the neck a second suspension loop, undoubtedly original. Unfortunately at Agaune nothing seems to be known about the early history of the bottle, which now acts as a reliquary, wax-sealed with the arms of the Abbey chapter and authenticated with a ticket specifying *Unus dens S. Mauritii* in what may be an eighteenth-century hand. The sides of the bottle are engraved with three winged dragons, with claw-feet and rapacious jaws, each with a tail growing into as many as three separate flowers; these flowers are trifoliate, breaking out of a central clasp or button. The dragons belong to the world of English pen-initials, particularly in Canterbury and Rochester manuscripts of *c.* 1120, where the bodies of the beasts are often decorated with the same hatched and dotted patterns.[24] What is more, the foliage is absolutely typical of English art; the hatching of the petals, the capping of the leaves and the basic trifoliate forms with central clasp, as well as the ribbed stems, can be paralleled, for instance, in the Mostyn Gospels and the somewhat later Josephus manuscript of *c.* 1130 (Cambridge, St John's College MS A.8). It is difficult to be precise about the pedigree and date of this foliage. It still occurs, accompanying similar dragons, in the Lambeth Bible of *c.* 1150, yet by the mid century far richer variations had already been played on this trifoliate theme, for instance in the Winchcombe manuscripts of *c.* 1130–40.[25] I would also invoke by way of comparison the dragons on some of the Reading and Winchester capitals of *c.* 1125–30, whilst a somewhat later carved shaft at Winchester is decorated with hatched and capped trifoliate flowers.[26] Even the little 'key' and meander patterns on the neck of the bottle have close parallels in English manuscript borders of this period.[27] Thus, the milieu in which the bottle was created was undoubtedly English, its date *c.* 1120–50. But these comparisons do not do full justice to this remarkable goldsmith. His control of line, the way he was able to accommodate his design to the curving sides of the bottle, represent a technical *tour de force*. The bottle is a *hapax*, not only a precious secular object of the second quarter of the century, but one affording a tantalizing glimpse of what levels of accomplishment nielloed silverwork in England was capable of reaching at this period.

At this point, all the problems take over. First I would like to offer some remarks on the vexed question: Lower Saxony or England? Ever since Georg Swarzenski's contribution on the subject in 1932,[28] the question has remained unresolved. I suspect that to many German scholars the problem has not seemed an important one, given the apparent integrity and self-contained development which can be traced for the metalwork of Lower Saxony itself. But the publication of one of the book-clasps of the great Durham Bible (pl. XIVc) raised the question again.[29] The Bible itself, in four volumes, was written and illuminated for Hugh du Puiset, Bishop of Durham (1153–95), probably *c.* 1170–80.[30] The two clasps of the first volume are now detached. They are identical one with the other. Each is formed of two copper-alloy plaques back to back with a central hole for the pin, attached through the leather strap of the book-fastening by four corner pins with spherical heads. The back plaque is modern. The front plaque is engraved with a grooved and beaded border, its central field inlaid with silver and filled with niello as background to a spiralling pattern of tightly coiled stems, which end in small tufted leaves. The copper surfaces framing the silver are gilded. The two clasps were almost certainly made for the Bible itself, although this can never be absolutely proved; a similar tightly coiled pattern was, though simplified, cut in metal on one of the stamps used for the original leather binding of Volume II of the Bible (pl. XVa).[31] So close is this nielloed scrollwork to the backgrounds of some Lower Saxon metalwork of the second half of the twelfth century, particularly on the St Oswald reliquary and on the St Laurence arm reliquary, that the similarity cannot be coincidental.[32]

The English elements in Lower Saxon metalwork seem to be second-hand, whether they involve comparisons of figure drawing, as Jane Geddes suggested, or the 'orchid-blossoms' on the St Laurence arm.[33] It is as if this Lower Saxon workshop translated certain English figures or foliage motifs into its own language. Thus, I would like to add to the Durham clasps several other English metalwork versions of this tightly scrolled foliage: nielloed on the handle of the Pevensey silver spoon (pl. XVb), dug up in Pevensey Castle (Sussex);[34] nielloed on one of two silver bands, set into a gilt copper-alloy mid twelfth-century crosier found in a bishop's tomb at St David's (pl. XVc);[35] engraved on two crosier-mounts, one of gilt copper-alloy from a second Bishop's crosier at St David's (pl. XVIa),[36] the other of silver found in a tomb at Bury St Edmunds (pl. XVIb), which was very likely that of the famous Abbot Samson (1182–1211);[37] and enamelled on the lid of the little English casket in Florence (pl. XVIc), of the late twelfth century.[38] Here is a formidable array of witnesses to the fact that this scrollwork, often nielloed, was at least thoroughly Anglicized. None of these objects, however, is dated. For this reason one more example is of great importance: the reverse of the seal-matrix of the Cathedral Chapter of Lincoln (pl. XVIIa), which first appears attached to a charter datable between 1148 and 1160.[39] My illustration is taken from an old engraving,[40] because the reverse of the matrix is at present hidden from view by a riveted silver plate, added in modern times. However, all accounts agree that the engraved figure of Christ (so sadly damaged) and the tufted scrollwork background were inlaid with niello. What is more, there can be no reasonable doubt about where the Lincoln seal matrix was made; the front is cut with an impression of the Virgin and Child (also shown on the engraving), which is in a wholly insular tradition.[41] We are thus faced with an indisputably English version of this nielloed scrollwork and, in addition, the matrix is firmly dated to a period earlier than any of the comparable Lower Saxon examples. Alexander Heslop has suggested that this scrollwork is ultimately Celtic-derived (from the hanging-bowl escutcheons), but this suggestion ignores the lack of examples in the later Anglo-Saxon period.[42] The Romanesque examples are vegetal; this is foliage, not pure pattern-making, even if some of the spirals (e.g. on the second St David's crosier (pl. XVIa) or the Trzemeszno chalice)[43] have been simplified to the point where the little foliage-tufts are omitted. It seems, therefore, more likely that this Romanesque scrollwork derives from late classical vine-scroll ornament, such as can also be found in Anglo-Saxon England, e.g. at Breedon and Bakewell.[44] But leaving aside the question of the insular origins of the motif, we must ask how it came to be adopted both in England and Lower Saxony at much the same time during the twelfth century. Political events are there to offer a possible explanation, with Duke Henry the Lion's close family ties to Henry II and with his English exile in the 1180s, but do we have any right as historians to batten onto the few events of which we have any knowledge and manipulate them to our own

PLATE XII

Photograph: Claude Blair, F.S.A.

b

a

Photograph: Antikvarisk-Topografiska Arkivet, Stockholm

a. Detail of silver drinking cup from the Dune treasure; English, 1180s. Statens Historiska Museum, Stockholm

b. Nielloed silver stud on the boss of the Gloucester candlestick; English, between 1107 and 1113. Victoria and Albert Museum

PLATE XIII

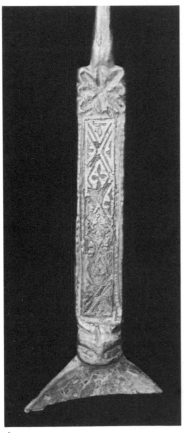

a

b

c

a. The six silver rings from the Larkhill hoard, deposited *c.* 1173–4. British Museum
b. Detail of one of the four Iona spoons; English, mid twelfth century. National Museum of Antiquities, Edinburgh
c. A second of the four Iona spoons; English, mid twelfth century

Photographs: a, British Museum; b–c, courtesy of the National Museum of Antiquities of Scotland

PLATE XIV

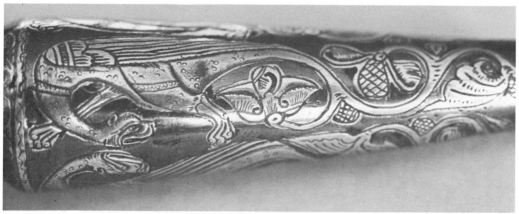

a

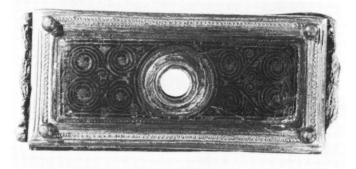

c

a. Detail of nielloed silver bottle; English, second quarter of twelfth century. St-Maurice d'Agaune

b. The nielloed silver bottle detailed in *a*

c. Nielloed silver book-clasp from Vol. I of the bible of Bishop Hugh du Puiset; English, *c.* 1170–80. Durham, Chapter Library

Photographs: a–b, by kind permission of the Chapter, St-Maurice d'Agaune; c, Janey Cronyn

b

PLATE XV

Photograph: National Museum of Wales

Photograph: British Museum

a

b

c

a. Tracing of stamped pattern on the leather binding of Vol. II of the Bible of Bishop Hugh du Puiset; English, c. 1170–80. Durham Chapter Library

b. Nielloed silver spoon from Pevensey Castle, Sussex; English, second half of twelfth century. British Museum

c. Head of a crosier, gilt copper-alloy with nielloed silver mounts; English, mid twelfth century. St David's, Cathedral Treasury

PLATE XVI

b. Silver-gilt mount from a crosier, perhaps from the tomb of Abbot Samson (1182–1211); English, last quarter of the twelfth century. Moyses Hall Museum, Bury St Edmunds

a. Gilt copper-alloy mount from a crosier; English, *c.* 1150–80. St David's, Cathedral Treasury

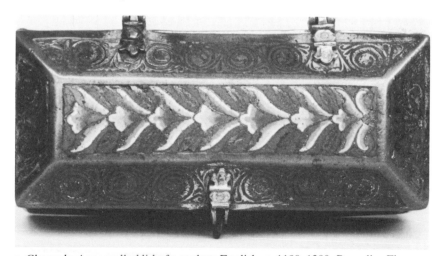

c. Champlevé enamelled lid of a casket; English, *c.* 1180–1200. Bargello, Florence

Photographs: a, by kind permission of the Dean and Chapter, St David's; b, Moyses Hall Museum

PLATE XVII

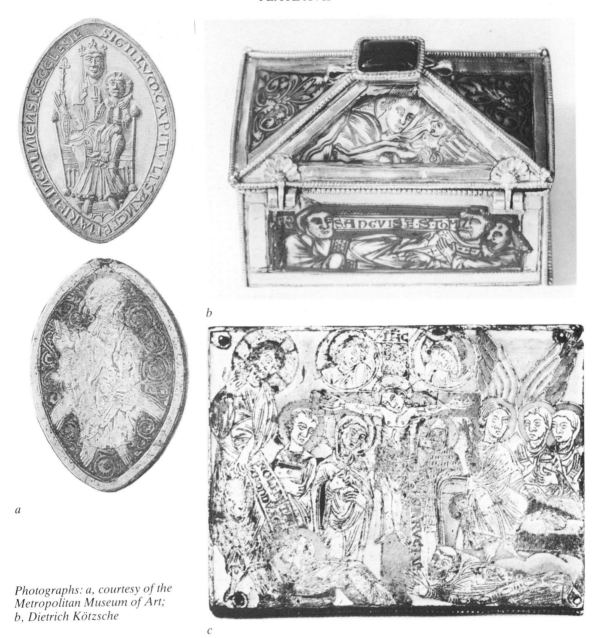

Photographs: a, courtesy of the
Metropolitan Museum of Art;
b, Dietrich Kötzsche

a. Seal matrix of the Cathedral Chapter of Lincoln: impression (top) and reverse, nielloed silver; English,
c. 1150–60. From an engraving, Society of Antiquaries

b. Nielloed silver casket; Rhenish (?), *c.* 1175. Metropolitan Museum of Art, New York

c. Detail of champlevé enamelled bookcover from the Bleidenstadt am Taunus necrology; Rhenish, *c.* 1160–70

PLATE XVIII

Photograph: M. Albert Lemeunier

b. Reverse of a phylactery from Waulsort; Mosan; c. 1160. Musée des Arts
Anciens du Namurois, Namur

Photograph: courtesy of the Metropolitan Museum of Art

a. Nielloed silver casket; Rhenish (?), c. 1175.
Metropolitan Museum of Art, New York

PLATE XIX

a. Stone relief; Rhenish, third quarter of twelfth century.
Schwarzrheindorf

Photograph: Antikvarisk-Topografiska Arkivet, Stockholm

b. Silver nielloed drinking cup from the Dune treasure (detail); Angevin
or Rhenish, last quarter of the twelfth century. Statens Historiska
Museum, Stockholm

PLATE XX

a. Silver nielloed drinking cup; Angevin or Rhenish, last quarter of
the twelfth century. Metropolitan Museum of Art, New York

b. Precentor's staff: detail of nielloed silver and gilt-silver embossed
mounts; Angevin or Rhenish, 1178. Domschatz, Cologne

c. Detail of a crosier (on loan from the Keir Collection); Limoges,
c. 1190. Nelson-Atkins Gallery of Art, Kansas City

*Photographs: a, courtesy of the Metropolitan Museum of Art; b,
Rheinisches Bildarchiv, Cologne; c, Trustees of the Nelson-Atkins
Gallery, by kind permission of the owner*

PLATE XXI

Photograph: Antikvarisk-Topografiska Arkivet, Stockholm

a. Detail of silver nielloed drinking cup from the Dune treasure: cast group inside cup; Angevin or Rhenish, last quarter of twelfth century. Statens Historiska Museum, Stockholm

Photograph: Dr Hanns Swarzenski

b. Cresting of the St Albinus shrine; Rhenish, *c.* 1186. St Pantaleon, Cologne

ends as 'explanations' of how works of art came into being? All that can be said with certainty is that artists, and metalworkers in particular, travelled widely. This brings me to the next problem, which is no easier of solution.

One of the earliest surviving Becket reliquaries (pls. XVII*b*, XVIII*a*) is the little silver-gilt nielloed casket in New York.[45] It is constructed from separate silver plates, soldered edge to edge, the framing strips and beaded borders gilded, the roof crowned by a glass 'jewel' backed by a copper foil, which gives it the appearance of a ruby, presumably as a reference to the blood of St Thomas's martyrdom. Even if we reject (and I think we must) Breck's fanciful interpretation of the inscriptions as referring to particular Canterbury monks involved in the martyrdom, the iconography of the slaying by the knights, who here are three in number, and of the Archbishop's burial suggest that the casket was made for somebody who knew well the details of the murder. Admittedly 'published' versions were circulating from the moment of Becket's death, but the casket cannot date from much later than the 1170s and in the circumstances there is every likelihood that it was made in England, the source of the Becket relic trade.[46] All the more puzzling is the total absence of stylistic parallels for its drawing style among English Romanesque works of art. I believe that the artist who made the casket, although very possibly working in England, was trained in a Mosan or German milieu. For the style there are general similarities to the group of mostly silver nielloed objects studied by Dietrich Kötzsche and centring on the Cologne niello chalice-bowl.[47] I illustrate here by way of comparison the entombment of St Thomas (in New York) (pl. XVII *b*), and a detail of the lost enamel bookcover from the Blcidenstadt am Taunus necrology (formerly in Berlin) (pl. XVII*c*).[48] Compare, for instance, the head of the New York roof angel with the head of the Bleidenstadt St John standing behind the Virgin Mary. As for the draperies, they are rendered with the same short parallel hatched lines and groups of V-folds. As to the two angels, or perhaps they are Virtues, on the ends of the New York casket (pl. XVIII*a*), they have no counterparts in English art, but are a standard iconographic formula with the Meuse-Rhine metal workshops: on the Waulsort phylactery alone (pl. XVIII*b*) no less than seven such frontal bust-length winged figures have survived, two enamelled on the front, five engraved on the back, not to mention the three beast-headed symbols of the Evangelists.[49] But what is particularly significant is that the symmetrical 'feathery' foliage on the two sloping ends of the roof of the New York casket (pl. XVIII*a*) has no English parallels, but numerous Mosan or Rhenish ones, both in metal[50] and in stone (pl. XIX*a*).[51] Kötzsche assigns his Rhenish group to the early 1160s–early 1170s, whilst the compatiblc Mosan works are usually dated in the third quarter of the twelfth century. Becket's murder on 29th December 1170 was followed by his formal canonization in 1173. Thus, if the New York casket is accepted as coming from the same general artistic milieu as these Mosan and Rhenish objects—and I would stress that the relationship is by no means one of identical 'hands', simply one of milieu—then it could well have been executed soon after 1173. This date is entirely plausible. Nor is it in any way unlikely that a Mosan- or German-trained goldsmith was active in England at such a time. For instance, we know that the Cologne merchants already had their own 'Guildhall' in London by some date in the reign of Henry II.[52]

Finally, there is the problem of the artistic origins of the group of silver nielloed pieces which includes one of the Dune drinking-cups (pl. XIX*b*), the New York bowl from a drinking-cup (pl. XX*a*) and the 1178 precentor's staff in the Cologne Domschatz (pl. XX*b*). I say 'the problem of the artistic origins of the group', because in the latter case it is probable that the nielloed parts of the staff were made for Cologne (the Hugo of the inscription may well be Hugo the Dean, provost of the church of S. Maria Ad Gradus, identified by Witte as active between 1166 and 1181),[53] even if in its present form it has additions of the second quarter of the thirteenth century,[54] the mid fourteenth century[55] and the nineteenth century,[56] and is anyway no longer necessarily assembled with the mounts in their original order.[57] The group could be enlarged to include a cup from Siberia in the Hermitage.[58] Other cups of similar shape have been found in Russia near Surgut in Siberia and in the Urals;[59] these vessels were apparently copied and traded over a wide area from the Baltic as far as Siberia (it is not certain whether the Basilewsky cup in New York was found in western Siberia or in Hungary,[60] but of course the Dune cup was dug up in a fourteenth-century context on Gotland[61]). However, to enlarge the group by taking in the simpler cups found in Russia does not help with the basic dilemma of its artistic sources. These are almost all 'Limoges' (pl. XX*c*). More or less every single motif on the New York and Dune cups is borrowed directly and literally from the ornamental repertoire of early Limoges: *vermiculé* backgrounds; fluted leaf borders; the lattice layout of the fields, sometimes with studs at the junctions of the lattice; grotesques, animals and figures caught up in foliage; tendrils ending in spidery blossoms; separately cast heads for the animals and figures.[62] What of course distances the group so emphatically from early Limoges is technique. But I wonder how far one can justify a rejection of the 'Limoges' label, just because the workshop is employing silver, using niello inlays and part-gilding, instead of cutting out the fields fully for *champlevé* enamel on copper. Given the 1178 date of the Cologne staff, which in terms of the mainstream Limoges production is very early, would it be possible to see this niello workshop as an offshoot of the very first generation of southern enamel workshops? Spawned perhaps before the enamel tradition of Aquitaine was fully developed and had settled into its own particular patterns of production? After all, it is only *c.* 1170 that the use of the term 'Limoges work' is first recorded.[63] Or is the workshop the product of a silver niello tradition, merely 'aping' early Limoges? The quality of the drawing on these engraved silver cups is too high for them to be regarded as mere pastiches, so that the former hypothesis is rather more probable. Since the town of Limoges was within the Angevin domains at the relevant period, 'Angevin' might be a possible way of describing this workshop. As to the Cologne staff (pl. XX*b*), nothing in Rhenish metalwork of the 1170s can explain its nielloed mounts and knop, but the enigma of the other four embossed mounts with apparently Lower Saxon flowers remains unresolved; they do not necessarily have to be contemporary with the niello-work, but it should be remembered that the cast group of the lion and dragon in foliage inside the Dune cup (pl. XXI*a*) also has close German parallels, e.g. on the Cologne St Albinus shrine (pl. XXI*b*).[64] Angevin and German elements are therefore found side by side on two out of the three main objects of the group. Be that as it may, I would be loath to attribute this group to England proper, although the repeating leaf motif on the rim of the Dune and New York cups and the fluted leaf pattern of the lattice borders are both reproduced on the crosier-mount from St David's (pl. XVI*a*). Compare also the foliage on one of the Iona spoons (pl. XIII*c*). It certainly cannot be excluded that some early Limoges was made in England: the Rusper chalice and the Rouen angel plaque?[65] The Nürnberg Christ?[66]

Where, then, does this brief survey of niello in England in the twelfth century leave us? With the evidence of an apparently popular technique, used on a range from humble to grand secular objects. With the certainty that the few survivals represent only the tip of an iceberg, irrevocably hidden. But with little knowledge of how niello was regarded by contemporaries. No enamelled silver survives from the Romanesque period. Perhaps the technical problems posed by enamelling silver, because its coefficient of expansion is so different from that of glass, defeated the twelfth century? If so, it may be that black niello combined with gilding provided the only current palette for embellishing silver. It is fair to assume that it was also used on gold, but no English examples of gold niello have survived from this period. As to the few survivors of English figured niello-work on silver, the St-Maurice bottle and the Lincoln seal matrix, they hardly do more than hint at lost glories. And did the technique continue to thrive in thirteenth-century England? There is the evidence of the St Albans jewels already mentioned. Again, the St Paul's Cathedral inventory of 1245 lists two large niel-loed silver altar candlesticks and a silver pyx with nielloed knops,[67] whilst its 1295 successor describes in detail several nielloed silver objects including no less than four figured book-covers.[68] But then these may have been imports.

Two separate decorative motifs (cross-patterns and spiral foliage scrolls) have been observed on both nielloed silver and enamelled copper objects. A stock repertory of minor motifs was apparently shared by metalworkers. This is what one would expect, since a competent artist would certainly have practised both techniques. What is more intriguing is the fact that this minor repertory is also shared with German Romanesque metalwork. Why is this? Is it possible that the mid eleventh century saw an injection of German elements into the native metalworking tradition? Goldsmiths with German names, Theodoric and Otto, occur in Domesday Book, and Edward the Confessor had Flemish and German friends about his court.[69] The Ottonian form and inconography of the Gloucester candlestick imply a knowledge of German metalwork, and if one accepts the foreign origins of the artist of the New York Becket casket, then here is a case where a Mosan or German metalworker was presumably active in twelfth-century England. There is nothing surprising about this, and there are other similar cases.[70] What is more, all the zinc calamine in England had, it seems, to be imported from the Maastricht-Aachen region. Where there is a trade in metal, the metalworker in person is likely to follow. But of course this does not imply that the native Anglo-Saxon tradition was dead by *c.* 1100. Far from it, as the exhibition showed abundantly clearly. Nevertheless, this survey of the surviving niello-work does suggest a close awareness in England of contemporary metal-work abroad and *vice versa*. The same is true of Mosan and English *champlevé* enamel from *c.* 1160 onwards.

NOTES

[1] Under the general editorship of Dr Dietrich Kötzsche and Professor Willibald Sauerländer, a group of essays was bound together and presented by friends to Hanns Swarzenski on the occasion of his 80th birthday, 30th August 1983, in Munich. This paper was written for that occasion. It is published here with minor modifications, made in the light of the exhibition *English Romanesque Art 1066–1200*, which has since taken place.

[2] W. A. Oddy, M. Bimson and S. La Niece, 'The composition of niello decoration on gold, silver and bronze in the antique and medieval periods', *Studies in Conservation*, xxviii (1983), 29–35; S. La Niece, 'Niello: an historical and technical survey', *Antiq. J.* lxiii (1983), 279–97.

[3] BM, MLA 98, 5–21, 1. Referred to as 'The Hugo Crosier' in Oddy, *et al.*, *op. cit.*, no. 18 on p. 31. See also La Niece, *op. cit.*, no. 121 on p. 293.

[4] H. Swarzenski, *Monuments of Romanesque Art* (London, 1954), fig. 262; catalogue of exhibition *Die Zeit der Staufer* (Stuttgart, 1977), no. 652 (Abb. 460). The niello was not sampled by Mrs La Niece. XRF analysis revealed a silver/copper sulphide inlaid on a copper/zinc/lead alloy: see La Niece, *op. cit.* (note 2), no. 111, on p. 293.

[5] Unpublished XRF analysis by Susan La Niece, by kind permission of the Dean and Chapter of Durham Cathedral.

[6] Theophilus, *De Diversis Artibus*, ed. and trans. C.R. Dodwell, NMT (1961), 80–1. Theophilus recommends two parts of silver, to one of copper, to half of lead.

[7] Almost without exception, all Gothic, Renaissance and post-Renaissance niello contains lead sulphide: see La Niece, *op. cit.* (note 2).

[8] A. Andersson, *Mediaeval Drinking Bowls of Silver Found in Sweden* (Stockholm, 1983), 25–9, 59–60 (no. 18), pls. 18A–I; *Catalogue*, no. 305. The English attribution of the cup is confirmed by comparing its combat scenes with those on the late twelfth-century enamelled casket in Florence, the lid of which is illustrated here as pl. XVIc, and its style with that of the sculpture of the Dunstable (Beds.) West Door of *c.* 1176–90.

[9] C. Oman, *English Church Plate 597–1830* (London, 1957), 299.

[10] Dr Jonathan Ashley-Smith, Keeper, Department of Conservation, Victoria and Albert Museum, has kindly confirmed that the studs are nielloed, not enamelled. For the dates of Abbot Peter of Gloucester, see D. Knowles, C. Brooke and V. London (eds.), *The Heads of Religious Houses. England and Wales 940–1216* (Cambridge, 1972), 52. The date of his death is often incorrectly quoted by art historians as 1114.

[11] A. Harris, 'A Romanesque candlestick in London', *JBAA*, 3rd ser. xxvii (1964), 32–52. See also *Catalogue*, no. 247. Peter Springer, in his recent *Kreuzfüsse*, vol. iii of the *Bronzegeräte des Mittelalters* (Berlin, 1981), does not know Harris's important article and repeats yet again (117–18) the wrongly conceived doubts about the origins of the candlestick.

[12] For Hugo and his various activities as a bronze-caster, bell-founder (?), carver of wood and illuminator of manuscripts, see M. R. James, *On the Abbey of S. Edmund at Bury*, Public. Cambridge Antiq. Soc., Octavo Series, xxviii (1895), 7, 128, 133–5, 199. The carved stone panels at Durham and the wall-painting of St Paul at Canterbury are so intimately related to the style of the Bury Bible that they are presumably by artists trained in Hugo's immediate artistic circle (workshop?). See *Catalogue*, nos. 154a and b, ill. p. 51.

[13] I owe this suggestion to my Laboratory colleague, Dr Paul Craddock, F.S.A. The analyses of the candlesticks were kindly provided by Dr Roger Brownsword, of the Coventry Polytechnic.

[14] J. Y. Akerman, 'Account of silver rings and coins discovered near Worcester', *Archaeologia*, xxxvi (1855), 200–2. Of the 229 coins in the hoard, 208 are of Henry II's first issue (1158–*c.* 1170), see *Catalogue*, nos. 319–20.

[15] F. Lindahl, 'Om Absalons gravklaedning', *Nationalmuseets Arbejdsmark* (Copenhagen, 1973), 149 (fig. 5).

[16] Swarzenski, *op. cit.* (note 4), figs. 234, 345.

[17] *Ibid.*, figs. 499, 447.

[18] BL Cotton MS Nero D.1, fos. 146–7. See C. C. Oman, 'The jewels of Saint Albans Abbey', *Burl. Mag.* lvii (1930), 80–2; *Catalogue*, no. 318. The short treatise on the rings and gems can be dated after 1250 (since it is followed by Matthew's written record of the works of art due to Richard the Painter between 1241 and 1250) and before Matthew Paris's probable date of death (1259).

19 cf. *Catalogue*, no. 315.

20 A. O. Curle, 'A note on four silver spoons and a fillet of gold found in the Nunnery at Iona . . .', *PSAS*, lviii (5th ser. x) (1923–4), 102–11; the *repoussé* gold hair-fillet found with the spoons is probably of the first half of the thirteenth century. The Benedictine nunnery at Iona was only founded in 1203.

21 C. M. Kauffmann, *Survey*, iii: *Romanesque Manuscripts 1066–1190* (London, 1975), ills. 144, 146.

22 The Pevensey spoon (BM, MLA 1931, 12–15, 1) was found in a pit under the stairs at the entrance to the keep of Pevensey Castle, Sussex; see R. S. Simms, *Antiq. J.* xii (1932), 73–4; *Catalogue*, no. 299. The Taunton spoon (Somerset County Museum OS.AA.4) was found in 1928 within the perimeter of the destroyed keep of Taunton Castle; see H. St G. Gray, *Antiq. J.* x (1930), 156–8; *Catalogue*, no. 297.

23 *Catalogue*, no. 296. The bottle is not included in E. Aubert, *Trésor de l'abbaye de St-Maurice d'Agaune* (1870–2), nor can it be identified with any of the objects listed in the early inventories published by Aubert.

24 Kauffmann, *op. cit.* (note 21), ills. 52, 55, 56. Similar dragons also occur in manuscripts of a later date and different provenance, e.g. Cambridge, Trinity Hall MS 4, a Josephus, perhaps from Hereford, of *c.* 1140.

25 Kauffmann, *op. cit.* (note 21), ills. 57 (Mostyn Gospels); 143–4, 146 (Winchcombe MSS). Most of the relevant initials in St John's A.8 are not published (e.g. fos. 29vo, 180vo), but see T. S. R. Boase, *English Art 1100–1216* (Oxford, 1953), pl. 12b, c; cf. also Cambridge, Trinity College MS B.3.13, fo. 4; Baltimore, Walters Art Gallery MS W.18, fo. 175. Again, for the Lambeth Bible, very few of the lesser initials are published, but for dragons see Kauffmann, *op. cit.* (note 21), ill. 194; C. R. Dodwell, *The Great Lambeth Bible* (London, 1959), pl. 6. For trifoliate leaves, see Kauffmann, ill. 195.

26 Very little of this sculpture is as yet published, but see *Catalogue*, nos. 127a (ill. p. 64), 128e(1), 147a.

27 Kauffmann, *op. cit.* (note 21), ills. 173–80; *Catalogue*, nos. 47–50.

28 G. Swarzenski, 'Aus dem Kunstkreis Heinrichs der Löwen', *Städel-Jahrbuch*, vii–viii (1932), 241–397, *passim*.

29 Swarzenski, *op. cit.* (note 4), fig. 487; *Catologue*, no. 301.

30 Kauffmann, *op. cit.* (note 21), no. 98; *Catalogue*, no. 77.

31 *Catalogue*, no. 474(27). My colleague in the British Library, Dr Mirjam Foot, F.S.A., took the rubbings from which pl. XV*a* is photographed.

32 Good illustrations in J. Sommer, 'Der Niellokelch von Iber', *Zeitschrift für Kunstwissenschaft*, xi (1957), 109–36, particularly pls. 9–11, 14–16, 21–23.

33 J. Geddes, 'The twelfth-century metalwork at Durham Cathedral', *BAA Conference Trans.* iii for 1977 (1980), 140–8. For the blossoms, O. von Falke *et al.*, *Der Welfenschatz* (Frankfurt, 1930), Taf. 68 (top, right).

34 See note 22.

35 *Catalogue*, no. 268. The silver nielloed bands are probably original and go not only with the crosier-head, but also with the original roundels engraved on the upper knop. But the lower knop of the crosier is thirteenth-century (not illustrated), and associated finds from the same tomb included a thirteenth-century gold and sapphire ring and a mid thirteenth-century silver chalice. J. B. Clear (in *Arch. Camb.* 3rd ser. xii (1866), 61, plan (Grave 2)) attributed the tomb to Bishop Richard de Carew (d. 1280).

36 *Catalogue*, no. 270. The mount comes from the stem of a crosier of *c.* 1150–80, crowned with a magnificent 'orchid' blossom of a type found in Camarillo (California), Doheny Library MS 7 (Kauffmann, *op. cit.* (note 21), ills. 247, 249). The crosier was found in 1844 in the grave of an unidentified bishop, without associated finds: see Clear, *op. cit.* (note 35), 63, ill.

37 *Catalogue*, no. 300. The tomb was on the site of the Chapterhouse, see *Bury Free Press*, 3rd and 10th January 1903.

38 See Swarzenski, *op. cit.* (note 4), fig. 489, where one of the ends of the casket is illustrated.

39 W. H. St J. Hope, *PSA*, xiv (1893), 13–15; K. Major (ed.), *The Registrum Antiquissimum of the Cathedral Church of Lincoln*, vi, Lincoln Record Society (1950), 169–70. The date of the charter cannot be earlier than 1148, or later than 1160, the date of death of Humphrey the Subdean (see John Le Neve, *Fasti Ecclesiae Anglicanae 1066–1300*, iii: *Lincoln*, compiled by D. E. Greenway (London, 1977), 21, 67, 79–80). The scrollwork on the Lincoln seal matrix

was drawn to my attention by Alexander Heslop, F.S.A., of the University of East Anglia: see *Catalogue*, no. 360. Dr Kathleen Major, F.S.A., kindly advised me on the dates of the charter.

[40] London, Society of Antiquaries, Kingsford Papers.

[41] T. A. Heslop, 'The Virgin Mary's regalia and twelfth-century seals', *The Vanishing Past, Studies . . . Presented to Christopher Hohler*, BAR S111 (Oxford, 1981), 53–62, pl. 5. 1–16.

[42] For non-vegetal scrollwork inlaid on a group of weapons found in Finland, see J. Leppäaho, *Späteisenzeitliche Waffen aus Finnland* (Helsinki, 1964), esp. Taf. 24, 40, 43, 57, 61. The British Museum scramasax from Southwark (London) belongs to this group and must at present be reckoned an import: see J. D. Cowen, *Antiq. J.* li (1971), 281–6, where it is called 'East Baltic' and dated within the period 1100–1300. I am grateful to my colleagues, Dafydd Kidd and Leslie Webster, F.S.A., for drawing these objects to my attention.

[43] G. Swarzenski, *op. cit.* (note 28), Abb. 332.

[44] R. Cramp, 'Schools of Mercian sculpture', in A. Dornier (ed.), *Mercian Studies* (Leicester, 1977), 191–233, esp. figs. 50, 60.

[45] J. Breck, 'A reliquary of St Thomas Becket made for John of Salisbury', *Bull. Metropolitan Museum of Art, New York*, xiii (October, 1918), 220–4; H. Swarzenski, *The Berthold Missal* (New York, 1943), 50, fig. 71; *id.* (*op. cit.*, note 4), fig. 490; *Catalogue*, no. 302.

[46] Admittedly William of Canterbury, writing in the period 1172/74 already refers to Becket relics in France, Flanders and Italy, but obviously Canterbury was always the major source of the relics: see e.g. H. E. J. Cowdrey, 'An early record at Dijon of the export of Becket's relics', *Bull. Inst. Historical Research*, liv, 130 (November, 1981), 251–3. In fact Breck's theory that the casket was made for two phials of Thomas's blood presented by John of Salisbury to Chartres is perfectly plausible, even if unprovable; the interior was formerly divided in two by a metal partition, and the casket is first recorded in France: see Alfred Darcel, *Gazette des Beaux-Arts*, xix (December, 1865), 508–10, engraving. The iconography of the New York casket is unique; this martyrdom is not related to the standard depiction of the scene as shown on the early Becket textiles and Limoges *châsses* (see *Catalogue*, nos. 492, 292).

[47] D. Kötzsche, 'Die Kölner Niello-Kelchkuppa und ihr Umkreis', *The Year 1200: a Symposium* (Metropolitan Museum of Art, New York, 1975), 139–62.

[48] *Id.*, 'Eine romanische Grubenschmelzplatte aus dem Berliner Kunstgewerbemuseum', *Festschrift für Peter Metz* (Berlin, 1965), 154–69.

[49] Swarzenski, *op. cit.* (note 4), fig. 426.

[50] e.g. on the enamelled colonnette in the Chicago Art Institute (inv. 1943.83), see M. R. Rogers and O. Goetz, *Handbook to the Lucy Maud Buckingham Medieval Collection* (1945), no. 32 (pl. XXXIII); and on numerous *vernis brun* objects of Mosan manufacture, e.g. the reverse of a phylactery in the Boston Museum of Fine Arts.

[51] The relief at Schwarzrheindorf is rephotographed from Dr H. A. Diepen, *Die romanische Bauornamentik in Klosterrath . . .* (The Hague, 1931), Taf. liii, 4.

[52] The charter, which refers to the Cologne hall, is printed in K. Höhlbaum (ed.), *Hansisches Urkundenbuch*, i (Halle, 1876), 8–9 (no. 14), where it is dated *c.* 1157. It is not in fact dated precisely within Henry II's reign and may well be of the 1170s, see C. N. L. Brooke and G. Keir, *London 800–1216: The Shaping of a City* (London, 1975), 268.

[53] F. Witte, *Die Schatzkammer des Domes zu Köln* (Augsburg/Cologne/Vienna, 1927), 13, Abb. 18. See also *Catalogue*, no. 307.

[54] Dr Roswitha Neu-Kock kindly studied the staff for me, prior to the exhibition. She suggested a comparison of the nielloed silver beasts on the reverse of the three-pronged stand at the top of the staff with thirteenth-century metalwork in the Oignies Treasury at Namur.

[55] The cast Adoration group which crowns the staff is attributable to Archbishop Wilhelm von Gennep (1349–62); the arms of Gennep and Eppstein (?) adorn the socle beneath the group: see most recently J. M. Fritz, *Goldschmiedekunst der Gotik in Mitteleuropa* (Munich, 1982), Abb. 109 (p. 200).

[56] Extensive repairs to the base of the top platform; modern mounts to one of the rock-crystals.

[57] Published photographs show more than one alteration to the way the twelfth-century mounts have been ordered since the 1930s.

[58] V. P. Darkevich, *Proizvedeniya Zapadnogo khudozhestvennogo remesla v Vostochnoi Evrope (X–XIV vv)*, Arkheologiya SSR—Svod Arkheologicheskikh Istochnikov El-57 (Moscow, 1966), no. 69 (pl. 19)—from the mouth of the River Ob, i.e. from beyond the Ural mountains.

[59] Ills. V. P. Darkevich, *Svetskoye Iskusstvo Vizantii. Proizvedeniya visantiiskogo khudozhestvee-nogo remesla v Vostochnoi Europe X–XIII vekov* (Moscow, 1975), 100 ff., 118 ff.; N. V. Fedor-ova, 'Dua Serebryanykh sosyda iz Raiona g Surguta', *Sovetskaya Archeologiya*, 1982/1, 183–94.

[60] *Catalogue*, no. 308. For the conflicting evidence, see *Collection Basilewsky. Catalogue raisonné, précédé d'un essai...*, by A. Darcel and A. Basilewsky (Paris, 1874), 65 (essai); 51 (no. 139), pl. xxi (catalogue): 'dit-on, trouvé en Hongrie'. See also Darkevich, *op. cit.* (note 58), 38–9 (no. 68): 'found on the lower banks of the river Ob'.

[61] Andersson, *op. cit.* (note 8), 55–6 (for the circumstances of the find); no. 16 (pp. 56–8). See also *Catalogue*, no. 306.

[62] For these various features, see E. Rupin, *L'Oeuvre de Limoges* (Paris, 1890), figs. 182–4 (lattice layout, cast heads, grotesque animals), 225 (fluted leaf motif); W. L. Hildburgh, *Medieval Spanish Enamels* (London, 1936), fig. 6d (closely similar *vermiculé*). See also J. J. Marquet de Vasselot, *Les Crosses limousines du XIIIe siècle* (Paris, 1941), pls. ii (no. 10), xxix (no. 17), xxx, xxxi. For the Limoges crosier, illustrated in pl. XXc, see M.-M. Gauthier and G. François, *Medieval Enamels. Masterpieces from the Keir Collection* (British Museum, 1981), no. 7. So specific is the Limoges repertory found on the cups that I cannot agree with Andersson (*op. cit.* (note 8), 21): 'these are simply the fashions of the time...'.

[63] The reference occurs in a letter of *c.* 1170 written by a certain John, attached to the circle of Archbishop Thomas Becket during his exile in France. See J. Labarte, *Histoire des art industriels au moyen âge...*, 2nd edn., iii (Paris, 1875), 133–6.

[64] cf. Swarzenski, *op. cit.* (note 4), fig. 528, with Andersson, *op. cit.* (note 8), pls. 16c–d.

[65] *Catalogue*, nos. 293, 294.

[66] *Catalogue*, no. 291.

[67] O. Lehmann-Brockhaus, *Lateinische Schriftquellen zur Kunst in England, Wales und Schottland vom Jahre 901 bis zum Jahre 1307* (Munich, 1956), no. 2735.

[68] *Ibid.*, no. 2901.

[69] C. R. Dodwell, *Anglo-Saxon Art. A New Perspective* (Manchester, 1982), 78, 270 (nn. 261–2).

[70] I have recently argued that the enamelled 'Henry of Blois plaques' are by a Mosan goldsmith working in England, see *BAA Conference Trans.* vi for 1980 (1983), 28–37, pls. x–xiii. See also *Catalogue*, no. 242 (the Rattlesden St John).

Seals as Evidence for Metalworking in England in the Later Twelfth Century

T. A. Heslop, F.S.A.

Although the statistical sample is small, a good case can be made for saying that between A.D. 1000 and about 1160 the majority of English seal matrices were of carved bone, ivory or stone. Most of them belonged to private individuals who have yet to be identified,[1] but some, for example the walrus ivory matrix of St Albans Abbey and the 'bone seal' used by the Dean and Chapter of Salisbury Cathedral until 1214, were made for important institutions.[2] It was not, therefore, merely a question of wealth determining the material used. In addition, there is a surviving stone matrix of an abbot's seal which was shown in the recent exhibition of English Romanesque Art, in London, which is probably late eleventh-century.[3]

With the single exception of a lead matrix of a late eleventh-century bishop of Chester,[4] we have no surviving early Romanesque seal-dies of metal. It is only from about 1140 that the evidence begins to accumulate. The silver seal matrix, now sadly untraceable, of Milo of Gloucester is known from casts, engravings and descriptions,[5] but the matrix, also silver, of Lincoln Cathedral is still extant.[6] There must once have been more metal matrices than this. All the great seals of the kings, from Edward the Confessor onwards, and all subsequent two-sided seals such as Waleran of Meulan's second seal, needed to be of metal, since only metal (though probably not lead) would have been strong enough to withstand the strain of a seal press, which two-sided seals needed to make an impression.[7] However, in order to control the statistical sample and compare like with like, we must restrict ourselves to the surviving or recorded material, so that, for the moment, two-sided seals will be left out of the reckoning. When that is done, it is noticeable that from a period c. 1000 to 1160 with three recorded metal matrices as against at least nine known bone, ivory or stone ones, we move to a period, at the end of the twelfth and beginning of the thirteenth centuries, with an overwhelming predominance of metal over all other media.

We know depressingly little about the makers of seals in this period. The earliest reference seems to be to a forgery. We are told in the *Gesta Abbatum* of St Albans that the abbot, Ralph Gubion (1146–51), discovered an uncut seal, *sigillum non insculptum*, on the metalworking table, *mensam aurifabrilem*, of the goldsmith Anketil, and, suspecting evil intent, he deposed the prior of the monastery, one Alcuin,[8] It is not until the end of the century and later that we have references to the commissioning of genuine seals from named individuals. Then, when we are given their titles, they too are called 'goldsmith'. Thus for a seal made for Richard I in 1194–5, William the Goldsmith was paid 2 marks, and Master Walter de Ripa, goldsmith, received 40*s*. in November 1218 for his work on Henry III's first great seal.[9] Interestingly, both men were reimbursed an additional 5 marks for the weight of silver used, and this suggests that they were wealthy enough to acquire raw materials on their own account rather than depending on the patrons to provide them from the outset. Surviving accounts from Canterbury Cathedral refer to Simon the Goldsmith, who made a seal in 1221, and a later charter mentions Nigel the Goldsmith *qui fecit sigillum*, almost certainly the large two-sided seal made in 1232 at a cost of £7. 6*s*. 8*d*.[10] It is not until the second half of the thirteenth century that we find consistent references to *sigillarius* or *factor sigillorum*, that is to people who seem to have been specialist seal-die makers. The rise of this craft, probably catering largely for the lower end of the market, reflects the increasing need for and use of seals during the thirteenth century[11]

Thus, so far as our evidence goes, it suggests that 'goldsmiths' made the metal seal-dies which became increasingly popular in the later twelfth and early thirteenth centuries. This is amply borne out by the surviving material evidence. The silver matrix of the capitular seal of Lincoln Cathedral, mentioned above, is engraved with an image of the Virgin and Child enthroned. On the back of the die was, until it was covered over with a silver plate which was riveted on at some point in the last ninety years, an engraved representation of Christ blessing, seated on the rainbow (pl. XXII*c*). The background to this image comprises niello scrollwork of a type closely comparable with such objects as the St Oswald's head reliquary at Hildesheim. This material has been discussed by Jane Geddes and Neil Stratford from the point of view of the likely places where the technique originated and was practised.[12] For the present purposes what matters is that it demonstrates that the matrix-maker was master of more than simply the technique of engraving and that this object would have required a workshop of sorts for creating and applying the metal sulphide.[13] Within current and medieval usage of the term this craftsman is entitled to be called 'goldsmith'.

Although the die side of the matrix is usually engraved at this period, the reverses sometimes show other techniques. The Exeter City silver matrix, signed by a metalworker called Lucas, who seems to have been based in the south-west, has a strap with a foliate-ended scroll to either side of it.[14] This was soldered on. A more elaborate version of this form is found on the reverse of the Chichester Cathedral matrix, probably dating from around 1220 (pl. XXII*b*).[15] This was possibly cast, but certainly engraved and soldered on. The surplus solder was filed away round the edge of the foliage and the leaves themselves also show signs of filing. The die side (pl. XXII*a*) is also filed, since very similar scratch marks appear on its surface, for example around the right-hand star, where a scratch is seen continuing on either side of a star point. The perfect alignment of the mark across the point suggests that it existed prior to the making of the star itself and this indicates that the star was cut into the matrix, not cast into it. Engraving is also very evident on the lettering, roof-tiles and stonework. It is worth noting that the mortar lines of the latter were originally marked out with a stylus in a different position from that which they now occupy. This demonstrates that much of the detailing, at least, was left until a fairly advanced stage in the production. It is possible that punches or drills were used for the dots in the punctuation, within the letters and on the finials of the building. For confirmation of the use of punches, however, by far the best evidence from the period exists on the matrix of Robert FitzWalter (pl. XXII*d*) which, to judge by the shape of his shield, with its rounded upper corners, and the helmet which curves under the chin towards the throat, probably dates from around 1215.[16] On this die we find punches used for the mail coat and, most clearly, the quatrefoils on the horse's caparison and in the punctuation. A single dot punch is also used. By the time Benvenuto Cellini wrote his treatise on goldsmithry in the mid sixteenth century, punches were used for the lettering on seals, but at this stage they seem to have been made only for tiny, often-repeated details.[17]

A final technical accomplishment required by at least some sealmakers was gem-setting. Those gem matrices I have examined are remarkably consistent in their construction. The stone is secured between a silver rim and a back plate which is soldered to it. Not infrequently, the reverses of such seals have decorative handles,[18] usually in the form of foliage, and these too are soldered on.

So far the discussion has centred on silver matrices, and there is an obvious reason: bronze seals are much less varied in their execution, being simply engraved at this date. A good example is the matrix of Payn of Chaworth which probably dates from *c*. 1202.[19] However, from the silver matrices mentioned in the preceding section we are in a position to say that their makers were used not only to engraving, but to niello, solder, stamped-work and gem-setting at least, and possibly casting as well.

However, the best reason for considering such people as versatile goldsmiths capable of, for example, making a large shrine, may lie in the quality of the figures, draperies and lettering executed on seals. The next section examines briefly nine seals which survive only as impressions. All the examples come from the period *c*. 1180–1200 and they have been chosen both because of the skill manifest in making the original matrix and the chance preservation of a good impression. The number could be considerably augmented, particularly if wax fragments of once beautiful seals were taken into account. In what follows the material is discussed in roughly chronological order.

In the case of two seals it is possible to reconstruct something of the terms of their commission. William de Mandeville, Earl of Essex, had a new seal made around 1180 (pl. XXV*a*) which is closely based on that used by Philip of Alsace, Count of Flanders, from 1168 (pl. XXV*b*).[20] This might be explained as no more than the sealmaker himself choosing an elegant and appropriate model were it not for the fact that William and Philip were comrades in arms who, in 1180,

PLATE XXII

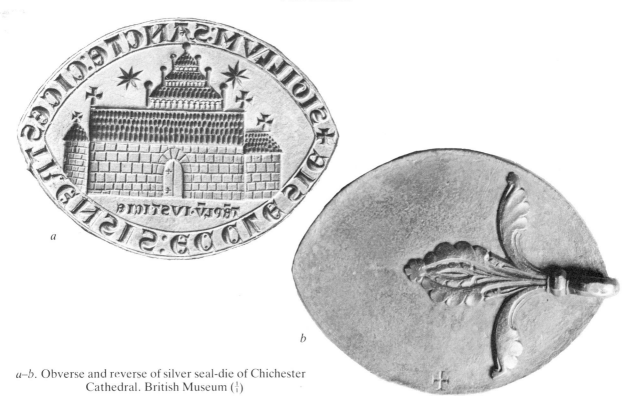

a–b. Obverse and reverse of silver seal-die of Chichester Cathedral. British Museum ($\frac{1}{1}$)

c. Reverse of the silver seal-die of Lincoln Cathedral (from a nineteenth-century photograph). Society of Antiquaries ($\frac{1}{1}$)

Photograph: British Museum

d. Silver seal-die of Robert Fitzwalter. British Museum ($\frac{1}{1}$)

PLATE XXIII

Photograph: Courtauld Institute of Art

a. Seal of Abbot Samson of Bury St Edmunds: cast ($\frac{1}{1}$)

b. Obverse of the great seal of King John: impression. Eton College ($\frac{3}{4}$)

c. Obverse of the first great seal of Richard I: cast. Society of Antiquaries ($\frac{3}{4}$)

d. Obverse of the second great seal of Richard I: cast. Society of Antiquaries ($\frac{3}{4}$)

PLATE XXIV

a. Seal of Waltham Abbey: cast ($\frac{1}{1}$)

Photograph: Ursula Edelman

b. Kneeling angel of gilt bronze. Liebighaus, Frankfurt ($\frac{1}{1}$)

c. Seal of Walden Abbey; cast ($\frac{1}{1}$)

Photograph: Bildarchiv Marburg

d. The Magi before Herod, detail from a silver ciborium. St-Maurice d'Agaune

PLATE XXV

Photograph: Sotheby's

a. Seal of William de Mandeville: impression.
Westminster Abbey, reproduced by courtesy
of the Dean and Chapter of Westminster ($\frac{3}{4}$)

Photograph: Warburg Institute

b. Seal of Philip of Alsace; cast. Archives
Nationales, Paris ($\frac{3}{4}$)

c. Obverse of the seal of St Augustine's,
Canterbury: cast ($\frac{1}{1}$)

d. Obverse of the seal of Westminster Abbey: cast.
Society of Antiquaries ($\frac{1}{1}$)

had recently returned from crusading together.[21] We may presume with some justification that William knew Philip's seal and that his admiration for it caused him to specify that its design should be used as a basis for his own. If anything, the derivative improves on the prototype. The flying ends of the surcoat and the implied twist in the riders waist, as well as the lively drawing of the horse, give William's image a sense of movement which is nascent in Philip's. Here, then, is the work of a craftsman of some independence and considerable skill.

The second instance concerns both the appearance of a seal and what a writer, Jocelin of Brakelond, says about it. He remarks that Abbot Samson of Bury St Edmunds required that his seal 'show him wearing a mitre, though his predecessors had not the like'.[22] It is probable that the matrix, which Jocelin tells was made in 1182, is that from which we have surviving impressions from later in Samson's abbacy (pl. XXIIIa). Jocelin, who seems to have been rather interested in seals, mentions only one seal being made for the abbot, though he lays great stress on the fact that Samson borrowed and used the prior's seal until his own was ready. The stocky, robust proportions of the figure may reflect the abbot's actual appearance since, like the straightsided head with salient cheekbones and hollow cheeks, they are sufficiently individual to suggest that the sealmaker knew his patron.[23] Certainly the head shown here does not strike one either as formulaic or as an idealized type. Thus some claim to a precocious interest in the naturalism associated with portraiture can be suggested on behalf of this artist.

It has to be acknowledged that neither of these seals can be proved to have had a metal matrix though, as argued above, their dates make this likely. Furthermore, William's is over 3 in. (7.6 cm.) across and hence too large to have come from a walrus tusk. Indeed no surviving English medieval matrix of this size is made of anything other than metal.

The next two seals to be considered, of Waltham and Walden abbeys,[24] can again only be assumed to have had metal matrices. However, in the case of Waltham's (pl. XXIVa) this assumption is virtually certain, since in the fourteenth century the original die was transformed from a pointed oval to a circle by the addition of traceried panels. These must surely have been of metal, presumably silver, and soldered onto the original core, since even the careful dowelling and glueing of bone or ivory would scarcely have produced an object strong enough to withstand the taking of countless impressions. Whatever the material, though, it is clear that the closest stylistic comparisons are with pieces of metalwork.

The angels on the Waltham seal clearly derive from Mosan representations in the tradition of the Liège font.[25] The naturalistic swathes of drapery drawn round the figure, with the folds of the sleeves, and of the cloak around the thighs, converging on the centre of the body, are very similar. Where they differ is in the depth of these folds and in the length and relative angularity of the profile heads. These details suggest a source in the second half of the twelfth century, the date usually assigned to a cast bronze angel now in Frankfurt (pl. XXIVb) which has the features of the seal which the font lacks.[26]

Walden Abbey's seal is rather different in style (pl. XXIVc). The drapery, for example, does not form self-consciously graceful loops. Indeed in places, such as around the hem of cloak and tunic, there is an angularity of line. These contrast with those parts where the cloth is pulled against the curving forms of the body. In its varied combination of fold types this seal is very close indeed to the scenes on a ciborium at St-Maurice d'Agaune.[27] Here, too, are the juxta-positions of angular and clinging folds, and also of broad, flat-topped pleats and finer curving corrugations. Even the loop of cloth in the saint's right hand has parallels, for example over Herod's wrist in the scene where he questions the Magi (pl. XXIV*d*).

The histories of the houses at Waltham and Walden in the later twelfth century have much in common. Both were elevated to the status of abbey, the former in 1184 and the latter in 1190, and both were, at those times, under royal patron-age.[28] It is tempting to suppose that their new seal matrices were produced, as part of the general aggrandizement they were experiencing, by goldsmiths who worked for the court. This possibility is borne out by a comparison of the Waltham seal (pl. XXIV*a*) and King John's great seal of 1199 (pl. XXIII*b*).[29] The letter forms used (for example R with a sharp angle high on its diagonal leg and uncial E and h), the spacing of the words and he use of a fine, solid bounding line are very similar. Furthermore, even though the figure poses can not be usefully juxtaposed, the configuration and gently swathing curvature of the draperies, the handling of relief and the assimilation of detail to overall structure indicate artistic priorities and predilections that are distinctive and indi-vidual enough to suggest that the two seals might be the work of one maker.

Like John's great seal, Richard I's are two-sided and of considerable size (about 10 cm. across), so their matrices will have been of metal;[30] indeed, as noted above, Richard's second seal is documented as being silver and weighing 5 marks. Rather than indulging here in a detailed comparison of the three royal seals, it will, I hope, suffice to reproduce the majesty side of each of them (pl. XXIII*b–d*). Here the variations in figure proportion, drapery style, quality of relief, character and form of lettering and punctuation, will be obvious enough. There is no hint that these three dies were cut by a single goldsmith.

A similar demonstration can be carried out with the two-sided seals of St Augustine's Abbey, Canterbury, made in 1198–9 (pl. XXV*c*), and Westminster Abbey (pl. XXV*d*).[31] If there were common craftsmanship involved it ought to be evident in the sides showing the dedicatory saints of the two houses: St Augustine and St Peter. Here again, though, it is the discrepancies which are striking. To take a small but symptomatic difference, the pallium worn by Augus-tine hangs straight around his neck and down his body, unmodulated by the folds of the chasuble over which it passes. On the other hand, St Peter's pallium hangs from his shoulders in a curve across his chest and then the descending strip undulates over the ridges of the garment beneath. Whatever one compares is different, whether halo and throne, lettering and bounding line (which is beaded in one case and unbroken in the other), or proportions and attitudes to symmetry.

By now we have examined, albeit briefly, nine seals which can be dated with some confidence to the twenty years between 1180 and 1200 and among them we have found only two for which common authorship seems even a possibility. The number surveyed could quite easily be trebled without our necessarily finding more than two or three cases where a single maker produced more than one seal. Of these nine seals, several have links with the court, perhaps through the shadowy institution known as the King's goldsmiths, of whom there seem to have been eight at any one time.[32] However, there were clearly more than eight seal-makers of considerable flair working in England in the last twenty years of the twelfth century who practised accomplished versions of the group of styles, still passing unhappily under the name of 'transitional', which was finding favour in north-western Europe at the time. Whatever the nationality of these artists, and there is no reason to suppose that they were not English, there was clearly a market for their work which was abreast of the latest fashions. The majority of the matrices made for wealthy individuals and institutions appear from the visual evidence to be unique survivals of their makers' work in this medium. The single instance (of the St-Maurice ciborium) where a seal can be positively compared with a rare, extant piece of English silverwork from the period serves to emphasize two general conclusions which may be drawn from this paper: firstly, that since they did not spend their time making lots of other seals, these craftsmen presumably made other types of object; and secondly, that if one wanted high-quality goldsmiths' work in late twelfth-century England, there were plenty of artists capable of providing it.

NOTES

[1] Hayward Gallery *Catalogue*, nos. 368, 369, 373–5; and see A. Way, 'Notice of a seal of bone discovered in the abbey church of St Albans ...', *Associated Architectural Societies' Reports & Papers*, i (1850–1), 208–12. A further, recently excavated, example is in the care of the Trust for Lincolnshire Archaeology, who kindly sent me a photograph. It bears the fragmentary legend SIGNO SIGILLATUR LEGATIO, so that its ownership by an individual is open to dispute.

[2] *Catalogue*, no. 363; and for Salisbury see O. Lehmann-Brockhaus, *Lateinische Schriftquellen zur Kunst in England, Wales und Schottland vom Jahre 901 bis zum 1307*, iii (Munich, 1955), nos. 6382 and 6387.

[3] *Catalogue*, no. 363, and now D. C. Cox and T. A. Heslop, 'An eleventh-century seal matrix from Evesham, Worcs.', *Antiq. J.* lxiv (1984), 396.

[4] Published by John Cherry in *Antiq. J.* lxv (1985), 472.

[5] Exhibited at the Society of Antiquaries of London in 1800 by the Bishop of Salisbury; *Archaeologia*, xiv (1808), 276 and pl. XLVII, 4, opp. p. 271. An electrotype of the matrix still exists at the Society.

[6] *Catalogue*, no. 360.

[7] On Waleran's seals see now E. King, 'Waleran, count of Meulan, earl of Worcester (1104–1166)', in *Tradition and Change in the Central Middle Ages: Essays in Honour of Marjorie Chibnall*, ed. C. Holdsworth, D. E. Greenway and J. Sayers (Cambridge, 1985), 166–8 and 171–6. for a photograph of a surviving early thirteenth-century seal press see T. A. Heslop, 'The Conventual seals of Canterbury Cathedral', *BAA Conference Trans.* v (1982), pl. XXVII, D.

[8] Lehmann-Brockhaus, *op. cit.* (note 2), no. 6376. For Anketil's career see C. C. Oman, 'The goldsmiths of St Albans during the twelfth and thirteenth centuries', *St Albans & Herts. Architect. & Arch. Soc. Trans.* (1932), 218–19, and O. Pächt, F. Wormald and C. R. Dodwell, *The St Albans Psalter* (1960), 172–6.

[9] For Richard's seal see Lionel Landon, *The Itinerary of Richard I*, Pipe Roll Society, n.s. xiii (1935), Appx. A, p. 178, and for Henry's, H. S. Kingsford, 'Some English medieval seal engravers', *Arch. J.* xcvii (1940), 158–9

[10] Heslop, *op cit.* (note 7), 94–5.

[11] Henry the Sealmaker (*Sigillarius*) occurs in R. R. Sharpe (ed.), *The Calendar of Letter Book A* (Guildhall Library and Museum, 1899), 226, and Adam the Sealmaker (*factor sigillorum*) in the same year in M. Weinbaum (ed.), *The London Eyre of 1276*, London Record Society, 12 (1976), no. 33. I would like to thank William Kellaway for these references.

[12] J. Geddes, 'The twelfth-century metalwork at Durham Cathedral', *BAA Conference Trans.* iii (1980), 142–5, and N. Stratford in *Catalogue*, no. 301, and in the present volume, p. 32.

[13] On the technique of niello see S. La Niece, 'Niello: an historical and technical survey', *Antiq. J.* lxiii (1983), 279–97.

[14] *Catalogue*, no. 378, and for a photograph of the reverse, Kingsford, *op. cit.* (note 9), pl. 1 opp. p. 176.

[15] A. B. Tonnochy, *Catalogue of British Seal Dies in the British Museum* (London, 1952), no. 794. I would like to thank John Cherry for showing me matrices in the British Museum and discussing them with me.

[16] G. Henderson, 'Romance and politics on some English medieval seals', *Art History*, i (1978), 33–8.

[17] *The Treatises of Benvenuto Cellini on Goldsmithing and Sculpture,* trans. C. R. Ashbee (New York, 1967), 65.

[18] From example P. Nelson, 'Some British medieval seal-matrices', *Arch. J.* xciii (1936), no. 28, pl. II, 6 and 11 and no. 30, pl. II, 12 and 13.

[19] J. Cherry, 'Two equestrian seal dies', in *Medieval and Later New Acquisitions 1976–1978,* BM Occ. Pap. x (1980), 31–2.

[20] *Catalogue*, no. 376, and for Philip, Count of Flanders, Stuttgart, Württembergisches Landesmuseum, *Die Zeit der Staufer, Geschichte-Kunst-Kultur*, i (1977), no. 67. The earliest extant datable example of William's second seal is probably that at Belvoir Castle on a charter of Easter 1181. Although I have not seen it, it is, to judge from the legend given in *The Manuscripts of his Grace the Duke of Rutland Preserved at Belvoir Castle*, iv, Historical Manuscripts Commission (1905), 6 (MANDE . . . ES ESSEXE), this seal and not his first, which reads SIGILLUM WILLELMI COMITIS DE ESSEX . . . For this first seal see W. de G. Birch, *Catalogue of Seals in the British Museum*, ii (London, 1892), nos. 6200–2 and pl. IX.

[21] On William's career see *The Complete Peerage*, v (1926), ed. V. Gibbs and H. A. Doubleday, 118–19, and for Philip's ineffectual crusading S. Runciman, *A History of the Crusades*, ii (Harmondsworth, 1972), 414–16.

[22] Lehmann-Brockhaus, *op. cit.* (note 2), no. 6379. On Samson's seal see R. H. C. Davis, *The Calendar of Abbot Samson*, Camden 3rd ser. lxxxiv (1954), viii. In addition there are impressions at Durham (see *Arch. Ael.* 3rd ser. xv (1918), 160, no. 3419), Westminster Abbey (Westminster Abbey Muniments 17315) and Canterbury (Cathedral Archives), whence the cast from which my plate was taken originated.

[23] Jocelin describes Samson as 'of middling stature, virtually bald, his face neither long nor round, his lips thick, his eyes as clear as crystal and with a watchful gaze, . . . his eyebrows increasing in length were often cut'. See H. E. Butler (ed.), *The Chronicle of Jocelin of Brakelond* (London, 1949), 39.

[24] *Catalogue*, nos. 361 and 362. As noted there, the earliest extant impression from Waltham is on a charter datable to 1184–1201, and from Walden on PRO DL 27/6, dating from the abbacy of Robert *c.* 1204–13.

[25] P. Lasko, *Ars Sacra 800–1200* (Harmondsworth, 1972), 162–3 and pl. 169.

[26] *Die Zeit der Staufer* (see note 20), i (1977), no. 547.

[27] *Catalogue*, no. 309.

[28] VCH, *Essex*, ii (1907), 111 and 167.

[29] *Catalogue*, no. 335.

[30] For Richard's seals, Landon, *op cit.* (note 9).

[31] W. de G. Birch, *Catalogue of Seals in the British Museum*, i (London, 1887), no. 2843, St Augustine's (where the date is wrongly given as 1188–9 for *recte* 1198–9, for which see the legend on the reverse), and nos. 4300–4 for Westminster. The earliest appearance of the latter is on Additional Charter 8473, the date of which is fixed by the abbacy of Ralph of Arundel (1200–14, see D. Knowles, C. N. L. Brooke and V. London, *The Heads of Religious Houses, England and Wales 940–1216* (Cambridge, 1972), 77). Westminster and St Augustine's are the first two English abbeys to use two-sided seals, and their comparable size and iconography may indicate direct rivalry and similar date. On the iconography see G. Henderson, 'The Damnation of Nero and related themes', in A. Borg and A. Martindale (eds.), *The Vanishing Past, Studies . . . presented to Christopher Hohler,* BAR S111 (Oxford, 1981), 39 ff. See also Heslop, *op. cit.* (note 7), 98.

[32] F. M. Stenton, 'Norman London', in D. M. Stenton (ed.), *Preparatory to Anglo-Saxon England* (Oxford, 1970), 43–4.

English Romanesque Book Illumination: Changes in the Field 1974–1984

C. M. Kauffmann

Of all aspects of English Romanesque art, the manuscripts have received most attention and the changes in the perception of the field have been less spectacular than in other areas. Nonetheless, there have been numerous publications, including three majestic tomes, which, taken together, present a formidable body of research. This survey is intended to provide a brief coverage of the material published since the completion of the Romanesque volume of the Harvey Miller *Survey of Manuscripts Illuminated in the British Isles* (1975). Not every contribution can be discussed here, but the bibliography (p. 68) provides a measure of support for the main argument.

Chronological survey

The fundamental question of whether narrative illustration survived the Conquest is raised in Malcolm Baker's work on the illustrations to Bede's Life of St Cuthbert (Oxford, University College MS 165: *Catalogue*, no. 15). In his view—supported by D. H. Farmer in a separate note—the absence of a second set of miracles added to the series shortly after 1100 and the lack of any mention of the translation of Cuthbert's relics fixes the date at *c.* 1100 and at any rate before the translation of 1104. From a comparison of University College 165 with the four later cycles (Cambridge, Trinity College MS 0.1.64, 1 drawing; London, BL Yates Thompson MS 26; Carlisle choir stalls; and York windows), Baker concludes that these cannot be directly dependent upon University College 165, but that both derive from a lost archetype. This must, by implication, date after the foundation of the Benedictine priory at Durham in 1083 and before *c.* 1100, the presumed date of University College 165. This conclusion, though incapable of direct proof, demolishes the general belief that there were no narrative cycles between the Conquest and the early twelfth century. Baker also discusses the Yates Thompson MS and demonstrates how the narrative scenes have been split up and converted into icon-like images of the saint, who is invoked to protect the monastic community in its struggles against the Bishop, Hugh du Puiset, which came to a head in 1195.

These conclusions are similar to those of Barbara Abou-El-Haj on the second great saint's life of twelfth-century England: the Life of St Edmund in the Pierpont Morgan Library, New York (MS 736: *Catalogue*, no. 20) though this is clearly a shrine book, with liturgical elements, whereas University College 165 was, according to D. H. Farmer, more probably made for private devotion. She links the selection of the text and the illustrative cycle, with its emphasis on the violation of the saint's shrine, very firmly with the attacks on the abbey by both Henry I, who kept the abbacy vacant from 1102 to 1121, and Herbert de Losinga, Bishop of Norwich. These arguments are very convincing and provide new insight into several of the miniatures; but it is a pity that the controversially early date, '*c*. 1125', based on copy letters bound with the manuscript, is accepted without discussion.[1]

Rodney Thomson's *Manuscripts from St Albans Abbey, 1066–1235* is one of the three major books to have appeared in the decade. He examines the production of manuscripts at St Albans as an indication of intellectual and artistic achievement. From the time of Paul of Caen, who introduced Norman monasticism after the Conquest and founded a scriptorium, through the high watermarks of the abbacies of Geoffrey Gorron (1119–46) and Simon (1167–83), Thomson discusses the content, script and make-up of non-illuminated as well as illuminated manuscripts. The very precise date, 1119–23, for the St Albans Psalter is abandoned in favour of a more general *c.* 1120–30 and the whole group of manuscripts is re-examined in codicological terms. For the mid century, the discussion centres on itinerant artists illuminating manuscripts for St Albans: the Lambeth Bible Master or a follower, the Winchester Master of the Apocrypha Drawings and Oakeshott's Entangled Figures Master. This discussion of itinerant workshops covers some of the ground traversed by Larry Ayres in his two articles on the 'Angevin style'. On the abbacy of Simon, Thomson stresses the importance of the arrival of *magistri*, trained in Paris, as part of an attempt to attract educated men to St Albans in face of competition from the cathedral schools and new universities. The result was immediately visible in St Albans manuscripts—the Ralph of Flaix Commentary on Leviticus (Cambridge, Trinity Hall MS 2: *Catalogue*, no. 70) was one of the very earliest copies of a Parisian commentary that was to become a standard text.

Well over a third of Thomson's book is devoted to a detailed descriptive catalogue of 106 manuscripts made at, kept at, or in some way linked with St Albans in the twelfth or early thirteenth centuries. It is a model of its kind, presenting complete textual, palaeographical, codicological and art-historical examination with a professionalism that will henceforth set the standard for such catalogues. The danger inherent in such detailed treatment of one centre is that the subject takes on an overriding importance: to the cursory reader everything appears to have originated at St Albans. Thomson, indeed, is very careful not to make exaggerated claims, yet many of the most famous manuscripts described in the catalogue—including the Shaftesbury and Copenhagen Psalters—have nothing to do with St Albans. All this highlights the problem of accommodating the itinerant artists, who dominate English illumination from the 1120s, in the treatment of single monastic centres, though it should not be taken as a serious criticism of Thomson's important book.

The scriptorium at Bury St Edmunds has been discussed in a series of articles by Elizabeth Parker McLachlan (1978a). George Henderson (1981) has examined the picture cycle of the Pembroke College New Testament (*Catalogue*, no. 21) and concluded that the sequence of scenes was influenced by liturgical factors: some scenes are shaken out of narrative order by readings and antiphons at liturgical hours. For the Bury Bible (*Catalogue*, no. 44), Thomson (1975) has managed to confirm the pre-1138 date by a close study of Bury charters, while Cahn (1982) suggests that the illuminated *incipit* page of Jerome's prologue is based on an Italian device, though the search for Italian stylistic sources continues to prove unproductive.

In a stimulating article on the Eadwine Psalter (*Catalogue*, no. 62), George Zarnecki (1981) has proposed that the great portrait belongs to a distinctly later stylistic phase than the Psalm illustrations and has adduced for comparison the wall painting of St Paul in the Anselm Chapel at Canterbury Cathedral (*c.* 1163) and the Copenhagen Psalter (*c.* 1170–5). He suggests that it is painted on an additional leaf and is not part of the original Psalter. However, Sydney M. Cockerell, who rebound the manuscript, is convinced that the last leaf, on which the portrait is painted, formed part of the original manuscript and this view is endorsed by Verfaillie-Markey (1983), who has carried out a codicological examination of the last two quires. Equally, it is unlikely that the portrait was painted on the verso of the last folio years after the manuscript was bound.

Yet Zarnecki is surely right to suggest that the Eadwine portrait is later than the date (*c.* 1145) usually given to the Psalter owing to the marginal reference to the comet of that date, even if his comparison with the Copenhagen Psalter is not entirely convincing. The extremely hieratic character of the Eadwine portrait belongs to an earlier, strictly Romanesque phase rather than the more sophisticated miniatures of the Copenhagen Psalter, which presage the transitional style. Such a late date, furthermore, hardly accords with what we know of Canterbury manuscripts of the later twelfth century. The Eadwine portrait certainly looks earlier than the picture of Dunstan in BL MS Royal 10.A.XIII (*Catalogue*, no. 71), which can be placed *c.* 1170–80. A likely solution is a date *c.* 1150–60 for the whole manuscript. The complex layout of the text and the decorated initials can hardly be placed before 1150 and the gloss, which Margaret Gibson suggests is related to Peter Lombard's, is also most probably of the 1150s. The fact that the Psalter illustrations look earlier can be explained by their close adherence to an earlier model (cf. Heimann 1975). At any rate we are now promised a full study and publication of the Psalter, to be edited by Margaret Gibson.

There have been several articles denoting work in progress on the Winchester Psalter (*Catalogue*, no. 61). Kristine Haney has rejected Hyde Abbey as the Psalter's probable home on the grounds of its partial demolition during the Anarchy and has argued firmly in favour of the Old Minster. Her study of the Psalter, to be published by Leicester University Press, is awaited with interest.

Patricia Danz Stirnemann's dissertation on the Copenhagen Psalter is, unfortunately, not widely available, but Jennifer Sheppard's on the Giffard Bible (Oxford, Bodleian Library MS Laud Misc. 752) will shortly be published by the Garland Press. She argues that it is French rather than English, not only from the script but also by comparing the three principal styles with French illumination. Most convincingly, the earliest hand, artist of the Solomon initial, is seen to be strikingly close to the initials in the Bible from Vendôme in Paris (Assemblée Nationale MS 2).

Walter Oakeshott's long-awaited *The Two Winchester Bibles* is the second of the major books to be considered in this survey. It is clearly impossible to summarize the contents of this important work in a few sentences, but worth highlighting some of the main arguments. The Winchester Bible (*Catalogue*, no. 64), begun in *c.* 1155–60 and partially illuminated by the Master of the Leaping Figures at that date, remained long unbound, at least until the period of the Master of the Morgan Leaf, which is placed *c.* 1170–80, and of the Isaiah initial, *c.* 1175–85. Oakeshott confirms Neil Ker's suggestion that the Winchester Bible was corrected from the Auct. Bible (Bodleian Library MS Auct. E. inf. 1–2: *Catalogue*, no. 63), which he identifies with the Bible given to St Hugh of Lincoln for his foundation at Witham in *c.* 1186. However, although the two great books were thus side by side at Winchester in the 1170s, Oakeshott argues that both the text and much of the decoration of the Auct. Bible are in a St Albans tradition and that it was produced not at Winchester but at St Albans. This remains controversial; at any rate Thomson does not accept the argument that the textual tradition necessarily proves a St Albans origin. The question of the decoration is bound up with Oakeshott's hypothesis that the Entangled Figures Master, the main decorator of the Auct. Bible (1160s), is the artist of the Shaftesbury Psalter (1130s) and that the principal peculiarities of his style are to be found in St Albans manuscripts. There can be no doubting the sharp insight of Oakeshott's observation and the general conviction of his argument: the links between the Shaftesbury Psalter and the Auct. Bible are now clear for all to see. On the other hand, it remains open to discussion whether we are dealing with a single artist or a clearly defined stylistic tendency possibly represented by more than one hand. The same caveat should be applied to Thomson's attribution of the two leaves at Corpus Christi College, Oxford, and the calendar illustrations of Bodley MS Auct. D.S.4 to the hand of the Lambeth Bible Master and, more generally, to the rapidly expanding production of the Simon Master. Tricks of style can easily be passed on from master to pupil and until we know more of the organization of itinerant workshops—how many assistants each master may have had—it is perhaps wiser to chart relationships than to attribute too firmly to individual hands. Above all, the danger of now ascribing every manuscript to St Albans is raised in Sandy Heslop's review of Oakeshott's book.

The third major publication of the decade is Christopher de Hamel's *Glossed Books of the Bible and the Origins of the Paris Booktrade*. Pontigny, he convincingly argues, was not the home of the Becket books. They were produced in Paris, where Herbert of Bosham lived from 1174 until 1178, and it was in the workshops of Paris that the new type of glossed book was created. In tracing the development of page layout in twelfth-century glossed texts, he analyses the new system of incorporating the gloss with the main text as typified in the

Becket books. Each page is designed as a single unit to contain a part of the text and the commentary and notes referring to it—no more and no less. The text is written against the left-hand column, with the gloss on three sides, the whole governed by a strict grid system of two lines of gloss allocated the same space as one of text. This layout was the designers' brilliant response to the problems of accommodating with striking clarity the new methods of study and teaching in the period from about 1170.

De Hamel's arguments are masterly and incontrovertible, yet the danger of Paris centricity is as great as that of St Albans in the earlier decades. The question of the English contribution to the white lion style and the tight coils of acanthus foliage of late twelfth-century decoration remains to be analysed. A good starting point could be Jennifer Sheppard's view that the white lion style has its direct forbear in the mid-century Lambeth Bible. Certainly it was England, rather than Paris, that provided a continuing tradition of inventive decoration in the twelfth century.

Trends, aims and methods

a. Monastic scriptoria, itinerant artists, texts

Much of the research carried out in recent years has followed tradition in concerning itself with individual monastic institutions, notably St Albans and Winchester, but Canterbury, Rochester, Bury, Durham and Worcester have also received attention in this way. Such work has confirmed the existence of monastic scriptoria producing books to a uniform pattern, though it does not answer the question of the proportion of monastic to professional scribes. There has been greater stress on the importance of itinerant workshops, in particular those active in France as well as in England, such as the workshops of the Master of the Apocrypha Drawings and the Simon Master. Ayres has ascribed this close Anglo-French relationship to the political circumstances of the Angevin empire, though the continuing monastic and intellectual ties doubtless remained equally important, as de Hamel has shown. The highlighting of these workshops, centred on some of the leading artists of the age, has produced important results, though there may be, as we have seen, a danger of over-enthusiastic identification of individual hands.

Analysis of style and discussion of workshops has been matched by more detailed study of texts. Sheppard's work on the Giffard Bible makes good use of the *Glossa Ordinaria*, the standard medieval compendium of commentary on the Bible, to help elucidate the iconography. This is a more textually based, less hypothetical interpretation than, for example, that of Wayne Dynes on the Stavelot Bible,[2] and it throws light on several of the more unusual illustrations. It does not, however, answer the question of programmes in illustrated Bibles and it may be that we should be satisfied with Walter Cahn's (1982) conclusion that the Bible is too varied to contain a tight programme comparable to those on the portals of the great cathedrals.

Close attention to variants in the texts of glosses, and especially in the prefaces to the books of the Bible, has also proved fruitful. Thomson gives individual references to Steegmüller's *Repertorium Biblicum Medii Aevi* (1940) for each preface in every Bible he catalogues, an invaluable aid to the grouping of manuscripts into textual families. However, a note of caution should be raised. How many manuscripts must there be to render such a textual comparison statistically viable? Thomson rightly criticizes Don Denny for placing the Lambeth Bible in Bury after comparing its prologues with the Bury Bible and Corpus Christi 48: an insufficiently wide comparison when there are other manuscripts of the same textual recension. He then proceeds to postulate a St Albans origin for the Lambeth Bible by adducing five other manuscripts, most of them made at St Albans, with a similar set of prologues. Clearly his evidence is stronger than Denny's, and yet is a comparison of five manuscripts essentially any more conclusive in statistical terms? Perhaps the model to be followed here is James Golob, who identified thousands of significant textual variants in 180 twelfth- and thirteenth-century psalters, which were then collated and processed by computer.[3] His results were disappointingly inconclusive, but the exercise serves as a warning to art historians not to draw too many conclusions from a comparison of five or six texts.

b. Historical context: broader themes

Monastic wealth as listed in Domesday Book has often been invoked to account for the artistic patronage of particular houses in the twelfth century, but there has been little detailed analysis of the economic basis of artistic flowering. In this respect, Brian Golding's paper[4] provides an illuminating insight into how St Albans, with an annual income of only £270 and twelfth down the list in Domesday Book, managed to occupy such a central position in the intellectual and artistic history of twelfth-century England. Certainly, the analysis of the effects of knight service in this connection indicates a hitherto untrodden path.

Art historians can also benefit from recent research into the expansion of learning and growth of literacy in the twelfth century and the extent to which these factors influenced the production, make-up and illustration of manuscripts. M. B. Parkes's essay on 'The influence of the concepts of *Ordinatio* and *Compilatio* on the development of the book',[5] tracing the change from monastic meditation, as a spiritual exercise, to scholastic *lectio*, a process of close study of the text, serves as an introduction to de Hamel's more detailed treatment of the glossed texts.

Another history book of fundamental importance to art historians is M. T. Clanchy's *From Memory to Written Record. England 1066–1307* (1979), which traces the growth of literacy in the twelfth century. It has long been recognized that the sophistication of the English administration at this period, with its standardized documentation, was second to none. Clanchy now draws a parallel between, for example, the unprecedented and unrivalled increase of royal letters and the rapid rise in the number of manuscripts produced, as twin signs of the same process. Certainly, the blossoming of book illumination in twelfth-century England and the wide variety of its manifestations is directly dependent on the growth of book production in a multitude of centres across the country.[6]   Following on Clanchy's book is Franz Bäuml's essay on 'Varieties and consequences of medieval literacy and illiteracy'.[7] Starting with St Gregory's letter ... *pro lectione pictura est*, he examines the close relationship of textual and pictorial communication in the twelfth and thirteenth centuries. His analysis of Romanesque art is very general and at times shows an unawareness of earlier trends. For example, the breaching of the picture frame in the later twelfth century is seen as an important innovation, yet there is no reference to the fact that most drawings of earlier centuries had no frame at all. Bäuml's essay is more thought-provoking for the thirteenth century, when he traces a parallel—if not a direct cause and effect—between the rise of vernacular languages and of greater pictorial realism.

This brings us to the 'new' art history, perhaps not quite as innovative as the claims made for it, but nevertheless with an often stimulating influence particularly from structuralist and Marxist studies. So far the influence on the study of English Romanesque book illumination has not been resounding. To an extent this is because medieval studies have always been more firmly rooted in historical and textual analysis and less dominated by style than the work of more recent periods. A knowledge of the Bible, of typological symbolism and of the liturgy has long been recognized as a more basic qualification for the study of book illumination than a grounding in Wölfflin.

An example of the productive use of new methods is Michael Camille's as yet unpublished study 'Seeing and reading: some visual consequences of medieval literacy and illiteracy'. St Augustine's view of the merely imitative role of pictures compared to the more rational process of reading is likened to the structuralist hierarchy of signs. Starting from Bäuml's discussion of literacy, Camille discusses several illustrations in some depth, for instance Henry I's visions in the Worcester Chronicle (Oxford, Corpus Christi College MS 157: *Catalogue*, no. 33). These are the earliest English chronicle illustrations and the only ones contained in this manuscript, and Camille interprets their purpose and their form as intending to explain the oral origin of the story. For this manuscript and for the other examples he chooses, which include the speechless king in the parable of the wedding feast in the Bury New Testament (Cambridge, Pembroke College MS 120: *Catalogue*, no. 21) and the bear taught to read his ABC in the Canterbury copy of Jerome's commentaries on the Old Testament (Cambridge, Trinity College MS 0.4.7: *Catalogue*, no. 42), his observation is acute and his analysis productive and stimulating. However, the wider claims for the application of structuralist methods to analyse the relationship of text and pictures at this period are, so far, unproven.

'Form is content' is now a familiar theme, but Madeline Caviness, in her paper on 'Images of Divine Order . . .' (1983), reminds us that it was first treated by Adolf Katzenellenbogen over forty years ago. Her own conclusion, that the governing principles which lay behind a variety of pictorial diagrams created a syntax for various means of expressing divinity, takes her far beyond the English material treated in this survey. However, the central example of Byrhtferth's diagram (Oxford, St John's College MS 17: *Catalogue*, no. 34) and its close relation to certain Majesty miniatures and similar compositional schemes, renders her discussion of particular relevance to English illumination.

For the use of historical evidence to elucidate pictures, the largest claims are made for Barbara Abou-El-Haj, whose study of the Life of St Edmund is subtitled 'A history of property, privilege and monastic art production'. She traces the direct influence of historical events on these illustrations, avoiding the pitfall of tracing parallel developments in political history and artistic output and then making a connection. It is an original and clearly argued piece of work, but the drum-beating subtitle should not disguise the fact that neither the method nor the conclusions are, as we have seen, very different to Malcolm Baker's study of the Durham manuscript of Bede's Life of St Cuthbert.

The best of the work surveyed stresses the need for a clearer understanding of historical circumstances and for a closer reading of our texts: laudable if not revolutionary proposals. Stylistic analysis, on the other hand, hardly appears at all. Oakeshott and Cahn, among others, successfully pursue stylistic traits in their attribution to individual hands, but there has been no stylistic analysis on the scale of Pächt's treatment of the St Alban's Psalter or of Garrison's dissection of the damp-fold.[8] This survey also shows us how many of the most basic questions remain unanswered. How many times, for example do we speak of Byzantine influence without a clue as to its mode of transmission (apart from that daily coach to Sicily)? Equally, the influence of religious drama on painting is still invoked, though there has been no resolution of the basic question posed in Swarzenski's review of Pächt: how can one prove that the influence did not move in the opposite direction?[9] And yet, in view of the relatively sparse number of practitioners, the results of the decade's work in this field are surely most encouraging and presage well for the future.

NOTES

[1] cf. *Survey*, 1975, no. 34.

[2] W. Dynes, *The Illuminations of the Stavelot Bible* (Garland Press, 1978), is an illuminating study, even though some conclusions are pressed too far, as is D. Denny, 'The historiated initials of the Lobbes Bible', *Revue Belge d'Archéologie et d'Histoire de l'Art*, xlv (1976), 3–26.

[3] J. Golob, 'The Glossed Psalter of Robert de Lindesey and Related Manuscripts', unpublished Ph.D. thesis, Cambridge, 1981.

[4] Below, pp. 107–17.

[5] M. B. Parkes, in *Medieval Learning and Literature: Essays Presented to R. W. Hunt*, ed. J. J. G. Alexander and M. Gibson (London, 1976), 115–41.

[6] Not all scriptoria produced illuminated books. Salisbury, for instance, a secular cathedral, built up a large library in the post-Conquest period, but its books were apparently written in a great hurry, untidily and on poor parchment, and there was no tradition of illumination there in the twelfth century. See N. R. Ker, 'The beginnings of Salisbury Cathedral library', *Essays presented to R. W. Hunt, op. cit.*, 23–49.

[7] *Speculum*, lv (1980), 237–65.

[8] E. B. Garrison, *Studies in the History of Mediaeval Italian Painting*, iii (London, 1958), 200–10.

[9] H. Swarzenski, *Kunstchronik*, xvi (1963), 77–85. Recently, Ursula Nilgen (1984), in discussing Heslop's identification of the twelfth-century ivory pyx in the Victoria and Albert Museum, has expressed total disbelief in the possibility of a medieval artist finding a play worthy of depiction. Similarities between pictures and drama, she implies, are due to their common source. For an introduction to the subject, see O. B. Hardison, *Christian Rite and Christian Drama in the Middle Ages* (Baltimore, 1965). He has significantly changed the accepted view of medieval drama in seeing it as an integral part of the liturgy.

BIBLIOGRAPHY

Twelfth-century English book illumination, 1974–84

Abou-El-Haj, B., 1983. 'Bury St Edmunds Abbey between 1070 and 1124; a history of property, privilege and monastic art production', *Art History*, vi, 1–29.

ALEXANDER, J. J. G., 1978. 'Scribes as artists: the arabesque initial in twelfth-century English manuscripts', *Medieval Scribes, Manuscripts and Libraries. Essays Presented to N. R. Ker* (London), 87–106.

AYRES, L. M., 1974. 'The role of the Angevin style in English Romanesque painting', *Zeitschrift für Kunstgeschichte*, xxxvi, 192–223.

— 1976. 'English painting and the Continent during the reign of Henry II and Eleanor', in Kibler, W. W. (ed.), *Eleanor of Aquitaine, Patron and Politician* (London), 116–45.

BAKER, M., 1978. 'Medieval illustrations of Bede's Life of St Cuthbert', with an appendix by Farmer, D. H., *JWCI*, xli, 16–40.

BATEMAN, K. M., 1978. 'Pembroke 120 and Morgan 736', *Gesta*, xvii, 18–26.

CAHN, W., 1975. 'St Albans and the Channel Style in England', *The Year 1200: a Symposium, Metropolitan Museum of Art* (New York), 187–230.

— 1982. *Romanesque Bible Illumination* (New York).

CAMILLE, M., 1982. 'Seeing and reading: some visual consequences of medieval literacy and illiteracy', unpublished paper, Cambridge. (Now *Art History*, viii (1985) 26–49.)

CAVINESS, M. H., 1983. 'Images of Divine Order and the Third Mode of Seeing', *Gesta*, xxii. 2, 99–120.

DE HAMEL, C., 1984. *Glossed Books of the Bible and the Origins of the Paris Booktrade* (Woodbridge).

ELEEN, L., 1982. *The Illustrations of the Pauline Epistles in French and English Bibles of the Twelfth and Thirteenth Centuries* (Oxford).

FLYNN, K., 1979. 'Romanesque wall paintings in the Cathedral Church of Christ Church, Canterbury', *Arch. Cant.* xcv, 185–95.

HANEY, K. E., 1980. 'The provenance of the Psalter of Henry of Blois', *Manuscripta*, xxiv, 40–3.

— 1981. 'The paint surfaces on the Psalter of Henry of Blois', *British Library J.*, vii. 2, 149–58.

— 1982. 'A Norman antecedent for English floral ornament of the mid twelfth century', *Scriptorium*, xxxvi, 84–6.

— 1982. 'The Immaculate Imagery in the Winchester Psalter', *Gesta*, xx, 111–18.

HEIMANN, A., 1975. 'The last copy of the Utrecht Psalter', *The Year 1200: a Symposium, Metropolitan Museum of Art* (New York), 313–38.

HENDERSON, G. D. S., 1980. 'Bede and the Visual Arts', *Jarrow Lecture*.

— 1981. 'Narrative illustration and theological exposition in medieval art', *Studies in Church History*, xvii, 19–35.

HESLOP, T. A., 1981. 'The Virgin Mary's regalia and twelfth-century English seals', in Borg, A. and Martindale, R. A. (eds.), *Studies . . . Presented to Christopher Hohler*, BAR S111, iii (Oxford), 53–62.

— 1982. Review of Oakeshott 1981, *Art History*, v, 94–100.

— 1984. 'Dunstan's Archiepiscopus and painting in Kent around 1200', *Burl. Mag.* cxxvi, 195–204.

KAHN, D., 1984. 'The structural evidence for the dating of the St Gabriel chapel wall paintings, at Christ Church, Canterbury', *Burl. Mag.* cxxvi, 225–9.

KAUFFMANN, C M., 1975. *Survey*, iii: *Romanesque Manuscripts 1066–1190* (London).

— 1978. 'Manuscript illumination at Worcester in the eleventh and twelfth centuries', *BAA Conference Trans.* i, 1975, 43–50.

LAWRENCE, A., 1981. 'The influence of Canterbury on . . . manuscripts at Durham in the Anglo-Norman period', in Borg, A. and Martindale, A. (eds.), *Studies . . . Presented to Christopher Hohler*, BARS S111, iii (Oxford), 95–104

—1982. 'Manuscripts of early Norman Canterbury', in 'Medieval Art and Architecture at Canterbury,' *BAA Conference Trans.* v, 1979, 101–11.

MCLACHLAN, E. P., 1975. 'The Pembroke College N T and a group of unusual English Evangelist symbols', *Gesta*, xiv, 3–18.

— 1978. 'The scriptorium of Bury St Edmunds in the third and fourth decades of the twelfth century', *Mediaeval Studies* (Toronto), xl, 328–48.

— 1978. 'The Bury Missal in Laon and its Cruxifixion miniature', *Gesta*, xvii, 27–35.

— 1979. 'In the wake of the Bury Bible, followers of Master Hugo at Bury St Edmunds', *JWCI*, xlii, 216–24.

MICHAEL, M. A., 1984. 'An illustrated Apocalypse manuscript at Longleat House', *Burl. Mag.* cxxvi, 340–4.

MORGAN, N., 1982. *Survey*, v: *Early Gothic Manuscripts*, i: *1190–1250* (London).

MURATOVA, X., 1977. 'Adam donne leurs noms aux animaux', *Studi Medievali*, xviii, pt. 2.

NILGEN, U., 1980. 'Thomas Becket as a patron of the arts', *Art History*, iii, 357–74.

— 1984. Review of the Arts Council 'English Romanesque Art' exhibition, *Kunstchronik*, xxxvii, 202–15.

OAKESHOTT, W., 1981. *The Two Winchester Bibles* (London).

— 1984. 'Some new initials by the Entangled Figures Master', *Burl. Mag.* cxxvi, 230.

PARK, D., 1983. 'The wall paintings of the Holy Sepulchre chapel' in 'Medieval Art and Architecture at Winchester', *BAA Conference Trans.* vi, 1980, 38–62.

PARKER, E. C., 1981. 'Master Hugo as sculptor: a source of the style of the Bury Bible', *Gesta*, xx, 99–109.

RICHARDS, M. P., 1981. 'A decorated Vulgate set from twelfth-century Rochester, England', *J. Walters Art Gallery*, xxxix, 59–67.

SHEPPARD, J., 1983. 'Oxford Bodleian Library MS Laud Misc. 752, The Giffard Bible', Ph.D. thesis, Bryn Mawr College.

STIRNEMANN, P. D., 1976. 'The Copenhagen Psalter', Ph.D. thesis, Columbia University.

TEMPLE, E., 1984. 'Some aspects of the iconography of the MS Douce 293', *Bodleian Library Record*, 211–19.

VERFAILLIE-MARKEY, D., 1983. 'Le dernier cahier du Psautier d'Eadwine', *Scriptorium*, xxxvii. 2, 245–58.

THOMSON, R. M., 1975. 'The date of the Bury Bible re-examined', *Viator* (Berkeley), vi, 51–8.

— 1982. *Manuscripts from St Albans Abbey 1066–1235* (Woodbridge).

ZARNECKI, G., 1981. 'The Eadwine portrait', *Études d'art médiéval offertes à Louis Grodecki* (Paris), 93–100.

Who Designed the Eadwine Psalter?

Margaret Gibson, F.S.A.

'Almighty and merciful God, I humbly beseech thee to grant that thy servant Eadwine may serve thee faithfully, persevere in good and die in grace. And may this Psalter "that I have sung in thy sight" be for the health of my soul and its eternal salvation' (fo. 262).

Eadwine's prayer is at the end of Psalm 150, in the main text hand. The Psalter that he has *sung in the sight of the Lord* evokes a mosaic of imagery: the waters of Babylon now, Jerusalem to come; the monastic life prefiguring the New Jerusalem.[1] His prayer is a scribal colophon referring to the greater part of the volume that is now Trinity College Cambridge R.17.1.[2] The entire volume is made up as follows:

(a) an early twelfth-century kalendar from Christ Church, Canterbury (fos. 1ᵛ–4)

(b) an illustrated Psalter (fos. 5ᵛ–262) with Canticles and other material following (fos. 262ᵛ–82ᵛ)

(c) a full-page picture of EADWINE PRICE OF SCRIBES (fo. 283ᵛ)

(d) two plans of the waterworks at Christ Church, Canterbury, in the time of Prior Guibert, 1152–67 (fos. 284–286)

The waterworks plans are not integral to the volume. The Christ Church kalendar and the picture of Eadwine have been cut down by a binder, in both cases along the top edge of the leaf. So they may not always have been part of the volume either.[3] They seem relevant: the kalendar confirms a Christ Church provenance attested by Prior Eastry's catalogue *c.* 1320, and indeed by Dean Nevile's donation of the manuscript to Trinity College;[4] and the portrait is of the very scribe whose prayer has just been quoted. But as it is uncertain how soon they were associated with the original manuscript,[5] I shall limit my remarks to what may still be called the Eadwine Psalter, namely fos. 5ᵛ–282ᵛ: the 150 Psalms, with Canticles following.

71

The Eadwine Psalter is set apart from the other great manuscripts of twelfth-century England by the extraordinary complexity of its *mis-en-page* (pl. XXVI). A text-page of the St Albans Psalter, the Bury Bible and the Lambeth Bible is a plain monastic quarto or folio, with no elaborate subdivision and little or no marginalia. By contrast, the Eadwine Psalter has ten elements to every Psalm. The Psalter text itself is tripartite: Hebraicum and Romanum on the inner side of each page, Gallicanum in the centre.[6] The Hebraicum has an interlinear translation in French, the Romanum an interlinear translation in Anglo-Saxon;[7] the Gallicanum, which has the dominant position, has a marginal and interlinear commentary in Latin. Preceding each Psalm is an illustration in the manner of the Utrecht Psalter, a collect[8] and one or more *tituli*. Finally, the Latin commentary has its own preface to every Psalm, normally preceding the 'Utrecht' picture. All these elements are normally found in one full spread of recto and verso. The disposition of the text requires that each be accessible, that none dominates, that nothing runs over and that there be no awkward blank spaces. It is a virtuoso performance by any standards.

Up to a point the designer had a model: either the ninth-century Utrecht Psalter itself, and/or Harley 603 (of the early eleventh century with later additions), and/or the recent postulate of a lost volume in the same tradition produced *c*. 1075–1100.[9] All these had pictures, collects and *tituli* for each Psalm. *Tituli* as such are the most ancient apparatus to the Psalter: DAVID SANG THIS WHEN HE WAS HIDING IN THE CAVE; DAVID SANG THIS WHEN THE TABERNACLE WAS COMPLETED. They relate the Psalms to events in the life of King David. They were taken into Christian tradition, explained by Augustine and Cassiodorus, and maintained in Carolingian exegesis.[10] The same series of ancient *tituli* is found in the Utrecht Psalter (the Gallicanum Psalter-text) and in Harley 603 (the Romanum Psalter-text). In Eadwine they are applied to the centrally placed Gallicanum; the now adjacent Hebraicum and Romanum have further *tituli* that often relate a Psalm to the life of Christ, or to the Church on earth. At Psalm 10, for example, 'I trust in the Lord', the central *titulus* is IN FINEM PSALMVS DAVID; the *titulus* to the Hebraicum (far left) reads VICTORI DAVID and that to the Romanum IN FINEM PSALMVS DAVID DE PASSIONE CHRISTI. Again Psalm 28, 'Ascribe unto the Lord', was sung WHEN THE TABERNACLE WAS COMPLETED; but IT REFERS NOW TO THE FINAL CONSUMMATION OF CHRIST'S CHURCH.[11] The pictorial tradition is adapted in the same direction. In the Utrecht Psalter and in the principal, early section of Harley 603 the deity is often shown above, attended by angels, rarely in the world below. Tentatively in the later section of Harley 603 and generally in Eadwine, Christ is associated with events in this lower world, to which the details of the Psalm refer. Cruciform haloes are worn throughout.

If the *tituli* of Hebraicum-Romanum and the modified 'Utrecht' pictures relate the Psalter more closely to the life of Christ, the Latin commentary relates it to twelfth-century society. This commentary is our best guide to the men for whom the Eadwine Psalter was first designed: to how they thought, and to the milieu in which they lived. It should be dated to *c*. 1150/60, for three reasons. The preface to each Psalm is cast as an *accessus*, treating the subject-matter (*materia*), how that matter is handled (*modus*) and the Psalmist's purpose (his *intentio*); formulae of this kind were current in the academic commentaries of

PLATE XXVI

Photograph: courtesy of the Master and Fellows of Trinity College, Cambridge

The Eadwine Psalter, Trinity College MS R.17.1, fo. 8

the mid twelfth century.[12] The commentary as a whole is related to the exposition of Peter Lombard, the definitive form of which was published *c.* 1160.[13] To clarify ambiguity or evade contradiction the commentator will use the *distinctio*—a tool not used, or not called by that name, before the second half of the twelfth century.[14]

To use the commentator's own term, he treats the *materia* of his text in four ways. 'Lord, how many there be that trouble me!' (Psalm 3). Here all the *tituli* run—DAVID WAS FLEEING FROM HIS SON ABSALOM. Historically David is being attacked by the son he has disinherited. Christ and the eleven Disciples withdraw to the garden of Gethsemane after Judas, the faithless son, has left them. (And Judas, like Absalom, died by hanging.) In personal terms, you or I are beset by evil desires, here personified. And finally it is the contemporary Church, close to shipwreck on the waves of the world, who cries to the Lord, 'How many there be that trouble me', and receives the assurance that her enemies—pagans, Jews and heretics—are all defeated: 'thou hast broken the teeth of the sinners'. The interpretations are historical, theological, personal and political; the central issue of twelfth-century politics was the status of the Church in society. Here and throughout the Psalter the *tituli* are sign-posts to the commentary, and the modified illustrations give visible form to passages in the argument. For the student of the Latin commentary the *tituli* and the 'Utrecht' pictures are the first resort in unravelling its fourfold complexity.

As to the *modus* of the Eadwine Psalter, how the manuscript was made, the physical sequence is clear. The designer began with a set of 'Utrecht' pictures, with the appropriate spaces intervening; this was the tramming on which he worked his tapestry.[15] Then the text was added, and lastly the major and minor initials. His *intentio* in creating so elaborate a display is best understood in terms of the Latin commentary, for these marginal glosses are not only tied into the rest of the page by their meaning, they have dictated the design as a whole. The Eadwine Psalter is a glossed biblical text, made at a time of wide and ingenious experiment in the disposition of such texts. The elegant solution, which prevailed, was a double-spaced central text, with half-spacing for the gloss on either side.[16] If the designer of the Eadwine Psalter does not achieve this simplicity, he has still made a solid contribution to a contemporary debate. That debate refers exclusively to school texts. We may argue over precisely which texts, in which schools, at what level, used by whom; but we cannot evade the proposition that these glossed texts of the Bible were made for formal, regular, academic study. The designer of the Eadwine Psalter had students in mind. Where were they studying? With what objective?

The former question does not yet admit of a confident answer. A substantial monastery no doubt, given the high cost of the volume; but not necessarily Christ Church, Canterbury. The kalendar is separate from the rest of the book; the *tripartitum psalterium Edwini* is first attested in Christ Church *c.* 1320; the major and minor initials (as distinct from the 'Utrecht' pictures) are scarcely characteristic of Christ Church illumination in the mid twelfth century.[17] Thus a Christ Church origin is a reasonable hypothesis, rather than a certainty. What were the students of the Eadwine Psalter studying for? A comprehensive reply would take many pages; but it may be said in a few concluding lines that the Benedictine monasteries of the mid twelfth century were under pressure *inter alia* from the leading French and English 'secular' schools. The monasteries had lost their near-monopoly of learning; they were in danger now of losing even their access to modern scholarship. New texts were coming into play, and new methods of study. The Eadwine Psalter is one monastic schoolmaster's response to this crisis. He presents a fundamental text with all the apparatus conceivable in the most modern form. The student who uses it will absorb the information and (far more important) grow adept in the scholastic methods current in Paris and Oxford, London and Poitiers. It is a noble vision, but it was cheaper and more convenient to send the student himself away to these schools, and in the next generation to university. To the lasting detriment of intellectual life in the monasteries, that was the option that would be chosen.

NOTES

[1] cf. Psalms 136–7 (Vulgate) and 'in conspectu deorum cantabo tibi' (Hebraicum 138 : 1).

[2] Facsimile by M. R. James, *The Canterbury Psalter* (London, 1935); see further C. M. Kauffmann, *Survey*, iii: *Romanesque Manuscripts 1066–1190* (London, 1975), no. 68, with further references, and *id., Catalogue*, no. 62.

[3] G. Zarnecki, 'The Eadwine portrait', *Études d'art médiéval offertes à Louis Grodecki* (Paris, 1981), 93–100.

[4] 'Tripartitum psalterium Edwini': M. R. James, *The Ancient Libraries of Canterbury and Dover* (Cambridge, 1903), 51, no. 323, among the 'libri de armariolo claustri'.

[5] See most recently the careful study by D. Verfaillie-Markey, 'Le dernier cahier du Psautier d'Eadwine', *Scriptorium*, xxxvii (1983), 245–58. Mme Markey fully demonstrates that the final quire (fos. 277–83) is 'xxxv^8 (wants 8)'—to use English terminology. Thus the Eadwine portrait is on a bifolium with the Magnificat and the Gloria. When the portrait was painted, and when and how often the volume was bound cannot be settled within the terms of her enquiry.

[6] The Hebraicum (H) is Jerome's translation from the Hebrew; it was not used liturgically. The Romanum (R) is Jerome's correction of the Latin version made via the Septuagint; it was used liturgically in Rome. The Gallicanum (G) is a Latin version made via Origen's *Hexaples*; it was in general liturgical use. Only the French psalters have been comprehensively surveyed: V. Leroquais, *Les Psautiers manuscrits latins des bibliothèques publiques de France* (Macon, 1940–41), 3 vols. They include tripartite texts from Chartres (HGR: s.x) and Rheims (GRH: s.xi) and even two quadripartite texts (GRH + Septuagint in Latin script: s.xii): Leroquais, *op. cit.* nos. 121, 387, 373, 457. None of these is an exact precedent for Eadwine (HRG).

[7] The French translation (ed. F. Michel, 1876) is currently being studied by Dominique Verfaillie-Markey: cf. note 5 above. The Anglo-Saxon translation is being studied by Patrick O'Neill, University of North Carolina, Chapel Hill; meanwhile see N. R. Ker, *Catalogue of Manuscripts Containing Anglo-Saxon* (Oxford, 1957), no. 91, with rcfs.

[8] For the collects see L. Brou, editing A. Wilmart, *The Psalter Collects*, Henry Bradshaw Society lxxxiii (London, 1949), 112–73, the so-called 'Hispana' series, MS E; critique by C. Mohrmann, 'A propos des collectes du Psautier', *Vigiliae Christianae*, vi (1952), 1–19. The *tituli* will be discussed by R. W. Pfaff in his forthcoming publication on the Eadwine Psalter. Meanwhile see *Biblia Sacra*, x: *Psalter*, ed. *monachi . . . sancti Hieronymi in urbe* (Rome, 1953), MSS U and D.

[9] For the Utrecht Psalter (816/35: Rheims) see E. T. de Wald, *The Illustrations of the Utrecht Psalter* (Princeton, 1932), and more recently S. Dufrenne, *Les Illustrations du Psautier de Utrecht* (Paris, 1979), with refs. For Harley 603 see E. Temple, *Survey*, ii: *Anglo-Saxon Illuminated Manuscripts 900–1066* (London, 1976), no. 64, with refs.; there is no facsimile edition or extended study. For the postulated volume and its bearing on the Eadwine Psalter see the forthcoming study by R. W. Pfaff.

[10] See successively Augustine, *Enarrationes in Psalmos*, ed. E. Dekkers and J. Fraipont, *CCSL* xxxviii–xl (Turnhout, 1956), Cassiodorus, *Expositio Psalmorum*, ed. M. Adriaen, *CCSL* xcvii–xcviii (Turnhout, 1958), and Remigius of Auxerre, *Enarrationes in Psalmos* (*PL* cxxxi. 133D–844C).

[11] Eadwine Psalter, fo. 19 (Psalm 10) and fo. 48 (Psalm 28).

[12] The terminology is ultimately Boethian. The nature and development of the *accessus*, or 'introduction', is most fully discussed, but not quite elucidated, by R. W. Hunt, 'The Introductions to the *artes* in the twelfth century', in *Studia Mediaevalia in Honorem R. J. Martin* (Bruges, 1949), 85–112.

[13] Peter Lombard, *Commentarius in Psalmos* (*PL* cxci. 55A–1296B). See further C. F. de Hamel, *Glossed Books of the Bible and the Origins of the Paris Booktrade* (Woodbridge, 1984) and [Brady's] valuable discussion in *Magistri Petri Lombardi Sententiae*, *Spicilegium Bonaventurianum*, IV (Grottaferrata, 1971), I.i.46*–61*.

[14] There is a lucid account by R. H. and M. A. Rouse, *Preachers, Florilegia and Sermons*, PIMS (Toronto, 1979), 7–11.

[15] From time to time the text overlaps the pictures, whereas the major and minor initials in their turn occasionally overlap the text.

[16] C. F. de Hamel dates the definitive solution to the 1160s (its invention) and the 1170s onwards (its general adoption): *op. cit.* (note 13), 24–5.

[17] I owe this observation to T. A. Heslop, who is currently engaged in a more detailed study of the illumination as a whole.

The 'Old Conventual Church' at Ely: a False Trail in Romanesque Studies?

Thomas Cocke, F.S.A.

Most of the buildings selected as key monuments of the Romanesque by eighteenth-century students of the style are still accepted as authentic, however much their precise date and significance have been reinterpreted. Such favourite examples as the cathedrals of Durham and Peterborough or the churches of Iffley, Tickencote and Barfreston remain important whatever their position in the chronology of Romanesque. The major exception is the so-called Old Conventual Church at Ely (pl. XXVII), which was agreed by all serious antiquaries to be founded by St Etheldreda in 673 and thus to be one of the earliest and best-preserved Saxon buildings in England, but which has been identified as simply the Infirmary of the Ely cathedral priory, built about five centuries later. The episode is worth investigating, since the antiquaries' error proceeded not from quaint fantasies but from their serious attempts to distinguish Saxon architecture from Norman, within the general context of the Romanesque style.[1]

The twelfth-century Infirmary at Ely is an impressive building even in its present ruined state. Originally it consisted of an aisled hall closed by a wall at the east end, beyond which was an aisled chapel, the length of the whole amounting to 191 ft. (58·2 m.).[2] In the later Middle Ages the aisles began to be divided off into separate units, a process completed after the Dissolution when the 'nave' was unroofed and became a lane serving a series of canons' residences built into the aisles and into the former chapel. The original fabric, in particular the piers and arches of the hall arcade, and the archway from hall to chapel remained clearly visible.

The first person to identify the building as Saxon, at least in print, appears to have been the antiquary Thomas Tanner, canon of Ely and later bishop of St Asaph. In the notes he supplied to Browne Willis for the latter's *History of Mitred Abbies*, published in 1718, Tanner suggested that 'some remains of St Ethelwold's church seem to be in the Arches and Pillars, that are still Visible behind the Lodgings of the First and Sixth and of the Second, Third and Fifth Resident canons. Where St Etheldreda's Foundation was I know not.'[3] Tanner's idea that the building belonged to the re-establishment of monastic life at Ely by St Ethelwold after the Danish Invasions was not ridiculous. Here was a large church-like building hard by the Norman cathedral, yet of a very different stylistic character. Considered as a church it could hardly be later than the cathedral which was known to have been founded in the late eleventh century, since there would be no point in building another so close. Ergo it must be earlier, and so pre-Conquest.

The amplification of this relatively slight notice of the building into a definite assertion of its Saxon origins must have been due to Ely's great historiographer, James Bentham. He was well versed in the documentary sources for the early period at Ely and he noted that St Ethelwold is recorded not as having built anew, but as having restored the church of the convent founded by St Etheldreda in 673 and later abandoned because of the Danes. So Bentham was able to push the date of the original structure back to 673. Since the foundress was known to have been assisted in her endeavours by that great patron of architecture, St Wilfrid, the early date for the 'Old Conventual Church' could be strengthened by association with the major buildings raised by St Wilfrid, such as Hexham, which were described in considerable detail in contemporary sources.[4]

The identification of the Ely Infirmary as St Etheldreda's Conventual Church was becoming generally accepted by the 1750s. William Stukeley listed it in a paper for the Antiquaries as one of St Wilfrid's buildings and noted that the 'major part' was still standing.[5] Stukeley, however, was inclined to date many Romanesque monuments too early, putting the Bishop's Chapel, Hereford, and St Alban's Abbey in the seventh century.[6] More important was the endorsement of the identification by Charles Lyttelton when he visited Ely in 1757 and, according to Bentham, acknowledged the Conventual Church as 'the most considerable Saxon building in England'.[7] Lyttelton, the virtual founder of Romanesque studies in England, acted as 'the centre in which the various informations on points of Antiquity from the different parts of the kingdom united, and the medium through which they were conveyed to [his fellows]'.[8] The Old Conventual Church thus became one of the standard examples of early Saxon architecture.

The canonical status of the building was confirmed by its mention in Bentham's own great work, the *History and Antiquities of the Conventual and Cathedral Church of Ely . . . from 673 to 1771*, published, after long delays, in the latter year. It included a lengthy introductory section on the successive styles of medieval architecture, which was soon accepted as authoritative.[9] A major part of it was directed to the questions of the extent and character of the architectural achievement of the Anglo-Saxons. Bentham illustrated his demonstration that the Saxons even in the seventh century built complex structures of stone, not only with literary examples from Bede and other early authors, but also with a large plate of the Old Conventual Church, shown in plan and in section (pl.

PLATE XXVII

Photograph: Fitzwilliam Museum, by kind permission of Prof. M. Jaffé

a. The 'Old Conventual Church' (*recte* former Infirmary) at Ely, from an engraving after T. Hearne, *c.* 1800

b. The same view today

PLATE XXVIII

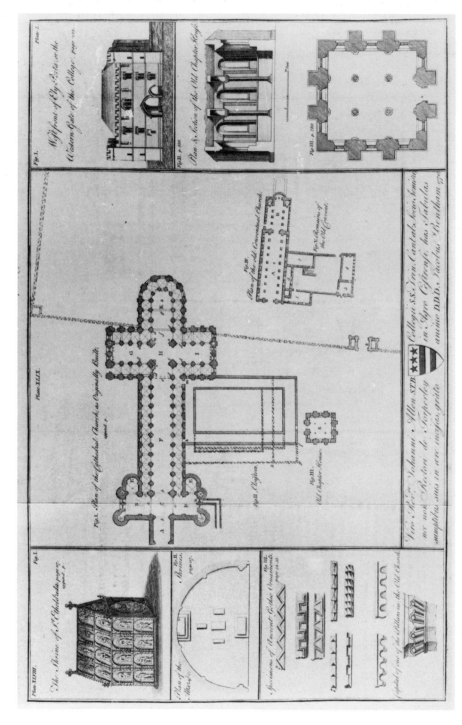

The plan of the Cathedral and 'Conventual Church' prepared by James Essex and published in Bentham's *Ely* in 1771

XXVIII). Curiously it was the only individual Saxon building that Bentham cited on his own authority in the whole of his excursus on Saxon architecture. For all his vigorous defence of it he commented cautiously that its 'Monuments . . . are very rare' and quoted Wren's list of them only to point out that Wren's examples were in fact all post-Conquest.[10] Bentham's absorption in documents rather than in the fabric of buildings is revealed by the contrast between the generalized discussions of architecture in his text and the detailed analysis of Romanesque ornament contributed by Thomas Gray in which such essential forms as the chevron and billet mouldings were described.[11]

In the second edition of Bentham's book, published in 1812, a detailed account of the Conventual Church was added by James Essex, the Cambridge architect and antiquary who acted as Surveyor to the Ely Chapter from 1757 until his death in 1784. Essex seems already to have been busy with the drawings of the building in 1757,[12] and in 1762 he made a measured plan.[13] He reconstructed the original form of the church as 'built by St Etheldreda about the year 673' with an apsed sanctuary and extensive conventual buildings to the south.[14] He attributed the present east end and the north doorway to the restoration under King Edgar. Essex did not adopt this view because he was a blind follower of Bentham in medieval architecture. He had studied with attention the major Romanesque monuments of his region, the cathedrals of Ely, Peterborough and Norwich and, in Cambridge, the 'Leper Chapel' at Barnwell and the Round Church and had used their evidence to define the style in his projected 'History of Gothic'.[15]

The Old Conventual Church continued to be upheld by the Ely historian of the next generation, George Millers, who devoted many pages to it in his popular books, first a *Guide* and then a *Description* of the Ely buildings (the former reprinted five times, the latter twice). In his *Guide* of 1805 Millers appears to have 'entertained no doubts' of the Conventual Church's antiquity and, he claimed, 'was not aware that they were entertained by others', but in his *Description*, published two years later, he felt obliged to defend the building vigorously.[16] The objections put to him were the 'vague and suspicious' nature of the early chronicles, the 'rigid caution' with which pretensions to high antiquity should be scrutinized, and the 'improbability' both of ruined buildings surviving so long and of such 'correct and elaborate' work belonging to 'a rude, and at least semi-barbarous age'.[17] Knowledge of authentic Saxon architecture was still so limited that the age of the Old Conventual Church could only be questioned on general, historical grounds, not on those of stylistic incompatibility. Millers countered the sceptics by reaffirming Bentham's arguments, with the concession that the building period might have been prolonged into the eighth century.

The eventual unmasking of the Conventual Church seems to have been swiftly accomplished. The Saxon theory, still maintained unaltered in the 1844 edition of Millers's *Guide*, was dismissed almost casually by D. J. Stewart two decades later. He pointed out how 'curious' it was of Bentham to have supported the 'popular error' about the building, since even in the documents Bentham knew so well there were two passages which disproved the idea.[18] Apparently Millers himself eventually 'became perfectly aware that the old theory was untenable'.[19]

Thus far the rise and fall of the Old Conventual Church appear simply as an amusing cul-de-sac in eighteenth-century antiquarianism. On a wider view, however, the episode had a positive value in the elucidation of the Romanesque. In particular it helped to establish what effect the Conquest had on English architecture and which, if any, of the Romanesque motifs being collected by contemporary enthusiasts could be ascribed to the Saxons and which to the Normans.

Seventeenth-century writers on medieval architecture, such as John Aubrey, Christopher Wren or Roger North, distinguished clearly between the round-arched and the Pointed styles, but within the former were not much concerned to isolate the Saxon contribution from the Norman. Aubrey, in the list of early medieval buildings in his *Chronologia Architectonica*, mentioned a church in Winchester as built by King Alfred and Corfe Castle as by King Edgar, but he did not set them up as examples of Saxon architecture. He claimed that in both cases the workmen were 'sent for . . . out of Italie'.[20] Wren and Roger North made no distinction amongst those buildings in the 'ancient . . . Manner . . . not much altered from the Roman' between those erected before and after the Conquest.[21] Wren called the style 'Saxon' and illustrated it by St John's chapel in the White Tower, the transepts in Winchester Cathedral and Christ Church Cathedral, Oxford, although as Thomas Gray and Bentham noted a century later, Wren must have known most of those buildings to have been built by the Normans.[22] North dated Durham Cathedral before the Danish invasions 'when the Saxon kings took to an humour of cloystering themselves'.[23] He, however, considered that there did not survive a 'house for dwelling so old as the conquest of the Normans', except possibly a castle such as Appleby, and that in general such ecclesiastical buildings as there were, were 'rude and lumpish, . . . I conclude all the prenorman buildings to be meer heaps of stone, and not worthy a minuter consideration'.[24]

It is thus not surprising that in the eighteenth century there were still many who doubted whether there had been any Saxon architecture worth the name. They followed the Stuart antiquary, Richard Somner, who, in his *History of Canterbury*, published as early as 1640, had suggested that the Saxons built in timber, not in masonry.[25] The tenacity of this not altogether erroneous opinion was such that in 1777 J. C. Brooke could still assert that 'the sacred structures of the Saxons were in general timber buildings, as might be easily shown'.[26]

Writers better versed in the documentary sources, particularly Bede, knew that such a sweeping dismissal of Saxon stone architecture was impossible. The problem was how to distinguish Saxon buildings from the later, but also round-arched, buildings of the Normans. William Stukeley boldly published a list of the churches which he considered Saxon. It included not only the Ely Conventual Church, Tickencote church, Hexham and Ripon ministers, but also as 'indubitably pre-Conquest' Rochester Cathedral and Waltham Abbey.[27] Charles Lyttelton approached the problem more prudently. 'About the year 1742' he 'remarked . . . the difference between the mode of architecture used by the Normans in their buildings, and that practised by the cotemporary [sic] Saxons in England' and formulated 'some rules whereby to distinguish' them.[28] As evidence he assembled over the years 'ye only collection of Saxon buildings that ever was made', a folio of drawings and prints of important churches such as Barfreston, Iffley and Stewkley, now of course recognized as twelfth century but then generally accepted as Saxon.[29]

The particular contribution of Bentham to the debate was to perceive that further progress was impossible until the nature of Saxon architecture was firmly established. If pre-Conquest churches were indeed of timber, then it was idle to expect much evidence to survive. Bentham successfully demonstrated by a wealth of texts and wordy argument that substantial buildings in stone were constructed by the Saxons from the seventh century onwards.[30] It only remained to associate the evidence derived from documentary sources with surviving structures. Ironically it was Bentham's correct understanding of the importance of late Roman sources in Saxon architecture that led him to regard the use of a basilican plan as a sign of early date and thus to see its appearance in the nave of the Ely Conventual Church as confirmation of its antiquity.

Once the authenticity was established of Anglo-Saxon stone architecture in general and of the Ely Conventual Church in particular, the Conventual Church could be used as prime evidence of the characteristics of Saxon, as opposed to post-Conquest, architecture. Here the consequences of the misidentification were at their most dangerous. The alternating round and diagonal piers of the 'nave', of relatively modest size, and the chevron enrichment of their arches formed a convincing contrast with the plain but massive cylindrical piers of the cathedral. Such a comparison also gave support to Bentham's interpretation of the 'novum aedificandi genus', introduced according to William of Malmesbury by the Normans, as meaning new 'massiveness and enlarged dimensions' in architecture, rather than an entirely new style.[31] Thus early Saxon churches were defined as relatively modest but elaborately decorated buildings with a basilican plan.

Bentham's analysis was sufficiently acute to convince some of the most prominent antiquaries among the architects of the time, one of them, as already mentioned James Essex, and the other, William Wilkins the elder, of Norwich. Essex put forward the Conventual Church as the 'most ancient example . . . in England' of a 'two-storey' basilican elevation[32] and included it as an illustration for the section on basilicas in his *History*, along with such grand models as Old St Peter's in Rome and the church of the Nativity in Bethlehem.[33] Essex also selected the Conventual Church to illustrate what he alleged was a Saxon and early Norman version of the Vitruvian masonry technique of 'opus insertum' [*sic*], where squared stones were used to make a regular bond through every course, instead of flat ragstones being used 'like bricks' to enclose a rubble core.[34] He indeed held the bulding up as a model 'correctly designed' and 'regular . . . in the Roman Architecture agreeable to the taste of the Saxons and Normans'.[35] Wilkins used many details from the Conventual Church in the illustrated list which he published in *Archaeologia* of specific examples of Saxon and Norman architecture. The tripartite arrangement at Ely of nave, chancel and sanctuary led Wilkins to consider as another early Saxon monument the church of St James's Hospital, Dunwich (Suffolk), a now vanished twelfth-century building of similar design, but with an unaisled nave.[36] In general he accepted and propagated Bentham's picture of the 'Saxon manner' as light and of rich execution, in contrast to the 'magnitude of design' of the Normans.[37]

The influence of the Conventual Church was most strikingly demonstrated at a meeting of the Society of Antiquaries in 1777, when H. P. Wyndham boldly dated the aisled barn, called King John's House, in Warnford (Hampshire) to the seventh century, almost solely by reference to the Ely building. He pointed to the similarities in the lightness of proportion and in the ornament and to the common influence of St Wilfrid, active in nearby Sussex as well as at Ely, and pronounced that 'there is such a striking conformity in the whole style of architecture of that church [at Ely] . . . and that of the Warnford ruin that a curious and judicious examiner would immediately declare them to have been formed upon the plan of one common architect'.[38] And indeed the two buildings would still be accepted as relating closely in date, although that date is in the late twelfth rather than the late seventh century.

It is not for modern scholars to be too condescending about their predecessors' mistaken evaluation of the 'Conventual Church'. Continuing uncertainties over the dating of such objects as the York Virgin or certain ivories, claimed in 1984 first by an exhibition of post-Conquest and then by another of pre-Conquest art, show the difficulty of establishing clear criteria in certain fields of early medieval art even after two further centuries of study. The researches which helped to create a mistaken function and date for the Ely Infirmary were not wasted. They established beyond doubt that the Saxons had built substantial stone structures according to coherent stylistic criteria which, within the overall context of the Romanesque, were to be distinguished from post-Conquest buildings. It was the establishment of this theoretical framework that made Rickman's recognition[39] of authentic examples of Saxon architecture possible and, ultimately, allowed the mature Romanesque of the Ely Infirmary to be accorded not only its stylistic character but its true date.

Acknowledgement

This essay is dedicated to George Zarnecki in grateful acknowledgement of his unfailing encouragement and support over the years.

NOTES

[1] In this paper 'Romanesque', a term not coined until 1819, is used for the style as it is understood today; 'Saxon' and 'Norman' to describe buildings considered in the seventeenth and eighteenth centuries to have been erected respectively before and after the Conquest. Alternative nomenclatures were current in the period, notably 'opus Romanum', a term derived from Bede but used to cover all round-arched architecture. It must be stressed that 'Saxon' as well as 'Norman' could be used in a stylistic as well as a chronological sense and could thus be applied to a building known to be post-1066, just as Covent Garden opera house could be called Grecian without implying that it was built by Greeks (J. Carter, *Gentleman's Mag.* lxxx (1810), i, 130). For a fuller discussion of the problems of style and period nomenclature, see T. H. Cocke 'Pre 19th-century attitudes in England to Romanesque architecture', *JBAA*, 3rd ser. xxxvi (1973), 72–5.

[2] Pevsner commented on the 'incomprehensible scale' of infirmaries such as Ely and Canterbury (250 ft. (76·2 m.) long): N. Pevsner, *Buildings of England: Cambridgeshire* (Harmondsworth, 2nd edn., rev., 1970), 376. The fullest recent account of the Ely Infirmary is given in T. D. Atkinson, *The Architectural History of the Benedictine Monastery of St Etheldreda at Ely* (Cambridge, 1933), 99 ff.

[3] B. Willis, *History of the Mitred Parliamentary Abbies and Conventual Cathedral Churches*, 2 vols. (London, 1718), i, 268.

4 J. Bentham, *The History and Antiquities of the Conventual and Cathedral Church of Ely . . . 673 to 1771* (Cambridge, 1771), 21–4.

5 W. Stukeley, 'The Sanctuary at Westminster', *Archaeologia*, i (1770), 43 (paper read 1755).

6 *Ibid.*, 44.

7 Letter of 25th August 1757 from Bentham to Dr A. C. Ducarel, who was paying for the engraving of the Conventual Church in Bentham's book (letter published in J. Nichols (ed.), *Literary Anecdotes of the 18th Century*, 9 vols. (London, 1812–15), iii, 487. It is significant that at this time the engraving was still 'captioned' A.D. 970, i.e. the date of St Ethelwold's refounding, rather than A.D. 673, as published: Nichols, *op. cit.*, 486.

8 From the eulogy of Lyttelton by his successor as President of the Society of Antiquaries, Jeremiah Milles (published in *Archaeologia*, i (1770), xliii). Lyttelton's role, hitherto much neglected, is outlined in T. H. Cocke, 'Rediscovery of the Romanesque', in *Catalogue*, 362.

9 It was extracted from the rest of the *History* and republished in 1800 by J. Taylor in his popular *Essays in Gothic Architecture*, together with relevant extracts from Wren, Warton, Grose and Milner. See also J. M. Frew, 'James Bentham's History of Ely Cathedral; a forgotten classic of the early Gothic Revival', *Art Bulletin*, lxii (1980), 290–2. Frew perhaps overstates Bentham's originality of mind.

10 Bentham, *op. cit.* (note 4), 31.

11 Bentham (*ibid.*, 34–5) quoted almost unaltered a letter sent by Gray after being shown the text of the *History* in draft, but was not otherwise indebted to him despite subsequent allegations. Gray prepared a longer account of Romanesque architecture, published posthumously as 'Architectura Gothica': T. Gray, *Works*, ed. T. J. Mathias, 2 vols. (London, 1814), ii, 98–103.

12 Nichols, *op. cit.* (note 7), iii, 487.

13 BL Add. MS 6764, fo. 7.

14 J. Bentham, *History and Antiquities . . . of Ely*, 2nd edn. (Cambridge 1812), Addendum 9. This published account differs greatly from Essex's draft 'observations' on the Conventual Church preserved as BL Add. MS 6764.

15 Essex worked on the project from *c.*1769 until his death and extensive drafts survive among his papers bequeathed to the British Museum in 1828 (see BL Add. MS 6768, fos. 55–69, for typical drawings of Norwich cathedral).

16 G. Millers, *A Description of the Cathedral Church of Ely with some account of the Conventual Buildings* (London, 1807), 118.

17 *Ibid.*, 119.

18 D. J. Stewart, *On the Architectural History of Ely Cathedral* (London, 1868), 270.

19 *Ibid.*, 271.

20 Bodleian MS top. gen, c. 25, fo. 154^v. For a general account of the *Chronologia* see H. M. Colvin, 'Aubrey's Chronologia Architectonica' in *Concerning Architecture*, ed. J. Summerson (London, 1968), 1–13, and for its importance in Romanesque studies see Cocke, *Catalogue*, 361 and 370.

21 S. Wren (ed.), *Parentalia* (London, 1750; Gregg Press repr. 1965), 296.

22 *Ibid.*, 296; T. Gray, *Correspondence*, ed. P. Toynbee and L. Whibley, 3 vols. (Oxford, 1937), ii, 862 and iii, 130.

23 R. North, *Of Building*, ed. H. M. Colvin and J. Newman (Oxford, 1981), 66.

24 *Ibid.*, 66.

25 W. Somner, *The Antiquities of Canterbury* (London, 1640), 156–7.

26 J. C. Brooke, 'An illustration of a Saxon inscription on the church of Kirkdale', *Archaeologia*, v (1779), 193–4. Brooke went on to admit that by the eleventh century there were masonry churches, such as the subject of his paper, Kirkdale, the dedicatory inscription of which he correctly dated to 1056–65. The Saxon timber church of Greensted in Essex had been published by the Society of Antiquaries in 1750 as *Vetusta Monumenta*, ii, pl. VII.

27 Stukeley, *op. cit.* (note 5), 44.

28 This summary of Lyttelton's role is from the dedication to him in A. C. Ducarel, *Anglo-Norman Antiquities Considered in a Tour through Part of Normandy* (London, 1767), i and ii.

29 MS note by Lyttelton as preface to the volume which was bequeathed by him to the library of the Society of Antiquaries.

30 Bentham was perhaps the first to identify correctly the meaning of the Saxon porticus: Bentham, *op. cit.* (note 4), 19 n. 6.

[31] *Ibid.*, 33.

[32] BL Add. MS 6762, fo. 15.

[33] BL Add. MS 6766, fo. 7.

[34] J. Essex, 'Remarks on the antiquity and the different modes of brick and stone building in England', *Archaeologia*, iv (1786), 97 (read 1774).

[35] BL Add. MS 6764, fo. 8.

[36] W. Wilkins, 'An essay towards...a history of the Venta Icenorum of the Romans, and of Norwich Castle; with remarks on the architecture of the Anglo-Saxons and Normans', *Archaeologia*, xii (1796), 166–7 (read 1791).

[37] *Ibid.*, 160.

[38] H. P. Wyndham, 'Observations on an ancient building at Warnford', *Archaeologia*, v (1779), 363. Essex, in spite of his interest in the Conventual Church, was not convinced and dismissed Warnford as an 'old barn': J. Nichols (ed.), *Illustrations of the Literary History of the 18th Century*, 8 vols. (London, 1817–58), vi, 371.

[39] Rickman's appendix on Saxon architecture, with a list of twenty authentic examples, was not added to his *Attempt to Discriminate the Styles of Architecture* until the 4th edn. of 1835, although he had already suggested the Saxon origin of St Peter's, Barton on Humber, in the 1st edn. of 1817.

The Bishop's Chapel at Hereford: the Roles of Patron and Craftsman

Richard Gem, F.S.A.

In a recent paper on Winchester Cathedral[1] it was argued that it was possible to induce from the design of a particular building the individual roles that the patron and craftsman must have played in the genesis of that design. Those arguments are ones that can be applied in some other cases, and the Bishop's Chapel at Hereford is a good example. The justification for doing this is more than a question of understanding the individual building, however: it has a wider relevance. The study of English Romanesque architecture has often proceeded on the assumption that every design idea is derivative; that every motif can be traced to a source in Normandy or elsewhere in France, Italy or Germany, or even further afield in Byzantium, the Levant, North Africa or Spain. It should not for a moment be denied that foreign influences were indeed significant, but to gain a true perspective they must be set alongside another factor: that English Romanesque architecture was itself innovative—that it created artistic forms which it did not copy from earlier exemplars elsewhere. It is in this creative process that the relationship between patron and craftsman may be seen as seminal.

The construction of the Hereford Chapel is fortunately recorded in a key passage of William of Malmesbury's *Gesta Pontificum*:

> Non multo post accepit sedem illam Rotbertus Lotharingus, qui ibi ecclesiam tereti aedificavit scemate, Aquensem basilicam pro modo imitatus suo.
> (Not long after Robert of Lorraine received the see, and he built there a church of elegant form, having copied for its design the basilica of Aachen.)[2]

Robert, who was Bishop of Hereford from 1079 to 1095, will be considered in more detail below. First, however, it is necessary to discuss the actual appearance of the chapel—a discussion which must be based in the first instance on

Drinkwater's earlier publication.[3] The principal evidence for the form of the building (which was mostly demolished in *c.* 1737) is: the surviving north wall; plans and views of the interior made by William Stukeley (pls. XXX–XXXI);[4] a vignette of the exterior shown on Taylor's 1757 map of Hereford (pl. XXIX*a*); and a plan and elevation commissioned by the Society of Antiquaries at the time of the destruction (pl. XXIX*b*).[5]

The chapel was a two-storeyed building, the principal part of which was square in plan, and which had a projecting rectangular sanctuary on the east and a projecting portal on the west. The *lower storey* had four free-standing cruciform piers with matching wall responds. These carried, without imposts, the transverse arches of a system of quadripartite groin vaults in the outer compartments. The central compartment, however, had pendentives which probably gave rise originally to an open octagonal well to the upper floor (but which by the eighteenth century supported a cupola). The north and south wide walls admitted light through simple double-splayed windows, while to the east opened the sanctuary— which was probably groin-vaulted. The west wall had a massive entrance portal of several rectangular orders, but with monolithic columns to the inner- and outermost orders. The portal was flanked by one or two spiral stairs leading to a tribune at upper-floor level; the latter was lit by a twin-light window above the portal.

The main *upper storey* had four free-standing, columnar piers of ashlar work, with lower monolithic columns forming responds against the walls. In a north and south direction the main piers were connected by arches springing from above imposts. In an east and west direction, however, the main piers and responds were connected by much lower arches, which fell onto the main piers at a height considerably below the imposts and simply died into the surface of the piers; these arches created the impression of an axial arcade of three bays. The east and west bays of this central 'nave' were covered by barrel vaults, but the central bay was carried up into a groin-vaulted lantern. In the north and south 'aisles' rampant arches rose from the responds to the level of the main pier imposts, and the bays between were covered by quadrant vaults. The form of the vault in the sanctuary and west tribune is not entirely certain.

In discussing the significance of this structure, different theories have been put forward by Bandmann[6] and Bony.[7] Bandmann took as his starting point William of Malmesbury's dictum that the chapel was modelled on the basilica at Aachen and, taking account of the limitations of what was meant by a 'copy' in medieval thought,[8] was able to list some striking points of resemblance: the octagonal well opening between the two storeys; the small, rectangular, two-storeyed sanctuary; the deep west portal flanked by spiral stairs leading to a tribune. He did not minimize the discrepancy, however, between the overall octagonal form of Aachen and the rectangular form of Hereford. On the other hand, it seemed that in Germany at an earlier date than Hereford the idea of incorporating certain features from Aachen into a two-storeyed, rectangular, four-pier chapel had already been developed. The earliest example seemed to be the chapel at the palace of Goslar built by Conrad II *c.* 1034–8. From *c.* 1080–90 dated the surviving chapel of Sts Martin and Emmeram at Speyer Cathedral. A later development (but with a rectangular, not octagonal well) is illustrated by the chapel of St Gothard at Mainz Cathedral built by Archbishop Arnold

PLATE XXIX

a. Vignette from Taylor's map of Hereford, 1757

b. Plan and elevation commissioned by the Society of Antiquaries
Hereford: former Bishop's Chapel
Photographs: RCHM (England)

PLATE XXX

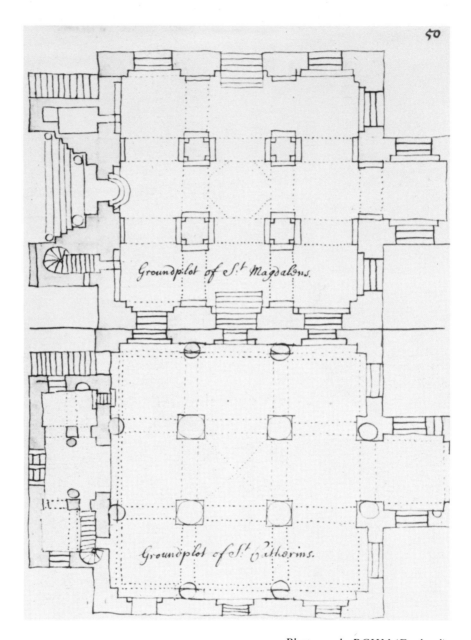

Photograph: RCHM (England)

Hereford, former Bishop's Chapel: groundplan by William Stukeley (Oxford, Bodleian Library MS top. gen. d. 13)

PLATE XXXI

a. Upper-floor chapel of St Mary Magdalene

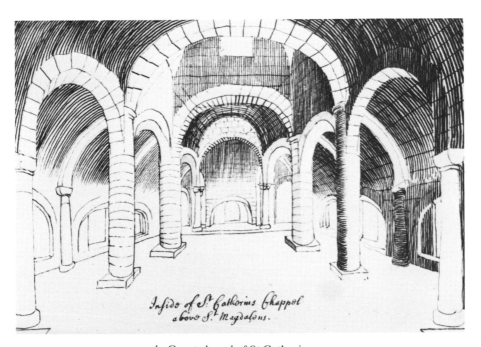

b. Crypt chapel of St Catherine

Hereford, former Bishop's Chapel: perspectives by
William Stukeley (Oxford, Bodleian Library MS top. gen. d. 13)

Photographs: RCHM (England)

I for his palace and burial (*ob.* 1137).

There can be little doubt that Bandmann's analysis of Hereford and its relationship with Aachen and the development of the double chapel in Germany is basically correct. This is suggested not only by the similarities between the German buildings and Hereford, but also by the fact that the latter seems to have been the sole occurrence of the form in England. Pre-Conquest buildings of Aachen derivation in England, as far as is known, retained the rotunda form of the prototype: that is, Abingdon; St Edmund's; St Augustine's, Canterbury.[9] Whereas no other recorded post-Conquest chapels belonged to the centralized tradition at all. The eleventh-century Bishop's Chapel at Durham was axially arranged and not centralized—though it probably was two-storeyed—and its form can be paralleled in Maine rather than Germany.[10]

Bony was not concerned with putting forward an explanation of the general form of the building, so much as with discussing its stylistic affiliations: his views, therefore, might have been complementary to those of Bandmann. Bony argued that various features of the building belonged to an essentially Burgundian and southern Early Romanesque (*premier roman*) tradition: several of these arguments, however, may be challenged. In the first place, where Bony saw as essentially Burgundian the use of a system of barrel and quadrant vaults in the upper chapel, it may be questioned whether these do form such a regular *system* (barrel vaults occur in only two bays), and it may be pointed out that barrel vaults and quadrant vaults individually had a wide use in late eleventh-century Anglo-Norman and Norman buildings.[11] Similarly, large-scale columnar piers need not have a Burgundian source at Hereford when they are of widespread occurrence in English buildings of the late eleventh-century—and of a technique of construction in regular ashlar masonary that is much closer to Hereford than most of the Burgundian examples.[12] Again, with the use of monolithic column shafts, Anglo-Norman buildings can provide precedents,[13] as they can also for piers continuing into arches without imposts.[14]

At first sight the most compelling comparison of Bony's is that for the arches coming from different directions to fall onto the columnar piers at different levels; something rather analogous happens, for instance, at Tournus. At Hereford, nonetheless, this feature is to some extent inherent in the actual form of the building itself: it is not the arbitrary choice of a wilful decorative motif. To make a convincing parallel with Tournus, therefore, it would be necessary to show that the architectural device in question had been adopted for the same reason in relation to the overall design of the building. But this was not the case—the device was adopted for quite different structural reasons in the two buildings, and the only point of similarity was that neither wished to abandon columnar piers in favour of compound ones to avoid the difficulty. It is best, therefore, to see the split-level springing from the piers at Hereford as an *ad hoc* device worked out to meet a particular situation, and to concentrate on understanding the problems that led to this solution rather than on possible Burgundian analogues.

One of the controlling factors of the Hereford design is the system of vaulting that is used, and this system suggests a formula that can be discerned elsewhere in Anglo-Norman buildings. According to this formula the crypt level of a building should be covered by uniform bays of groin vaulting, while at the main high level there should be groin vaults in the central bays, but barrel vaults in the forebays to the sanctuary and other chapels, and quadrant vaults over the gallery to buttress the high vaults. The system is here reduced to a miniature scale, but it is not applied to the sort of four-storeyed (that is, four storeys including a crypt) basilican structure in which no doubt it was first devised. Instead it has been applied to a centralized structure for which a different formula would have been appropriate. All this suggests that the technical expertise and the centralized concept came from different directions to the mason responsible for the construction.

The fact that much of the constructional expertise of the Hereford Chapel can be paralleled elsewhere in late eleventh-century Anglo-Norman architecture suggests that the mason was a man who had himself received his training in that school, but it is difficult to be very specific about his formation. The first major Anglo-Norman Romanesque monument in the south-west Midlands was Worcester Cathedral, begun in 1804,[15] and this in turn seems to have been dependent upon the design of St Augustine's Abbey, Canterbury, begun in the early 1070s.[16] However, it is unclear whether the Hereford Chapel was earlier or later in date than the start of Worcester and, moreover, only fragments of Romanesque Worcester survive. It is not easy, therefore, to speculate on the closeness or distance between the Hereford mason and this particular current. On the other hand, there is one feature that perhaps argues for the mason being an Englishman (rather than a Burgundian) trained in an Anglo-Norman workshop, and that is the use of double-splayed windows. Such windows were common in late Anglo-Saxon architecture, but elsewhere had largely fallen out of use by the late eleventh century except in domestic contexts.[17]

In contrast, an Anglo-Norman ancestry is not credible for the general form of the chapel: its centralized plan with four supports on each of two storeys, and the open well between the storeys. These on the contrary point to the German source argued for by Bandmann. An additional point that may be made at this juncture is that a recurrent feature in the German chapels of this group is the use of columns at first-floor level, no doubt as a deliberate reminiscence of the splendid columns of Aachen. This suggests that the use of columns was one of the necessary features of the Hereford design, and helps explain why the mason did not revert to the use of compound piers to avoid the expedient of the split-level springings.

If the source for the concept of the chapel was German, however, while the mason was Anglo-Norman, it must be asked how the two currents actually came into conjunction at Hereford. One solution that seems *prima facie* unlikely is that the mason himself had travelled in Germany and had picked up the idea of such a chapel to add to his artistic repertoire. If this had been the case it is difficult to understand why Hereford is not a more literal copy of the German models, or why the mason involved himself in such difficulties by trying to translate the German original into an Anglo-Norman vocabulary. Much more likely does it seem that the concept of the chapel was imposed on the mason as part of the patron's brief—which brings attention back to Robert of Lorraine.

William of Malmesbury, indeed, attributes to Bishop Robert the copying of the Aachen chapel and, whereas this statement on its own might be no more than the conventional attribution of a work of art to the patron rather than the artist, in this case it probably means more. Not only was Robert a Lotharingian, and hence in a good position to know not only Aachen but also the four-pier chapel type derivative from it, but also he was, as William tells us:

> A man most skilled in all the liberal arts, researching principally into the abacus, into lunar computation and into the course of the heavenly constellations.[18]

The last of these accomplishments is illustrated by Robert's declining to travel to Lincoln for Bishop Remi's planned dedication of the cathedral there in 1092 because he read in the stars that the ceremony would not take place.[19] His interest in computation is witnessed principally by his introduction to England of the *Chronica* of Marianus Scotus, of which he made an *Excerptio* in 1086, including additional material among which was his own calculation for correcting the date of the era.[20] As for the abacus, he may have had a key role in the introduction of this also into England and, since the abacus provided the origin of the system of accounting used in the royal exchequer, this may mean that he was an important figure in the royal administration.[21] The latter role is only hinted at, however, by the fact that Robert was a royal chaplain before his appointment, and that still only a few months before his death he was hearing pleas at court.[22]

Bishop Robert, judging from his particular learning, seems very likely to have had an interest in the significance of architectural form and to have valued the abstruse reference to Aachen made by the type he adopted for his episcopal chapel. He therefore may be supposed to have formulated the brief for the building and to have given it to his mason to translate into concrete form. The mason, not having seen this type of building for himself, sought to adapt his own training in the Anglo-Norman tradition to meet the patron's wishes. This was not carried out without difficulty, and resulted in a building with several idiosyncratic features: most notably in the relationships between the columnar piers and the arches springing from them at different levels.

But what was achieved at Hereford, for all its idiosyncracy, was not a dead end: the architectural synthesis of the chapel opened up new design possibilities. It was Bony who suggested that the mason who designed the Hereford Chapel was the same man who designed Tewkesbury Abbey only a few years later at most—and this seems entirely plausible. The splendid west façade of Tewkesbury shows the transposition into a major key of the Hereford west portal; but more significant was perhaps the earlier elevation of the east arm of Tewkesbury. The east arm may have combined (though this is not uncontroversial[23]) a giant order of columns and a low main arcade dying into the piers: that is, what happened on a small scale at Hereford. If, as has been suggested here, this feature at Hereford was an independent solution to a particular problem and was unrelated to Burgundy, then Tewkesbury (all the main features of which stand firmly in an Anglo-Norman architectural tradition) need look no further than Hereford as its source for this element—while Tewkesbury in turn prepared the way, perhaps, for designs like Romsey Abbey. This brings the argument of this paper back to its starting point: that the interrelationship between patron and craftsman in late eleventh-century England led to the genuine *creation* of new artistic ideas which were not derivative from Continental precedents.

That individual eleventh-century masons could be creative artists and not merely passive creatures of an abstract momentum towards architectural progress may seem obvious, but often it has been accepted only with reluctance. Perhaps this has been as a result of the myth created by the Renaissance that individual genius and self-expression were the distinguishing characteristics of modern art and that, *per contra*, medieval art must be marked by the absence of these qualities. Yet the truth is that the Renaissance architect, without ceasing to be a creative individualist, was strongly influenced by tradition and precedent[24]—as well as conditioned by social, economic and technological factors. And the same was true of the medieval mason: he started from a received craft tradition which he used to solve the practical problems that were set him by his patrons; but in doing so he was able to bring his own creative impulses to fruition. The Bishop's Chapel at Hereford was in its own terms as much a 'work of art' as Michelangelo's Laurentian Library vestibule.

NOTES

[1] R. D. H. Gem, 'The Romanesque cathedral of Winchester: patron and design in the eleventh century', *BAA Conference Trans.* vi (1983), 1–12.

[2] William of Malmesbury, *Gesta Pontificum*, ed. N. E. S. A. Hamilton, Rolls Series lii (1870), 300.

[3] N. Drinkwater, 'Hereford Cathedral, the Bishop's Chapel', *Arch. J.* cxi (1954), 129–37, and cxii (1955), 74–5.

[4] Oxford, Bodleian Library MS top. gen. d. 13.

[5] *Vetusta Monumenta*, i (1847), pl. XLIX.

[6] D. Bandmann, 'Die Bischofskapelle in Hereford', in *Festschrift für Herbert von Einem* (Berlin, 1965), 9–26.

[7] J. Bony, 'La chapelle épiscopale de Hereford et les apports lorrains en Angleterre après la conquête', in *Actes du XIXᵉ congrès international d'histoire de l'art* (Paris, 1958), 36–43.

[8] See R. Krautheimer, 'Introduction to an "Iconography of Mediaeval Architecture"', *JWCI*, v (1942), 1–33.

[9] R. Gem, 'Towards an iconography of Anglo-Saxon architecture', *JWCI*, xlvi (1983), 8–12.

[10] e.g. in the castle chapel at Laval (see M. Pré, 'Le château de Laval', *Congrès Archéologique de France: Maine* (1961), 353–72). This parallel may favour the attribution of the chapel to Bishop William of St-Calais (Maine) *c.* 1080–8. The chapel is anyway secondary to the curtain wall constructed probably *c.* 1072.

[11] Barrel vaults: St John's chapel, Tower of London; Lastingham priory, crypt, forebay to apse; Bayeux Cathedral, west towers; Le Mont St-Michel Abbey, transepts. Quadrant vaults: Caen, St Stephen's Abbey, nave galleries; Gloucester Abbey (Cathedral), presbytery galleries.

[12] Westminster Abbey; St John's chapel, Tower of London; Winchester Cathedral; Gloucester Abbey; Shrewsbury Abbey; Durham Cathedral, etc.

[13] Bernay Abbey, transept chapels; Jumièges Abbey, presbytery; St Augustine's Abbey, Canterbury, crypt (free-standing); Worcester Cathedral, slype and (free-standing) crypt.

[14] St John's chapel, Tower of London; Christ Church, Canterbury, dormitory undercroft; Gloucester Abbey, in several contexts.

[15] R. D. H. Gem, 'Bishop Wulfstan II and the Romanesque cathedral church of Worcester', *BAA Conference Trans.* i (1978), 15–37.

[16] *Id.*, 'The significance of the eleventh-century rebuilding of Christ Church and St Augustine's, Canterbury', *BAA Conference Trans.* v (1982), 1–19.

[17] See *id.*, 'An early church of the Knights Templars at Shipley, Sussex', *Anglo-Norman Studies*, vi (1983), 238–46.

[18] *Omnium liberalium artium peritissimus, abacum praecipue et lunarem compotum et caelestium cursum astrorum rimatus*: William of Malmesbury, *Gesta Pontificum*, 300.

[19] *Ibid.*, 313.

[20] A. Cordoliani, 'L'activité computistique de Robert, evêque de Hereford', in *Mélanges offerts à René Crozet* (Poitiers, 1966), 333–40.

[21] C. H. Haskins, 'The abacus and the king's curia', *English Hist. Rev.* xxvii (1912), 105–6.

[22] *Annales Wintoniae*, ed. H. R. Luard, *Annales Monastici*, Rolls Series xxxvi (1864-9), ii, 32. William of Malmesbury, *Gesta Pontificum*, 302. *Id.*, *Vita Wulfstani*, ed. R. R. Darlington, Camden Society xl (1928), 62.

[23] See most recently P. McAleer, 'The Romanesque choir of Tewkesbury Abbey and the problem of a "colossal order"', *Art Bulletin*, lxiv (1982), 549–63. Also, *BAA Conference Trans.* for 1981, forthcoming.

[24] To illustrate this one might cite two cases where famous designs have been interpreted by some commentators as particular evidence of the innovative inspiration of their architects, whereas in fact both are dependent apparently on Antique precedent. The recessed columns of Michelangelo's Laurentian Library vestibule are likely to have been inspired by the second-century tomb of Anna Regilla in Rome, while the crowning volutes of Bernini's baldacchino for St Peter's must owe something to its Constantinian (and subsequent?) predecessor. Neither design is absolutely 'original' in these respects: but each is still a brilliant work of art for other reasons.

Postscript

Since the above paper was written the following has appeared: C. Wilson, 'Abbot Serlo's church at Gloucester (1089–1100): its place in Romanesque architecture', *BAA Conference Trans.* vii (1985), 52–83. Wilson regards Bilson's analysis of the Hereford chapel as convincing and even 'unassailable', but he does not discuss Bandmann's paper. While Wilson thus reiterates Bony's thesis (and discusses its implications for the design of Gloucester), I believe that the thesis remains open to the objections raised above.

The Role of Musicians at Court in Twelfth-Century Britain

Laurence Wright

In examining the role of musicians at court in Britain up to 1200, I propose to draw fairly heavily on Old French literary references. There are two justifications for this approach. First, necessity: source materials on this subject are hard to come by for the twelfth century. We do not have the plentiful documentary evidence that is available for the fourteenth and fifteenth centuries, such as records of payments to minstrels in Household accounts or in those of the Westminster Feast of 1306.[1] The only 'historical' evidence we have is the occasional remark by a chronicler. In contrast, references in French poetry are relatively abundant. The second reason is that the courts of twelfth-century Britain were French-speaking, that innovations in literature and music came mainly from France, and above all that the notion of the court and of *courtoisie* was founded on French ideas. Some of the material which I will use was written in Britain; some is Continental, but not necessarily inappropriate, since the aristocracy kept close cultural links with France.[2]

Examples of how minstrels were employed

Royal courts were not the only courts: indeed, we must remember that in twelfth-century England many castles were centres for literary (and probably musical) activity. However, kings and queens are better documented, and the English royal court played a central role in maintaining close links between Britain and France, introducing French influence and sometimes exporting British products, such as the lay, as well. Evidence for the employment of musicians is scarce, but let us take a few examples, isolated though they are.

(a) *Taillefer*. In 1066, as the chroniclers relate,[3] Duke William brought with him a minstrel named Taillefer, who performed before the Norman army just before the Battle of of Hastings and then struck the first blow, killing the first Englishman. On this, the sources are in broad agreement. But was he a musician or just a juggler? Opinions differ. According to three chroniclers (Gaimar, Guy of Amiens and Henry of Huntingdom) he juggled with a lance or with swords, terrifying the English, according to the two last-named writers (Guy also states ambiguously that Taillefer exhorted the French with words, which might refer to speech or song). But according to two other chroniclers (William of Malmesbury and Wace) he sang part of the *Chanson de Roland* in order (says William) 'that the example of a man of war might excite the warriors'. Wace's statement has an air of unreality:

> Taillefer, a great singer,
> Preceded the duke on a fast-moving horse
> Singing of Charlemagne and of Roland
> And of Oliver and of the vassals
> Who died at Roncevaux.

Any man who can sing to a whole army (perhaps accompanying himself on the fiddle, as was usual when performing a *chanson de geste*) whilst riding a horse at speed deserves immortality! True or false, the references by William of Malmesbury and Wace to the song underline three facts relevant to this paper: first, the Norman invasion brought an invasion of French music; second, *chansons de geste* were very popular in twelfth-century Britain (the sole surviving manuscripts of some of them were copied there); third, Taillefer appears to have combined two roles, those of soldier and musician.

(b) *Maud*. Of Queen Maud, the first wife of Henry I, William of Malmesbury speaks bitterly of her generous patronage:

> Her one love was of hearing divine service; and therefore she recklessly provided for sweet-singing clerks, speaking well of them all, making generous gifts, promising more. Thence, as news of her liberality spread world-wide, clerks famed in song and poetry flocked thither; he who charmed the queen's ears with the novelty of song considered himself lucky. She contributed payment not only to these, but also to all kinds of men, especially foreigners: so that, having accepted the rewards, they might sing her praises in all lands.[4]

The 'foreigners' were most probably from France, given that the aristocracy was French-speaking: if so, we have one example of how French music was imported into Britain, and English courts kept up to date on cultural developments across the Channel. Also, we note that the musicians were intended to increase the monarch's prestige: we shall return later to the importance of this function. William adds: '. . . For the desire for glory is so innate in the minds of men that scarcely anyone eager for the precious fruits of a good conscience, if he has done any good, does not find it sweet to be extolled to the crowds.'

(c) *Henry II and Eleanor of Aquitaine*. At Henry's court there was, according to Peter of Blois[5] in a letter to the court chaplains, a large number of minstrels and other hangers-on. He complains:

> If the king has announced that he will go early next morning to a certain place, the decision is sure to be changed: and so you know he will sleep till midday. You will see pack-animals waiting under their loads, teams of horses

standing in silence, heralds sleeping, court traders fretting, and everyone in turn grumbling. One runs to whores and pavilioners of the court to ask them where the king is going. For this breed of courtier often knows the palace secrets. For the king's court has an assiduous following of entertainers (*histriones*), female singers (*candidatrices*, which I take as a mistake for *cantatrices*), dice-players, flatterers, taverners (*caupones*), waferers (*nebulatores*), actors (*mimi*), barbers—gluttons the whole lot of them!

(d) *Richard the Lionheart.* Not only do we know of this monarch's close links with the troubadours but also we know the name of one of his minstrels, Blondel, thanks to the well-known anecdote related around 1260 by the Minstrel of Reims.[6] According to this account, the king, imprisoned by the Duke of Austria in 1193–4 whilst returning from the third crusade, was located by his minstrel Blondel, and then ransomed. Whatever the authenticity of the story, it contains details which must at least have been credible, and are informative to us. Firstly we read: 'Now it happend that the king had raised from infancy a minstrel named Blondel of France, from the region of Arras.' Thus the minstrel (usually identified with Blondel de Nesle) came from across the Channel, and the fact that he was raised by the king implies a close relationship and a position of privilege.

Next, when the king espies Blondel through his prison window, we are told:

> ... he wondered how he might get Blondel to recognize him; and he remembered a song which they had composed between them, and which nobody else knew. And he began to sing the beginning loud and clear, for he was a good singer.

So the king himself composed and sang (several of his compositions are preserved) and collaborated in this with a minstrel.

Thirdly, Blondel not only collaborated in composition, but played several instruments, if we are to believe the statement that he 'went and fetched his fiddle and his instruments', although the only instrument he actually plays in the story is the fiddle.

Certain other aspects of the minstrel's life come out in this anecdote: travelling long distances (from England to Austria and back); and temporary employment with another patron: he offers his services to the castellan, is 'retained' by him, stays all winter and up to Whitsun, when he asks to be allowed to leave. The castellan reluctantly grants leave, and gives him a horse and a new robe. The expressions 'retain' (*retenir*) and 'grant leave' (*otroier congé*) occur in other French literary references to minstrels,[7] and illustrate how the so-called 'wandering minstrel' might often be resident in one house for many months or even years, and have what was virtually a steady job under contract. We may safely assume that other minstrels working at English courts absented themselves from time to time to work elsewhere.

Another role was played by minstrels during Richard's absence. According to one chronicler,[8] his regent William Longchamp, 'in order to enhance and increase his reputation enticed singers and minstrels from France with gifts, so that they might sing of him in public places'. Unfortunately, no songs about William Longchamp survive, so we do not know what type of song was involved, but we can guess that the text was in French.

(e) *Renard the Fox.* An episode in the fictional *Roman de Renart*[9] in which the hero masquerades as an English minstrel is instructive. Renart, made unrecognizable because he fell into a vat of yellow dye, goes up to his old enemy Ysengrin the Wolf and tells him (in atrocious French which is a parody of Anglo-Norman) that he has become separated from his companion, has sought him throughout England and France, and is now on the way to Paris to improve his French. He asks for news of the king of France, saying that nobles often give hospitality to minstrels such as him, and boasts of all the lays which he knows. He persuades Ysengrin to steal a fiddle for him, and is engaged as musician for the wedding of Poincet and Renart's own wife, but, needless to say, thwarts their plans.

Many interesting aspects are illustrated in this incident: Anglo-Norman minstrels travelled in France and were understood (or at least appreciated) by French audiences; they sought hospitality at the courts of the nobility; the lays and *chansons de geste* which Renart boasts of knowing can be taken as typical of the British repertoire; lastly, a minstrel was essential for a wedding:

> Poincet would have married her
> If he had been able to find a minstrel.

The reason why one was essential is the same as the reason why minstrels were present at court: prestige. We will develop this point in a moment.

To sum up what can be gleaned from these scattered references to the employment of minstrels, it is clear that their role was not confined to giving pleasure by entertaining: their songs could be functional, serving to embolden soldiers' hearts (as at Hastings), to glorify magnates (such as Maud and Wiliam Longchamp), or simply to lend prestige to an occasion. They might also perform other tasks: fighting (like Taillefer), spying and carrying messages (like Blondel), or doing the work of waferers.[10] Furthermore, minstrels helped to promote French culture in Britain, thereby increasing the standing of the new aristocracy.

The symbolical function of minstrels

To judge by the majority of references in poetry, the most important reason for employing minstrels was not because they entertained or performed useful secondary roles, but because they symbolized joy which in turn symbolized honour—and honour was an essential part of the very notion of a court. The equation music = joy = honour seems to have been an axiom of medieval poets. Entertainers of all types, including musicians, and especially musical instruments, are the elements which poets stress most frequently in their descriptions of celebrations. Dancing by courtiers and ordinary people also has the same symbolism. Let us take one such description in *Erec et Enide* written (possibly for the court of Henry II[11]) by Chrétien de Troyes:

> The archbishop of Canterbury
> Who had come to the court
> Blessed them as he should.
> When all the court was assembled
> There was not a minstrel in all the land
> Who could offer any entertainment

Who did not flock to the court.
Great was the joy in the hall:
Each performed his service:
One leaps, one tumbles, one conjures,
One tells tales, the other sings
One whistles, the other plays tunes
This one plays the harp, this the rote,
This the *gigue*, this the fiddle,
This the flute and this the shawm.
Maidens carol and dance.
All strive to make joy.
There is nothing that can make joy
Which was not present that day at the wedding.[12]

So far we have seen an illustration of the first part of the equation (music = joy), which some poets take so literally that they speak of *seeing* joy and *hearing* joy. Now for the second part of the equation (joy = honour). Joy and honour are often mentioned together as if they were practically synonyms. To take one example from elsewhere in the same poem:

He made great joy and great honour for them;
He loved them for the sake of his son Erec,
And granted them the castle.[13]

Notice the words 'for them': joy is made *for* someone, to give them honour, Poets are conscious of the fact that the entertainments at feasts have a specific purpose: giving honour to someone. And the more jugglers, instruments, etc., the more joy and hence the more honour. Hence the stress on quantity and diversity.   A note of caution: the poetical descriptions identifying music with joy and honour all relate to large-scale feasts and public celebrations. It would be misleading to imply that this went on every day. I have no firm evidence that the same symbolism was valid in the long quiet periods between such festivities. However, the identification of musical instruments with joy, if not honour, does appear to have been constant. One manifestation of this is the way that *absence* of music was treated as a sign of sadness. When describing scenes of mourning, poets convey sadness by commenting on the lack of music. For example in *Horn*, when Egfer dies. 'Never that day was there song, fiddle or dance',[14] and in the *Roman de Rou*, when Duke Richard is taken prisoner,

Throughout the land there was much weeping and grieving:
There were no fiddles, no rotes, no *rotruenges*, no songs.
Even the children weep in many houses.[15]

If the absence of music had this significance, it would seem obvious that no court of repute could afford to be without minstrels, otherwise it would be a place of sadness. A magnate could no more afford to dispense with minstrels than he could afford not to indulge in hunting, hawking and wearing fine clothes. Putting it another way, the presence of minstrels in any household increased the honour of that house. Far from being an unnecessary luxury, they contributed positively to the honour and prestige which was essential to the very concept of the court and of *courtoisie*.

It is an interesting thought that representations of musicians in secular wall-paintings and stonecarvings (e.g. those in the twelfth-century hall of Oakham Castle, see pl. XXXII) may have had the same symbolical function and similarly brought honour to their owners.

A particular British interest: harp-playing

It would be wrong to give the impression that courts in Britain were carbon copies of their French counterparts. As regards the use of music, I would single out a pronounced interest in the music of the harp or sometime the rote (a similar plucked instrument) rather than that of the fiddle, which was the favoured instrument in France. We find some very fine harps depicted in English carving and manuscripts of the period (e.g. pl. XXXIII), and it is too much of a coincidence that three literary works containing outstandingly detailed and beautiful descriptions of harp-playing were probably written for the court of Henry II.

The first work in question is the *Tristan* poem[16] written by Thomas after 1155. Harp-playing features at several points in the story, notably the following: when the young Tristan comes to the court of Cornwall and amazes all by his playing; when he goes to Ireland and teaches Isolt; the episode of the harp and the rote, in which an Irishman wins Mark's wife by his harp-playing and Tristan wins her back by his rote-playing; and the lay sung by Isolt after Tristan is banished. Unfortunately only the last survives in the original French, and we have to reconstruct the others, which are in the parts of the poem now lost, from subsequent translations, particularly that by Gottfried von Strassburg. Even allowing for embellishments by Gottfried, we can see that the original descriptions must have been quite lengthy, and some of Gottfried's technical terms (e.g. *noten, ursuoche*) seem to be translated from French. Not only are the descriptions long and detailed: they show a particular reverence for music not found in continental French poems.

The second is *Horn*, written around 1180 by Thomas (not the same Thomas as the one who wrote *Tristan*, although it is an odd coincidence). The harping scene in *Horn* is well known. The two sons of the king of Dublin ask their sister to play some lays on the harp; then each in turn plays, for, as the poet explains: 'In those times everyone was proficient on the harp.' Finally Horn (under the assumed name of Gudmod) performs a beautiful lay. This is how the poet begins his lyrical description:

> Then he takes up the harp to tune it.
> God! anyone who watched how well he handled it,
> How he plucked the strings, made them tremble,
> Sometimes sound the tune, sometimes the chords,
> Would have been reminded of the harmony of heaven . . .[17]

The passage also contains the most complete surviving description of how a lay was performed, with instrumental prelude, retuning, singing the lay, then instrumental postlude.

The third author is Giraldus Cambrensis, who came of a Norman French family in South Wales, and who became chaplain to the court of Henry II. He includes the same description of harp-playing in both the *Topography of Ireland* (c. 1186)

PLATE XXXII

a. Unidentified musician playing the fiddle. Oakham Castle, *c.* 1180

PLATE XXXIII

a

a. Animals playing an unidentified wind instrument and a harp. Canterbury Cathedral, crypt, *c.* 1120

b. David harping, from a psalter from Westminster Abbey, late twelfth century (British Library MS Roy. 2.A. XXII, fo. 14[b])

b   *Photograph: British Library*

and the *Description of Wales* (*c.* 1188). This could be because the Irish and Welsh played in the same manner (perfectly conceivable, given that the Welsh had learned from the Irish) or simply because the passage found favour with Gerald's audience, namely Henry's court. He writes:

> It is remarkable how, with such rapid and complex snatching with the fingers, musical harmony is preserved; and with consummate artistry, through clusters of melody and intricate chords, with such sweet rapidity, such balanced imbalance, such discordant concord, the melody is rendered and fulfilled harmoniously. Whether the strings sound in fourths or fifths, they always start from a B flat, and return to the same, so that the whole may be fulfilled in the sweetness of cheerful sonority. They begin and end their phrases with such skill; so pleasantly playing the tinkling slender strings against the deep sound of the thicker string, so stealthily ravishing, so sweetly soothing, that the essence of the art is to conceal art.[18]

It does not matter for our pursposes that Celtic music may not have been common at courts in England, or that some of the technical terms remain highly obscure to us; what matters is that the passage must have been comprehensible and interesting to Gerald's readers. In other words, there must have been at the court of Henry II a public of musical *cognoscenti* with a taste for descriptions of harp-playing such as those in the three works cited above. It is also likely that they had a taste for the actual music of the harp, which means that among the types of minstrel so disparagingly listed in the earlier-quoted letter by Peter of Blois there were probably some harpists of the highest standard whose music was appreciated to a degree far beyond what is conveyed in the somewhat summary references so often found in poetry and in chronicles.

Conclusion

Despite the paucity of relevant documentary evidence for the twelfth century, we can build up some sort of picture of the role, or rather roles, played by musicians at court. The reasons for employing them were several: some provided music which was appreciated at the highest level by sensitive audiences; some brought prestige to their patrons and to French-speaking culture in general; some performed secondary functions. All contributed to the honour of the courts where they worked. Their role was a positive one: they may have been regarded by their detractors as hangers-on, but they can also be seen as one of the pillars of the court and courtly life.

NOTES

[1] C. Bullock-Davies, *Menestrellorum Multitudo* (Cardiff, 1978); C. Wright, *Musicians at the Court of Burgundy, 1364–1419* (Henryville/Ottawa/Binningen, 1979); for the earlier period see E. Faral, *Les Jongleurs en France au moyen âge*, 2nd. edn. (Paris, 1971).
[2] M. D. Legge, *Anglo-Norman Literature and its Background* (Oxford, 1963), 139.
[3] *Widonis carmen de Hastingae proelio*, in F. Michel, *Chroniques Anglo-Normandes* (Rouen, 1836–40), iii, 18; *Henrici Huntendunensis Historia Anglorum*, ed. T. Arnold, Rolls Series 74 (London, 1879); Gaimar, *Estorie des Engleis*, ed. T. D. Hardy and C. T. Martin, Rolls Series

91 (London, 1888–9), 202–3; H. Andresen, *Maistre Wace's Roman de Rou et des ducs de Norman-die*, 2 vols. (Heilbronn, 1877–9), ii, vv. 8035 ff.; William of Malmesbury, *De Gestis Regum Anglorum*, ed. W. Stubbs, 2 vols. Rolls Series 90 (London, 1887-89), ii, 302.

4 William of Malmesbury, *op. cit.*, 494.

5 *PL*, ccvii, col. 49.

6 N. de Wailly, *Récits d'un ménestrel de Reims au treizième siècle* (Paris, 1876), 41–5.

7 e.g. *Le Roman de Silence, by Heldris de Cornuälle*, ed. L. Thorpe (Cambridge, 1972), vv. 2698, 3217, 3234, 3353 and 3482.

8 Roger de Hovedene, *Chronica*, ed. W. Stubbs, 3 vols. Rolls Series 51 (London, 1868–71), iii, 143.

9 *Le Roman de Renart, première branche*, ed. M. Roques (Paris, 1967), vv. 2393–2962.

10 For an explanation of this term, see C. Bullock-Davies, *op. cit.* (note 1), 44–50.

11 M. D. Legge, *op. cit.* (note 2), 74.

12 My translation of Chrétien de Troyes, *Erec et Enide*, ed. W. Foerster (Halle, 1909), vv. 2032–2051.

13 *Ibid.*, vv. 1900–1902.

14 Thomas, *The Romance of Horn*, ed. M. K. Pope, 2 vols. (Oxford, 1955–64), v. 3563.

15 Wace, *op. cit.* (note 3), vv. 2349–2351.

16 J. Bédier, *Le Roman de Tristan par Thomas*, 2 vols. (Paris, 1902–5); B. H. Wind, *Les Fragments de Tristan par Thomas* (Geneva / Paris, 1960); English translation in Gottfried von Strassburg, *Tristan, with the Surviving Fragments of the Tristran of Thomas*, trans. A. T. Hatto (London, 1960).

17 *Horn* (see note 14), vv. 2830–2834.

18 Translated from Giraldus Cambrensis, *Opera*, ed. J. S. Brewer and others (London 1861–91), v, 153–4, and vi, 186–7.

Wealth and Artistic Patronage at Twelfth-Century St Albans

Brian Golding

In the twelfth century the intellectual, literary and artistic life of St Albans 'surpassed that of all the other monasteries of England'.[1] It would indeed be ludicrous to pretend that St Albans was not a leading, perhaps the leading, *foyer* of English Benedictine artistic production during the twelfth century: surviving works such as the St Albans Psalter and the description in the *Gesta Abbatum* of others, now destroyed, such as the great shrine of St Alban, testify to the first 'golden age' of the abbey, while the extensive surviving work of abbot Paul's late eleventh-century church is amongst the finest early Romanesque structures in England.

What made this flowering possible, who or what provided the stimulus for the work and how was it achieved? The accepted orthodoxy is that the personal initiative of the abbots of St Albans during this period was responsible for the abbey's artistic achievements. Thus, for example, Michael Kauffmann has written: 'it is not surprising that the richest monasteries should have been the greatest patrons, but wealth had to be matched by the personalities of the abbots and priors.'[2]

In the first half of this paper I wish to focus in a little more detail on these abbots to whom so much is attributed before going on to suggest that there might be other more structural and less 'personal' reasons for St Albans' artistic development and pre-eminence during this period. The chief source for the history of the abbey during this period is the *Gesta Abbatum*, which in many ways is the most impressive monastic chronicle of medieval England.[3] Yet the *Gesta* is not only a chronicle, it also had a didactic function for the monks of mid thirteenth-century St Albans for whom it was compiled. Matthew Paris had a number of objectives when he produced this quasi-official history of his abbey; not least was his intention that monks and abbots read his account of their predecessors as *exempla* for themselves. This accounts, at least in part, for the layout of the work, in which praise and blame is accorded to individual abbots in turn. Unlike most, if not all, other monastic chronicles the *Gesta Abbatum* is self-consciously the 'Deeds of the Abbots', not the 'History of the Abbey'. The activities of the monks and the policies of the community are revealed only in so far as the activities and policies of the abbot impinged upon them. The implications of this sort of historical writing for an analysis of the monastery at this time are obvious. Firstly, there is a danger that historians may ascribe to the abbots rather more initiative and responsibility for developments in the abbey than they in fact had, and that conversely the role and activities of the obedientiaries and lesser officials may be understated. Secondly, the arrangement of the *Gesta* as essentially a series of biographical studies may lead later commentators, too, to divide artificially the development of the abbey by reference to the individual careers of the abbots, thus making the evolutionary pattern of St Albans' history hard to recover.[4]

With this caveat, it is time now to consider the abbots in more detail, to examine their origins and perhaps to look rather more closely than has been the case before at their shortcomings as described in the *Gesta*. It is clear that, like most English abbeys, St Albans suffered severely in the post-Conquest era. According to the *Gesta*, William I laid waste its manors, lands, houses and possessions.[5] After the disgraced abbot Frederick's death William took the abbey into his own hands, heavily exploited it, and, if the *Gesta* is to be believed, would have destroyed it completely had not Lanfranc intervened. It was Lanfranc, too, who gained the appointment of his kinsman Paul as abbot.[6]

Paul was undoubtedly one of the greatest of the Anglo-Norman abbots. His origins are unclear: as a close kinsman of Lanfranc he must have been at least in part of Lombard origin and he is certainly not known to have had aristocratic Norman connections. Indeed, the fact that the *Gesta* accuses Paul of granting many lands to his kinsmen suggests that he may have used his position to advance his family.[7] It is clear that Paul owed his position to Lanfranc: he had been a monk at Caen under Lanfranc; Lanfranc obtained his appointment, and throughout Paul's abbacy he seems to have kept a close eye on developments at the abbey.[8] In particular he provided books, ornaments and vestments for the abbey and he gave the considerable sum of 1,000 marks for the rebuilding of the church begun in 1088.[9]

Perhaps more importantly, Lanfranc used his influence to recover for St Albans estates that had been seized or otherwise alienated in the difficult years preceding Paul's abbacy. Such recoveries cost money and it seems likely that Paul's priority was to recover the estates and then to rebuild the church.[10] This policy would explain the eleven years' delay between the commencement of his abbacy and the beginning of the rebuilding programme. Yet Paul was not wholly successful in his attempt to regain lost estates. The *Gesta* blames him for granting too much land in farm, particularly to his kinsmen, who are scorned by the chronicler as illiterate and ignoble.[11] Some lands were granted for 'legitimate' reasons: Robert the Mason gained Sarratt and another manor together with a house in St Albans rent-free as a reward for his work in the monastery.[12] Other alienations were less justifiable, but equally explicable grants to powerful lay magnates, such as Peter de Valognes, and the recovery of these lands, were to occupy several generations of abbots.[13] Yet it would perhaps be going too far with the *Gesta* in the condemnation of Paul. By the mid thirteenth century the prevailing economic orthodoxy was that lords should cultivate their lands themselves and produce for the market: many abbeys were going to great trouble and expense to recover lands that had been demised in fee farm in earlier years. In the late eleventh century, however, the leasing of estates was an acceptable response to contemporary economic conditions and Paul was doing no more than many of his fellow abbots.

On Paul's death in 1093 there was a vacancy for four years, during which time the abbey was in the hands of William Rufus, who seems to have over-exploited the estates and to have reduced the community to near penury.[14] This ensured that Paul's successor Richard would have to spend much time restoring the abbey's resources, which may account for a comparatively fallow period as far as the abbey's artistic and architectural productions are concerned. Richard's abbacy did see the dedication with great splendour of the new abbey church, but there is little evidence that he himself was responsible for further building.[15] He is also said to have given two reliquaries, vestments, tapestries and many volumes to the house and he allegedly granted two-thirds of the tithes of the abbey's churches to the scriptorium.[16] By comparison with those of his immediate predecessor and successor, Richard's abbacy marked time: as suggested above, one reason may have been the need to recover from Rufus's administration. There are other reasons, however. During this period St Albans established three cells, at Wymondham, Tynemouth and Binham, and it may be that the abbey's energies were concentrated in the development of these daughter-houses.[17] Certainly, too, comparatively few benefactions were received by the mother-house during this period. Just as Paul had been before him, Richard was accused of alienating lands to his Norman kinsfolk and of having leased lands in fee farm to local lay families. One such lease, that of the manor of Saratt, once held by Robert the Mason, was particularly censured, for this was made not only against the wishes and order of the community but also against the advice of lay magnates who supported the abbey.[18]

On Richard's death he was immediately succeeded by his protégé, the then prior, Geoffrey de Gorron, whom Richard had brought from Le Mans to head the grammar school at St Albans.[19] Geoffrey's achievements were as remarkable as those of Paul. He provided a new guest-hall, an infirmary with infirmary chapel and a chamber known as the Queen's chamber, a lodging for the queen, the only woman allowed to stay in the house.[20] He gave books and vestments to the abbey and above all he commenced the construction of a magnificent new shrine for the relics of St Alban, a work on which he spent the not inconsiderable sum of £60.[21] Though the body of the saint was translated with great solemnity in 1129, the shrine was incomplete at the time of Geoffrey's death. The first interruption to the work came when the abbot (who had a considerable reputation for his care for the sick and the poor) sold off the precious materials that had been assembled for the shrine in order that food might be bought for the starving poor during a famine in which the price of corn reached 20*s.* a quarter.[22] The work then appears to have been resumed, but was again frustrated because of the 'many emergencies which the increasing evil of the world daily encouraged'.[23] This rather cryptic statement is explained a little later when we are told that during the civil war of Stephen's reign the Earl of Warenne, William de Ipre, the Earl of Arundel and William Martel (all supporters of Stephen) threatened to burn down the town of St Albans. Geoffrey was obliged to melt down precious fittings of the church in order to buy the magnates off.[24] In spite of the obvious disruption caused at the abbey by the anarchy, it is noteworthy that, in contrast to Paul and Richard, Geoffrey is not accused of alienating lands to his kin. In general he appears to have been successful in the temporal organization of his abbey: he augmented conventual revenues, he was active in the land market, established the leper hospital of St Julian and set aside some revenues especially for the provision of ornaments for the church, making over the church of Rickmansworth to the sacristan for this purpose.[25] There does seem, therefore, to be a clear correlation between the economic and artistic activities of St Albans during this period. Can a similar pattern be seen in the short abbacy of Geoffrey's successor, Ralph Gubion (1146–51)?

Ralph's policy is rather ambiguous. The *Gesta* states that he was a lover of books and had been in charge of the scriptorium.[26] He was also a learned man, having been instructed in the Scriptures by the Italian master Guy while he was in the household of Alexander, Bishop of Lincoln.[27] Ralph gave a number of volumes to the abbey and provided two fine altar cloths, one worth 9, the other 11 marks.[28] He also built chambers for the abbot and a garderobe luxuriously covered with oaken tiles.[29] At the same time, however, the abbot's chief concern seems to have been the restoration of the economic fortunes of his house. He is praised for having quickly restored the abbey's losses during the difficult times of the civil war. He also increased the stock on the abbey's manors and above all left the abbey totally debt-free: we can only assume that such debts had been incurred during the rather more flamboyant abbacy of Geoffrey.[30] It is symbolic of the different attitude of the two abbots that in order to raise money to purchase the manor of Brantfield Ralph stripped the still incomplete shrine of St Alban of its gold plates and sold them along with other ornaments and jewels, and he also allowed an extremely costly chasuble, fringed with gold and jewels, to be destroyed, presumably in order that these items could be sold.[31]

Unfortunately, after Ralph's death there was little opportunity to build on the firm foundations he had provided. The third quarter of the twelfth century, when the abbey was ruled first by Robert de Gorron (d. 1167), the nephew of abbot Geoffrey, and then by another Englishman, Simon, was dominated by attempts to gain freedom from the episcopal jurisdiction of the bishop of Lincoln. In this the abbey was ultimately successful, but such efforts cost money. No new benefactions to the abbey are recorded at this time and it is hardly surprising that the abbey was now reckoned to be 600 marks in debt, both to Christian and Jewish money-lenders.[32] Matthew Paris indeed explains this indebtedness as the result of the expenses of negotiations (presumably at the Roman Curia) and also as a result of Robert's favour to his kinsmen and compatriots.[33] Similar criticisms were levied at Simon, who left the abbey more than 600 marks in debt to the Jews at his death, and more than 200 marks in debt to Christian money-lenders.[34] It was during Simon's abbacy that Aaron of Lincoln made his celebrated boast that he had been responsible for providing a shrine for the homeless St Alban.[35] Like Robert, Simon was also condemned for favouring his relatives, not only the poor and the indigent, but also knights and magnates.[36] But the abbey was not only in difficulties through indebtedness and unwise favouritism: alienations continued at a high level and it is clear that St Albans was facing a problem encountered by virtually all Benedictine houses in twelfth-century England—lands leased to lay tenants were proving extremely difficult to recover.[37]

During this period, when the house's attention was focused on constitutional matters, it is hardly surprising that little building work was carried out, since the abbey's finances were required for other purposes. Abbot Robert made some repairs to the abbey church and he is said to have rebuilt the chapter house, where he was buried at the feet of abbot Paul, from its foundations, though it is not wholly clear whether this rebuilding occurred while Robert was abbot or while he was still sacristan.[38] No building works at all are recorded during Simon's abbacy, though he did increase the endowment of the scriptorium, which he also repaired 'because it was at this time almost *disused* [my italics] and in poor repair', and this may further suggest that in the preceding generation the monks were more concerned with the establishment of their constitutional liberties than they were with the production of manuscripts.[39]

It cannot be denied that some at least of the abbots of twelfth-century St Albans were artistic patrons of the highest order. Most were themselves learned men; some had already gained experience in the scriptorium before they became abbot. Though none, perhaps, matched the individual achievements of a Baldwin of Bury St Edmunds or a Gilbert Crispin of Westminster, collectively they were an impressive group. It was one thing, however, to provide the initiative for the production of works of art, quite another to finance them. How was this done? The abbots were not personally of great wealth. Though abbot Richard may have been a member of the important Norman family of d'Aubigny and Geoffrey and Robert de Gorron were of aristocratic descent and had ties with the Lucy family, all three were condemned for favouring their relatives, who are described in terms which suggest that they at least were not of high social standing.[40] The origins of the Englishmen Ralph and Simon are unknown, but though these men were scarcely likely to be of peasant stock they are equally hardly likely to have been members of influential magnatial families.[41] If the patrons did not have resources of their own, what resources did they use?

In 1086 St Albans had an assessed gross income of *c.* £270.[42] This was a large corporate income, but it is important to place this figure in the context of the other great Benedictine abbeys. Amongst these it only ranked twelfth, far below Glastonbury, the wealthiest house of all assessed at *c.* £830, or St Albans' rival for the relics of the martyr, Ely, at *c.* £700. If, therefore, a prediction had been made at the end of the eleventh century as to which monasteries were to emerge as cultural leaders in the following century, basing this prediction on wealth alone, St Albans would have been a far from obvious choice. It is, I think, possible to explain this apparent paradox in three ways.

There can be no doubt that the English monasteries suffered very heavily in the generation following the Conquest. Even if St Albans did not experience the same disturbances as troubled Glastonbury, Peterborough or St Augustine's, Canterbury, Domesday testifies to the scale of losses and illegal seizure of lands suffered by the community.[43] Of course these disruptions were only temporary: recruitment rapidly picked up and the Old English abbeys survived to dominate the religious life of the country until the Dissolution. There was, however, a longer-term consequence of the Conquest for the English abbeys. A new Norman aristocracy tended to favour Norman rather than English monasteries. Their spiritual as well as temporal roots lay across the Channel, in monasteries founded by their fathers or grandfathers. These monasteries were usually the *foci* of their benefactions; it was in these houses that the first generation at least of Norman magnates chose to be buried and in them that oblates from the family were placed.[44] The extent to which Norman monasteries were favoured is demonstrated by the fact that in 1086 the assessed income of Fécamp from its English lands was £200, only £70 less than St Albans and derived from land acquired in only twenty years.[45] English monasteries could not hope for much temporal support from the new aristocracy. St Albans, however, may have been an exception. An analysis of the benefactions recorded in the *Gesta* and the so-called 'Golden Book' suggests that this monastery at least continued to prove attractive to Norman benefactors, among the more surprising of whom is Robert of Mortain, who doubled both as a despoiler and patron of the house![46] Benefactions seem to have been particularly lavish during the last years of the eleventh century. Some of these grants were for specific needs, such as the well-known grant made by an educated knight of two-thirds of his demesne tithes in Hatfield for the support of the scriptorium.[47] Many grants, like that one, were of tithes or churches, which represent the most common type of grant to religious houses during the eleventh and twelfth centuries, but there were also substantial grants of lands.[48] Thus, while many other Benedictine houses were marking time and re ceiving few benefactions, St Albans was continuing to expand its holdings and revenues.

There was another unusual feature of post-Conquest St Albans that I believe was fundamental to the twelfth-century development of the community and which has been largely ignored by commentators. Sometime after the Conquest the obligation to provide knights for royal military service was laid upon the Old English abbeys. Just when this imposition was made is a matter of debate, but most historians would still agree that it occurred early in William I's reign, probably *c.* 1070, the year in which, according to Roger of Wendover, William ordered the bishops and all abbots who held baronies, and who had held them free from all secular service until that date, to perform military service. Such service was imposed arbitrarily by the king (*pro voluntate suo*).[49] The placing of the *servicia debita* on the abbeys had serious implications: they now had to maintain knights at their own expense. As is well known, the usual initial solution was to keep the knights in the household itself, but the drawbacks of this arangement led to the subinfeudation of monastic lands in order that the knights might be provided with estates of their own.[50] This development was doubtless less harassing to the monastic community and perhaps less expensive as well, but it could result in a serious diminution of income from landed estates: for some it could be 'a permanent source of very real hardship'.[51] Not only was land lost permanently to the knights, but it could prove difficult to enforce the required service, which could then bring the abbot into conflict with the crown.[52] Even worse from the abbey's point of view was the fact that royal taxation and exactions were normally assessed on the basis of the number of knights' fees, and though, of course, the abbeys could attempt to recoup some of these demands from their own tenants, it is clear that those abbeys with the highest knightly quotas suffered the highest taxation demands.[53]

Now, as we have seen, William is said to have imposed the *servicia debita* in an arbitrary fashion. This becomes even more apparent when the wealth of the abbey is correlated with its quota, when it becomes immediately clear that there *is* no correlation. It is true that the wealthiest abbey, Glastonbury, had the highest quota (60 knights), but the same quota was imposed on Peterborough, with an assessed income only about 40 per cent that of Glastonbury.

One of the most striking examples is that of St Albans: with its assessed income of £270, it only had to provide six knights.[54] The reasons for this low assessment have never been satisfactorily explained. Knowles hazarded a suggestion that it was significant that both St Albans and Ramsey (which also had a low assessment) 'long held aloof from the new régime and received Norman abbots only in 1077 and 1087 respectively'.[55] However, it is likely that St Albans *did* have a Norman, or at any rate a non-English, abbot before 1077.[56] Whatever the reasons for St Albans' good fortune it is probably to the low assessment that we should look for an explanation of its later prosperity.

In one of his most lapidary phrases, David Knowles, comparing St Albans with Bury, wrote: 'The Athenian vivacity of the one is a contrast to the Boeotian atmosphere of the other': whereas Bury concentrated on estate organization and administration, St Albans concentrated on letters and the arts.[57] The contrast is a real one, but the reason does not, I think, lie as Knowles would have it, primarily in the different characters of the abbots of the two houses: after all, Baldwin and Anselm stand comparison with any of the abbots of contemporary St Albans. The contrast is not a matter of personalities, but of opportunities. Bury had to provide forty knights to St Albans' six, or put in very crude statistical terms, one knight for every £16 of assessed income. St Albans had to provide one knight for every £54. We have only to read Jocelin's Life of Samson to see how much trouble the great abbot of Bury experienced in the recovery of estates lost to the knights of the abbey or in the attempts to force these knights to perform their service.[58] This sort of problem was not experienced by the abbots of St Albans. Thus, during the twelfth century, though they did not have as large a gross income as did Benedictine abbeys like Bury or Glastonbury, they did possess great freedom to do as they pleased with their estates and they were subject to fewer demands for royal taxation.

There is one other possible factor to be considered. During the twelfth century there was an increasing tendency for the revenues of abbot and convent to be divided.[59] Such a division raises an important constitutional question: how far did the abbot of a Benedictine house have access to the revenues of his community for his own needs and projects? There is not a great deal of evidence to answer this question either way, though a close reading of Jocelin of Brakelond suggests that by the end of the twelfth century the theory was established that in normal circumstances the abbot should not interfere with the revenues of the obedientiaries.[60] I am not sure that this was the case, however, in twelfth-century St Albans. Though it is clear that in the thirteenth century a full obedientiary system obtained, the pattern of organization in the preceding century is obscure.[61] Certainly, the abbot appears to have had considerable authority in the disposition of all monastic revenues and the *Constitutions* of Lanfranc adopted by abbot Paul gave the abbot important powers: 'All the ordering of the monastery shall depend upon his will'.[62]

The *Gesta* makes it clear that by the time of abbot Paul the estates of St Albans were divided into the abbot's and the convent's lands: it also mentions several obedientiaries during the twelfth century, notably the cellarer, almoner and sacristan, but they never appear to have taken any independent action in the running of the abbey's affairs.[63] As was normal in Benedictine houses, the cellarer was the most important official. According to the *Constitutions* his role above all was to provide for the monks' food and to have charge of the kitchens.[64] It is interesting that when the cellarer is mentioned in twelfth-century St Albans it is always in connection with the community's food allowances, but it is also clear that it was the abbot who made the dispositions and alterations to these allowances.[65] It may be that at St Albans the abbot retained rather more control of monastic resources than in some other houses and there are some indications in the *Gesta* to support this hypothesis. In the famous passage describing the knight Robert's grant to the scriptorium, abbot Paul ordered food allowances to be given to the scribes from the brethren's revenues and from the cellary and then, as if recognizing his high-handed behaviour, Paul increased the almoner's allowance 'to salve his conscience'.[66] The scriptorium was certainly the responsibility of the abbot during the twelfth century, as abbot Simon's augmentation of its revenues makes clear.[67] It has already been seen how Paul alienated the manor of Sarrett to Robert the Mason and Westwick to Humbold, though both were part of the monks' demesne. Indeed, virtually every succeeding abbot of the century was condemned for alienating property that belonged to the community's *mensa*.[68] Moreover, it appears that this was a worsening trend which reached a climax during the abbacies of Warin (1183–95) and John de Cella (1195–1214). When Warin took monastic property to establish the hospital of St Mary de Pré the *Gesta* was quite explicit: 'all this would have been laudable and of merit and to the eternal praise of abbot Warin if it had been established from *his* patrimony or from acquisitions, but almost everything was taken from the church of St Albans for that insignificant little church to the damage and diminution of the monastery.'[69]

There can be little doubt, therefore, that the twelfth-century abbots frequently acted in a high-handed manner in using the property of the monks for their own ends. To what extent such action was actually 'unconstitutional' is hard to assess: clearly to Matthew Paris, looking at the previous century's history through the eyes of a thirteenth-century monk, it was unjustifiable. And yet the *Constitutions* of Lanfranc, as we have seen, allow considerable authority and freedom to the abbot. Before any certain conclusions can be reached it will be necessary to make comparative studies of the organization of the other Benedictine houses during this period. Preliminary investigations do, however, suggest that the abbots of St Albans did indeed possess an extraordinary degree of freedom at this time which gave them access to resources to promote their own projects. Among such projects must of course be reckoned their cultural and artistic policies. I would suggest that St Albans' exceptional place among the great abbeys of England was indeed the result of the 'election of learned and cultivated abbots without break or exception', but that these abbots were both ruthless and fortunate in obtaining the necessary resources: ruthless in that they were able to override their convent's views if necessary, fortunate in that their abbey's lands continued to grow after the Conquest and that royal demands upon the house were comparatively slight.[70]

NOTES

[1] D. Knowles, *The Monastic Order in England*, 2nd edn. (Cambridge, 1963), 311; cf. 186–9. See also the more recent comments of C. M. Kauffmann, *Survey*, iii: *Romanesque Manuscripts, 1066–1190* (London, 1975), 12, 13: R. M. Thomson, *Manuscripts from St Albans Abbey: 1066–1235*, 2 vols. (Woodbridge, 1982), i, *passim*, esp. p. 2, and D. Kahn, 'Recent discoveries of Romanesque sculpture at St Albans' in F. H. Thompson (ed.), *Studies in Medieval Sculpture*, Soc. Antiq. London Occ. Paper, new ser. iii (1983), 71–89.

[2] Kauffmann, *op. cit.*, 12, where he compares the unfortunate experiences of the wealthy, but disastrously led, Glastonbury with the poorer, but well-governed, St Albans. See also Knowles, *op. cit.*, 523 and Thomson, *op. cit.*, i, esp. 69, 78–9.

[3] For the *Gesta* see A. Gransden, *Historical Writing in England, c. 550–c. 1307* (London, 1974), 374–7 and R. Vaughan, *Matthew Paris* (Cambridge, 1958), 182–9.

[4] A clear example of this approach is to be found in vol. iv of VCH, *Hertfordshire*, where the history of the abbey is described solely in terms of its abbots.

[5] *Gesta Abbatum Monasterii Sancti Albani a Thoma Walsingham* (A.D. *793–1401*), ed. H. T. Riley, 3 vols., Rolls Series, 25 (London, 1867–9), i, 46, 50.

[6] *Ibid.*, i, 51.

[7] *Ibid.*, i, 64. For a brief account of abbot Paul and the rebuilding of the abbey, see C. N. L. Brooke, 'St Albans: the Great Abbey', in R. Runcie (ed.), *Cathedral and City: St Albans Ancient and Modern* (London, 1977), 46–53.

[8] *Gesta Abbatum*, i, 54, 58, 61.

[9] *Ibid.*, i, 54.

[10] Properties were recovered from Odo of Bayeux and Remigius, Bishop of Lincoln and the good offices of Lanfranc were used to regain possession of the important estates of Redbourn and Childwick (*ibid.*, i, 53–4).

[11] See above, note 7.

[12] *Gesta Abbatum*, i, 63–4. In addition the manor of Westwick was granted to Humbald 'out of love for Lanfranc' from the monks' demesne.

[13] *Ibid.*, i, 63. See also i, 159–66.

[14] *Ibid.*, i, 65.

[15] *Ibid.*, i, 70–1.

[16] *Ibid.*, i, 69–70, 76.

[17] *Ibid.*, i, 68–9.

[18] *Ibid.*, i, 72.

[19] *Ibid.*, i, 73.

[20] *Ibid.*, i, 79–80.

[21] *Ibid.*, i, 93–4, 80.

[22] *Ibid.*, i, 82–3. For the translation of the relics see i, 85.

[23] *Ibid.*, *loc. cit.*

[24] *Ibid.*, i, 94.

[25] *Ibid.*, i, 73–8. He was accused of endowing a new church, Holy Trinity de Bosco, with tithes taken from the abbey's own churches against the will of the convent and of having granted two estates which belonged to the monks' endowment to two lay men (one a kinsman) by his own impulse 'to the great damage of and prejudice to the church' (*ibid.*, i, 95–6).

[26] *Ibid.*, i, 106.

[27] *Ibid.*, *loc. cit.*: *English Episcopal Acta*, i: *Lincoln, 1067–1185*, ed. D. M. Smith (London, 1980), p. xli.

[28] *Gesta Abbatum*, i, 107.

[29] *Ibid.*, *loc. cit.*

[30] *Ibid.*, *loc. cit.*

[31] *Ibid.*, i, 109.

[32] *Ibid.*, i, 183.

[33] *Ibid., loc. cit. Pace* Rodney Thomson, who states that the fact that 'no such complaint [of favouritism] is voiced about Robert says something for his probity' (Thomson, *op. cit.* (note 1), 44).

[34] *Gesta Abbatum*, i, 193.

[35] *Ibid.*, i, 193–4.

[36] *Ibid.*, i, 194.

[37] *Ibid.*, i, 181–2.

[38] *Ibid.*, i, 179, 182. See esp. Kahn, *op. cit.* (note 1), *passim*.

[39] *Gesta Abbatum*, i, 192.

[40] *Ibid.*, i, 66, 71 (Richard), 72–3, 95–6 (Geoffrey), 110–11, 183 (Robert). For Geoffrey see also *The Chronicle of Battle Abbey*, ed. E. Searle, OMT (Oxford, 1980), 142.

[41] *Gesta Abbatum.*, i, 106, 184.

[42] Knowles, *op. cit.* (note 1), 702.

[43] See, e.g., the manors of Gread Gaddesden and Titeberst in Hertfordshire (*Domesday Book*, ed. A. Farley, 2 vols. (London, 1783), i, 133, 139–139ᵛ).

[44] On this topic see C. Harper-Bill, 'The piety of the Anglo-Norman knightly class' in *Proceedings of the Battle Conference on Anglo-Norman Studies*, ii, 1979, ed. R. A. Brown (Woodbridge, 1980), 63–77.

[45] Knowles, *op. cit.* (note 1), 703.

[46] *Gesta Abbatum*, i, 55–6: for Robert of Mortain's grant see BL MS Cotton Nero D. VII, fo. 92; for his spoliation see *Domesday Book*, *op. cit.* (note 43), i, 135b.

[47] *Gesta Abbatum*, i, 57–8.

[48] Ibid., i, *passim*, esp. 55–6. Many of these benefactors are listed in BL MS Cotton Nero VII (the Golden Book of St Albans), fos. 89 f.

[49] For Roger of Wendover see Matthew Paris, *Chronica Majora*, ed. H. R. Luard, 7 vols. Rolls Series, 57 (London, 1872–83), ii, 6. A controversial recent reinterpretation is J. Gillingham, 'The introduction of knight service to England' in *Proceedings of the Battle Conference on Anglo-Norman Studies*, iv, 1981, ed. R. A. Brown (Woodbridge, 1982), 53–64.

[50] H. M. Chew, *The English Ecclesiastical Tenants in Chief and Knight Service* (London, 1932), 112–22.

[51] Knowles, *op. cit.* (note 1), 607–12.

[52] Eadmer, *Historia Novorum in Anglia*, ed. M. Rule, Rolls Series, 81 (London, 1884), 78.

[53] See Chew, *op. cit.* (note 50), *passim*.

[54] Incomes and quotas are conveniently listed in Knowles, *op. cit.* (note 1), 702–3. The total *servicium* remained constant as long as this system of military service lasted.

[55] *Ibid.*, 611.

[56] See D. Knowles, C. N. L. Brooke and V. C. M. London (eds.) *The Heads of Religious Houses, England and Wales, 940–1216* (Cambridge, 1972), 66.

[57] Knowles, *op. cit.* (note 1), 311.

[58] *Ibid.*, 702; *The Chronicle of Jocelin of Brakelond*, trans. H. E. Butler, NMT (London, 1949), 28–9, 65–8.

[59] M. Howell, 'Abbatial vacancies and the divided *mensa* in medieval England', *J. Ecclesiastical History*, xxxiii (1982), 173–92 and bibliography there cited.

[60] *Jocelin of Brakelond* (see note 58) 27, 87–90.

[61] The *Taxatio Ecclesiastica* of 1291 clearly reveals the existence of a large number of obedientiaries with responsibility for their own estates: *Taxatio Ecclesiastica*, Record Commission (London, 1802), esp. 37b, 52b.

[62] *The Monastic Constitutions of Lanfranc*, trans. D. Knowles, NMT (London, 1951), 74: *Gesta Abbatum*, i, 52. See also Knowles, *op. cit.* (note 1), 123.

[63] *Gesta Abbatum*, i, 74–5, 107 (cellarer), 76 (almoner), 199 (sacristan).

[64] *Constitutions* (see note 62), 85.

[65] See especially *Gesta Abbatum*, i, 74–5.

[66] *Ibid.*, i, 57–8.

[67] See above, p. 111.

[68] See above, p. 108 and note 12.

[69] *Gesta Abbatum*, i, 202–5. For John de Cella's gift of 140 marks from the abbey treasury to a kinsman in order that he be made a knight, see *ibid.*, i, 252–3.

[70] Kauffmann, *op. cit.* (note 1), 12 13.

Bestiaries: an Aspect
of Medieval Patronage

Xenia Muratova

The Pierpont Morgan Library's MS 81,[1] a sumptuously decorated English bestiary of the last quarter of the twelfth century, contains a more or less contemporary inscription[2] concerning the donation of the manuscript. On the verso of the first leaf appears an inscription which can be expanded as follows (pl. XXXIV*a*):

> *Anno MCLXXXVII ab incarnatione Domini in vigilia sancti Mathei apostoli Philippus Apostolorum canonicus Lincolniensis Ecclesie donavit Deo et Ecclesie sancte Marie et sancti Cuthberti de Radeford ad edificationem fratrum ipsius Ecclesie in perpetuum: unum optimum psalterium glosatum et quatuor evangelistas glosatos in uno volumine elegantissimo et Genesim glosatam et Meditationes Beati Anselmi Cantuariensis archiepiscopi et Bestiarium et Mappam Mundi. Et ad peticionem ipsius Philippi consensu Anchet'[3] prioris et omnium fratrum excommunicati sunt candelis accensis et stolis acceptis ab omnibus sacerdotibus et canonicis predicte ecclesie quicumque aliquem de predictis libris elongaverit extra septe curie sancti Cuthberti ex quacumque causa. Quisquis ergo aliquem de predictis libris extra curiam sancti Cuthberti commodaverit vel commodatum acceperit, deposuerit vel depositum acceperit, pignori dederit vel acceperit, donaverit vel donatum acceperit vel quocumque titulo alienationis alienaverit vel acceperit vel vi vel clam abstulerit vel precario cuiquam concesserit, noverit proculdubio se iram et indignationem omnipotentis Dei incursurum.*

(In the year 1187 from the Incarnation of Our Lord, on the eve of St Matthew the Apostle's day,[4] Philip Apostolorum, canon of the church of Lincoln, donated to God and to the church of St Mary and St Cuthbert of Radford [i.e. Worksop Priory, Notts.], for the edification of the brethren of the aforesaid church, in perpetual use: an excellent book of Psalms with glosses, the four Gospels with glosses, in one most elegant volume, a Genesis with glosses, the Meditations of the Blessed Anselm, Archbishop of Canterbury, a bestiary and a map of the world. And upon the request of the aforesaid Philip and with the assent of Anchetil, the prior, and of all the brethren, whoever removes any of the aforementioned books without the precincts of the house of St Cuthbert, whatever be the cause [of such removal], is hereby excommunicated by the priests and canons of the aforesaid church, candles being lit and stoles put on. Anyone, therefore, who lends or accepts the loan of, deposits or accepts the deposit of, pawns or receives, donates or accepts the gift of, or, whatever may be the title of the alienation, alienates or assents to [such alienation]— whether by force or by stealth—takes away or allows the temporary use of any of the aforementioned books out of the house of St Cuthbert, let him know for certain that he shall incur the wrath and indignation of Almighty God.)

Among medieval documents concerning donations[5] or custody of manuscripts, one sometimes comes across references to the value of a manuscript and warnings against thieves, such thefts evidently not being rare events in medieval libraries.[6] But it is seldom that one encounters this kind of description of the value of a manuscript and warning against thieves expressed in such a solemn and categorical form.

On the one hand, this curious text is drawn up in terms displaying a combination of language used in legal documents and standard formulae against alienation— the terms *alienatio, commodatum, precarius* and *concessio* being used in various medieval charters and documents concerning the transfer of property. All the possible parties to such a theft are enumerated: the man who steals the books, his accessaries and anyone who receives the stolen goods are considered equally guilty. The inscription has all the appearance of an official document drawn up in legal terms. It might serve for scholars as an interesting, though extreme, example of twelfth-century attitudes to property rights and theft.

On the other hand, one is struck by the strongly expressed personal attitude of the donor towards his cherished manuscripts. *Optimum psalterium*, 'an excellent book of Psalms', and *volumen elegantissimum*, 'the most elegant volume' of Gospels,[7] are expressions which reveal Philip as a passionate bibliophile, highly appreciative of the beauty of illuminated manuscripts.

The threat of excommunication appears quite often in English documents of the twelfth to thirteenth centuries, in cases concerning disobedience to ecclesiastical ordinances, misappropriation of estates,[8] misuse of prebends,[9] and other infringements. But it is rare that such a punishment is threatened against a book thief. It is also rare that the solemn procedure of excommunication (*candelis accensis et stolis acceptis*) is described in all its details for a relatively minor crime.[10]

Properly speaking, the curse on thieves who might steal manuscripts from Canon Philip's collection is an important example of the principles of medieval copyright: it not only expresses the value of these manuscripts and attests to the popularity of the bestiary among English cultured circles in the twelfth century; it also includes a prohibition against giving them into a stranger's hands for copying. The existence of the Leningrad bestiary (Leningrad Library MS Q.v.V.I), which is a sister-manuscript to the Morgan bestiary and probably its predecessor,[11] makes the story of Philip's manuscript even more interesting. But we shall never know whether all the books donated to Radford Priory by Philip included a similar dedication, or whether it appears only in the Morgan bestiary. We shall never know what effect Philip's copyright had on the flourishing production of illuminated bestiaries at the end of the twelfth century.

Philip's inscription enables us to date the Morgan bestiary before or *c.* 1187. It is important evidence for the presence of an illuminated bestiary in the Lincoln area, for the circulation of models for bestiaries, and probably that Philip's manuscript was produced in this area. But it also gives us an idea of the cultural milieu in which this kind of illustrated scientific and moralizing literature found favour. It allows us to suggest that a cultured élite centred on Lincoln and on its cathedral school was one of the likely promoters of the production of illuminated manuscripts of bestiaries, providing a close integration of text and illustration.

The fact that a bestiary, together with other books, was donated to an Augustinian house *ad edificationem fratrum* is also significant. It can be interpreted as indirect proof of the importance, for the Augustinian order in Lincolnshire, of the bestiary as an instrument of moral education.[12]

Thus, our inscription implies that bestiaries were used as teaching aids by two of the important intellectual agents responsible for education in England in the second half of the twelfth century: the secular and the regular canons.

When one reflects on the popularity of bestiaries in England in the twelfth to thirteenth centuries, and asks oneself about the people who favoured this genre of literature and its illustrations, one thinks, of course, in the first place of the tenacious tradition of animal lore, going back to the Anglo-Saxon past and, further, to Celtic folklore, with its particular sensitivity to the marvels of nature. The first translation of the *Physiologus* into the vernacular was made in Anglo-Saxon England, and the presence of *Libri Bestiarum* in English libraries is evidenced in the tenth century.[13]

After a gap in the eleventh century, when there is no mention of bestiaries in England, the twelfth and thirteenth centuries produce, suddenly, a great number of illuminated bestiaries, some of which are masterpieces of English medieval illumination. As is well known, the earliest surviving illuminated bestiary, dating to the first half of the twelfth century, is included in the Bodleian Library MS Laud Misc. 247.[14] In this manuscript the text of the *Physiologus*, of the B version,[15] contains important additions from the Etymologies of Isidore of Seville. The manuscript is decorated with unframed pen drawings. Their direct iconographical sources are not clear, but they undoubtedly go back to much more ancient models. Some identical iconographical types can be found in the Carolingian MS 318 of the Bern City Library[16] (cf. fo. 13ᵛ: Siren and Onocentaur, where the Siren is represented as half-fish, as in MS Laud Misc. 247, fo. 147; or fo. 18: the Antelope, where the animal is represented alone, without a hunter—the same occurs in MS Laud Misc. 247, fo. 141ʳ). Others occur in the Greek eleventh-century manuscript produced in southern Italy, MS E.16 sup. of the Ambrosiana Library, Milan[17] (cf. fo. 34ʳ, where the Serra is represented as a winged dragon, as in MS Laud Misc. 247, fo. 141ᵛ, and not as a fish, as in the Bern *Physiologus*, nor as a mermaid, as in the tenth-century Carolingian MS 10067–74 of the Royal Library, Brussels, fo. 142[18]).

The iconographic and compositional schemes of the cycle of MS Laud Misc. 247 are of special importance because they are one of the sources of the later development of bestiary illustration in England. Such schemes are used in works of art from various social and historical contexts in twelfth-century England.

I have already had occasion to note that the increasing interest in bestiaries was connected in some way with the royal entourage; the bestiary served as entertaining and moralizing reading for the royal ladies.[19] The first bestiary in French verse, that of Philip de Thaon, written between 1121 and 1135, probably in the 1120s, originated at the court of Henry I.[20] It was dedicated by the author to Queen Aelis (Adela), wife of Henry I from 1121. In one of the three extant manuscripts of this work[21] (Oxford, Merton College MS 249, of the thirteenth century), the name of Queen Aelis was altered to that of Alienor (Eleanor of Aquitaine). The poetical text of the bestiary by Philip de Thaon shows that the author intended it to be accompanied by illustrations. Examination of the cycles of illustrations in the extant manuscripts of this work, and the study of the poetical descriptions of animals by Philip, brings one to the conclusion that Philip de Thaon was able to base his descriptions on a cycle of bestiary illustrations analogous to that of MS Laud Misc. 247.[22]

The sculptures decorating the Norman doorway of the church of St Mary at Alne in North Yorkshire (*c.* 1160–70) are based on a cycle of illustrations extremely close to that of MS Laud Misc. 247.[23] Other representations derived from bestiaries which occur in several churches in Yorkshire, although they do not present an entire bestiary cycle as in the church at Alne, witness the wide diffusion of the bestiary repertory in this region during the second half of the twelfth century.[24] It is tempting, remembering the important role played by bestiaries in Cistercian teaching in this region, especially in the work of St Aelred of Rievaulx, to link the appearance of representations from the *Physiologus* cycle in the sculptural decoration of Yorkshire with the influence of the Cistercians, perhaps from Rievaulx.

As was shown by J. Morson,[25] the sermons of St Aelred of Rievaulx are particularly rich in the use of imagery and allegories from the *Physiologus*;[26] the sermons of Gilbert of Holland, abbot of the Cistercian house in Swineshead in Lincolnshire (d. 1172), also abound in references to the *Physiologus*.[27]

Thus, the royal entourage on the one hand, and the Cistercian circles of Yorkshire, Lincolnshire and the north of England on the other,[28] are the cultural milieux which could be suggested as having contributed in particular to the diffusion, and to the didactic use, of the *Physiologus* and the bestiary during the first three-quarters of the twelfth century.

The appearance, in the 1180s, of the Morgan and Leningrad bestiaries marks a turning point in our knowledge of the diffusion and production of bestiaries. The two earliest known bestiaries decorated with painted miniatures, they are also the first manuscripts of the 'transitional group' of bestiaries,[29] and include, instead of the thirty-six or thirty-seven chapters of the *Physiologus* of the B version, 110 chapters. Most of the new material is borrowed from the Etymologies of Isidore of Seville and from the *Collectanea rerum memorabilium* of Solinus (in particular, the exotic animals: the Bonacon, the Leucrota, the Manticore, the Parandrus, the Yale and others), and goes back indirectly to Pliny. Several texts derive from St Ambrose. All the chapters on animals are illustrated. This raises the question of the source of the animal illustrations, which appear for the first time in England in these manuscripts. Illuminated manuscripts of the twelfth book of the Etymologies are unknown;[30] the extant illuminated manuscripts of Solinus[31] are far removed from the pictorial tradition apparent in the English bestiaries. The majority of these illustrations draw on an extensive repertory of animal representations going back to the zoological tradition of the

Hellenistic-Roman period,[32] a tradition which was preserved through the Middle Ages, as witnessed by the eleventh-century manuscript of the Rabanus Maurus Encyclopaedia in Montecassino Abbey , MS 132 (pl. XXXV*a*).[33] The other intermediaries in this pictorial tradition have not survived.[34] Thus, not only the use of textual material and of information going back to antiquity, but also the use of a cycle of animal representations going back to late antiquity, show bestiaries to be peculiar manifestations of the twelfth-century Renaissance.[35]

The Morgan and Leningrad bestiaries were undoubtedly produced in related artistic circles. The pictorial technique, the stylistic approach to the representation of figures and forms, and the typology of forms used in these manuscripts, are close to those appearing in illuminated manuscripts usually associated with the north midlands.[36] In the cycles of their illustrations, identical iconography is interpreted with slight variations in detail and colour (pls. XXXIV*b*, XXXV*b*). But different additions in each of the manuscripts to the basic text give to each of them a different didactic bias and determine their different purposes and programmes.[37]

The Morgan bestiary begins with extracts from Honorius of Autun's *De Imagine mundi*, about the form of the Universe (I. 1–2),[38] and from Genesis on the Creation (without miniatures). It includes, at the end, Isidore's texts on Worms, Plants, Nature and the Ages of Man (XII. v; XI. i–ii; XVII. vi–vii) and the regions of the Earth (XIV. ii. 1–3; XIV. iii. 1–15; XIV. ii. 1–8; XIV. V. 1–7).[39] It also includes (fos. 29, 31–31ᵛ), in the section on wild animals, extracts from the *Cosmographia* of Bernardus Silvestris on the properties of animals (III. 205–14, 217–32).[40]

The Leningrad bestiary does not include most of these additions, but begins with extracts from Genesis on the Creation, accompanied by miniatures. The fact that the former manuscript becomes a kind of encyclopaedia of nature and that the latter is focused on the glorification of the Lord and on the relationship between the Creator and Creation bears witness not only to a constant reworking of the bestiary in the circles in which these two manuscripts were produced, but also to the fact that the same treatise could serve different purposes, according to the wishes of the client and the destination of the book.

It is in this milieu that the old practice of enriching the *Physiologus* with text (and illustrations?) borrowed from Isidore of Seville and other authors[41] may have been applied in order to transform the ancient book on the allegorical significance of the animals of the Bible into a medieval encyclopaedia of the animal world, in accordance with ideas on knowledge of the material world leading to knowledge of God: ideas which were widely current among English scholars of the twelfth century.[42] It is in these circles that the various programmes of the treatise, much enriched, might be elaborated, and their particular aspects emphasized. It is in this milieu that the use of the allegorical imagery of the *Physiologus* in sermons and moral teaching, characteristic of the Cistercians of Yorkshire and Lincolnshire towards the middle of the twelfth century, is adopted and developed.

The additions from the works of Honorius of Autun and Bernardus Silvestris in the Morgan bestiary are worth discussing in detail, even if this does not contribute to our knowledge of the manuscript's origin. The works of Honorius and Bernardus Silvestris had a wide diffusion in twelfth-century England. Bernardus was cited and used especially by those authors concerned with the study of the Universe: Gerald of Wales and Alexander Nequam.[43] The use of passages from Honorius and Bernardus in the Morgan bestiary could serve as another indication of the school environment, with its didactic and educational bias, as the milieu which produced the manuscript. Of course, the use of the same passages from Bernardus Silvestris by Alexander Nequam and by the compiler of the Morgan bestiary[44] is more a testimony to the success of the *Cosmographia* in England than to a direct connection between the Morgan bestiary and Alexander Nequam.[45] Alexander acknowledges his debt to Bernardus, while the compiler of the Morgan bestiary, who borrowed much larger extracts from the *Cosmographia*, does not. But Alexander, who undoubtedly used the bestiary in his work,[46] might well have had access to a manuscript of a bestiary with these additions. The work of Alexander and the elaboration of bestiary treatises were carried out in a common atmosphere of study and research where the same sources were circulating and where the same authors were in fashion.

The historical relationship of the Morgan bestiary with Lincoln, the artistic connections between the Morgan and Leningrad bestiaries and the tradition of illumination in north-east England, in particular in Durham, Lincoln and York, as well as the special interest in the bestiary manifest among the educated classes of Lincolnshire and Yorkshire in the twelfth century, permit one to attribute to this area an important centre of production of illuminated bestiaries, based on the reworking of existing manuscripts and new imported models. In particular, it produced luxury manuscripts for individual clients, but its range anticipates the wide scale of production of the thirteenth century.[47]

Let us return once more to our Lincoln canon, Philip Apostolorum. We find his name in various Lincoln charters and documents dating to between 1160 and 1203,[48] spanning more than forty years spent under Robert de Chesney (1148–66), Geoffrey Plantagenet, bishop-elect (1173–82), Walter of Coutances (1183–4) and St Hugh (1186–1200). He was probably born at Lincoln and lived there, but his prebend has not so far been identified.[49] We do not know exactly what his relations were with the Augustinian house at Radford (Worksop) in Nottinghamshire, historically linked with York,[50] but belonging to the Lincoln Chapter.[51] But it is important to note that Worksop in the 1180s experienced a period of great cultural activity, expressed first of all in the rebuilding of the church of St Mary and St Cuthbert,[52] which has some features of the transitional style. In 1194 Worksop was chosen as the meeting place of Richard I with the King of Scots.[53] The gift of manuscripts to Radford, not as a bequest, but *ad edificationem fratrum*, hints that Philip was a kind of spiritual patron of this priory. At any rate, he chose to make a gift of his manuscripts to the Augustinians of Radford, or perhaps even ordered them specially for the house, rather than leave them to Fulk, his son and heir,[54] or to the Lincoln Chapter library.[55] But the fact that Lincoln Cathedral and the related chapter buildings were seriously damaged by an earthquake in 1185 may have influenced him.

Philip's inscribed dedication is the first document to name him as canon, no title being mentioned in earlier documents.[56] His name appears without title, together with the names of many other eminent Englishmen of the period, among the debtors of the famous Aaron the Jew, between 1191 and 1203:[57] this is not surprising for someone who enjoyed owning and donating precious illuminated

PLATE XXXIV

a. New York, Pierpont Morgan Library MS 81, fo. 1ᵛ (detail)

b. Leningrad, State Public Library MS lat. Q.v.V.I, fo. 18 (detail)

PLATE XXXV

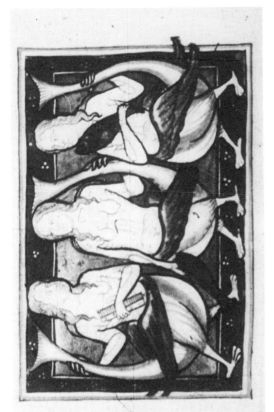

a

Photograph: by permission of Montecassino Abbey

b

a. Montecassino Library MS 132, p. 189
b. New York, Pierpont Morgan Library MS 81, fo. 17 (detail)

PLATE XXXVI

b. Aberdeen, University Library MS 24, fo. 1

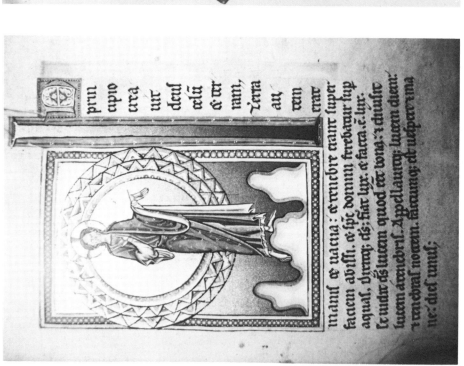

a. Oxford, Bodleian Library MS Ashmole 1511, fo. 4

PLATE XXXVII

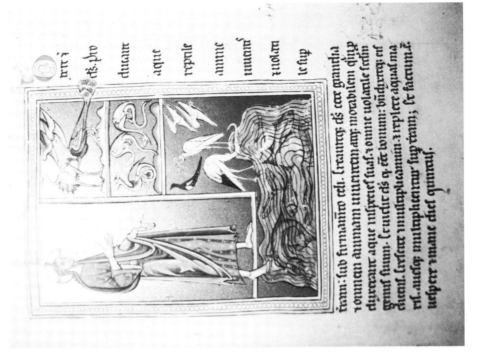

b. Oxford, Bodleian Library MS Ashmole 1511, fo. 6

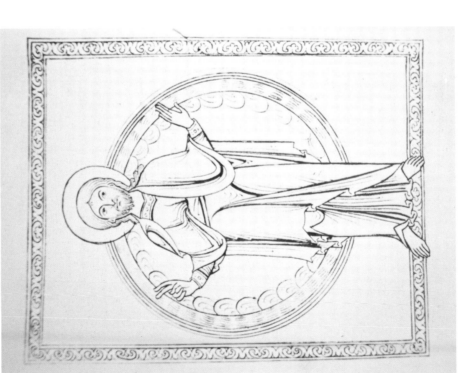

Photograph: Bayerische Staatsbibliothek, Munich

a. Munich, Staatsbibliothek MS Clm 14399, fo. 14

PLATE XXXVIII

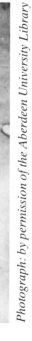

b. Creation of birds and fishes: Cappella Palatina, Palermo

Photograph: by permission of the Aberdeen University Library

a. Aberdeen, University Library MS 24, fo. 2

PLATE XXXIX

Photograph: Leiden University Library

b

a

a. Oxford, Bodleian Library MS Ashmole 1511, fo. 12 (detail)
b. Leiden, University Library MS 76A, fo. 19

PLATE XL

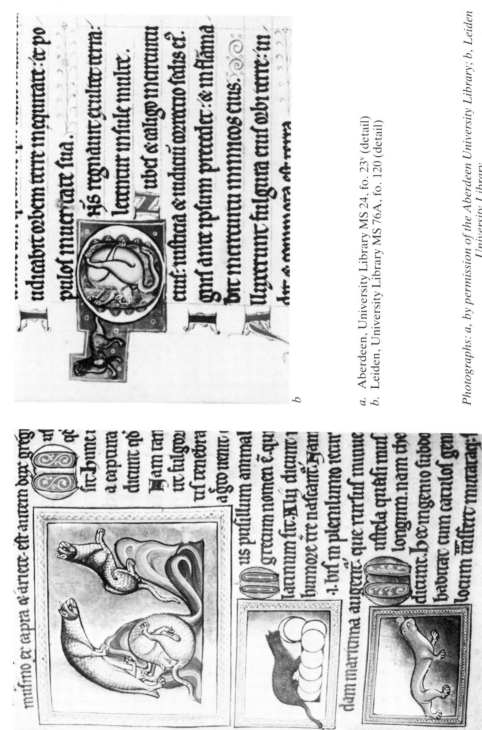

manuscripts. In the majority of Lincoln documents mentioning his name, Philip features as a witness.[58] There is no mention of him in connection with the cathedral school, though his collection of manuscripts and concern for them show him to have belonged to the cultured élite of the Chapter.[59] The glossed manuscripts indicate a preacher and scholar, while the map of the world reveals his interest in natural history.

The last quarter of the twelfth century saw the flowering of Lincoln Cathedral's theological school, which enjoyed close connections with the theological school at York[60] and with Oxford scholars,[61] and extended its influence to the neighbouring monasteries.[62] Its bishops—Geoffrey Plantagenet (*literarum vero studiis et liberalibus disciplinis a pueritia datus*, according to Gerald of Wales[63]), Walter of Coutances (*vir affabilis et liberalis, literarumque studiis affatim eruditus*[64]) and St Hugh—were anxious to assemble in Lincoln *viros sapientes*, scholars and famous intellectuals of the period.[65] On becoming Archbishop of York, Geoffrey continued to encourage theological studies in Lincoln. In a letter dating to the 1190s, adressed to the Lincoln master Robertus Blondus, Geoffrey rates the importance of Lincoln as equal to that of the Paris, Bologna and Oxford schools.[66] Like other members of the English royal family and prelates of the English Church he could largely enjoy the services of masters.[67]

In this school, the theological teaching was undertaken by masters and by secular and regular canons, who were undoubtedly in close cooperation. Many masters were themselves Augustinians; many of those who had studied in Paris (and there were many[68]) were Victorines or influenced by them. The whole Chapter greatly revered Gilbert of Sempringham, and was in constant contact with Gilbertines.[69] The main *raison d'être* and, at the same time, the result of this intense scholarly activity, was the evolution, on a very large scale, of the art of the sermon.[70] It was above all as a collection of instructive examples appropriate for sermons that the bestiary attracted the attention of English masters and canons.

Philip's donation of the bestiary to Radford Priory in September 1187 roughly coincides with a number of important cultural events in England which were of significance in the development of studies in natural history and in the subsequent reworking of bestiaries. The first version of the *Topographia Hibernica*, by Gerald of Wales, had been completed by this date. It was read publicly at Oxford, possibly as early as the autumn of 1187 and in 1188.[71] Gerald of Wales retired to Lincoln *c.* 1192–4, finding it a more propitious place to resume his studies of nature.[72] It was possibly under the influence of the Lincoln school that Gerald enriched his work with various allegorical moralizations.[73] In 1187 Alexander Nequam was probably already writing *De Naturis Rerum*.[74] The Augustinian Peter of Cornwall had finished, *c.* 1188, his *Pantheologus*:[75] extracts from it would often be added to later bestiaries.[76] And just a year earlier, in September 1186, St Hugh of Avalon had been installed in Lincoln, arousing everyone's curiosity with his pet swan.[77]

More or less at the same time, a famous master of theology, William de Montibus, arrived at Lincoln. Originally from Lincoln, he studied and taught on the Mont-Ste-Geneviève in Paris in the 1170s, and earned the admiration of Alexander Nequam, Gerald of Wales and many other contemporaries.[78] His name began to appear in the Lincoln records *c.* 1189,[79] first as a master, and, from

1191, as the Chancellor of Lincoln Cathedral.[80] Among his duties as Chancellor were the care and enrichment of the library, involving the selection and correction of books, the running of the cathedral school, and the nomination of masters.[81] His numerous works—*Speculum Penitentis, Distinctiones, Similitudinarius, Summa 'Qui bene presunt presbiteri...', Versarius*, and *Numerale*—were the fruits of his chief concern, to elucidate for his pupils the principles of current pastoral theology.[82] Neither contemplative nor speculative theology was apparently his strong point. In his search for examples for moral instruction, he had recourse to bestiaries, which provided him with infinite possibilities for moral interpretation.

In his use of imagery from the bestiaries he goes further than St Aelred. A noticeable feature of his *Summa* (I refer to MS 774(495) of the Bibliothèque Mazarine in Paris) is his reference to animals not only from the *Physiologus* but also from the sections of the bestiary derived from Isidore of Seville. Naturally, he speaks about the resurrection of lion-cubs in relation to the Resurrection of Christ (fo. 14 v) and mentions the Elephant in connection with the 'concupiscentia carnis' (*ibid.*). But he endeavours to provide a moral interpretation of animal behaviour which had received no allegorical explanation in the bestiary. Animal metaphors are his principal tool in discussing the opposition of virtues and vices. He speaks about 'scorpio' and 'dipsa' in relation to the vices of 'superbia' and 'luxuria' (fo. 21). The passages on the unnatural 'adulterina commixtio' of species hark directly back to the Isidore extracts included in the bestiaries.[83] Considering the capital vices, he mentions not only the Lion, the Serpent, the Onager, the Fox, the Hedgehog, the Ostrich, the Owl, the Peacock, etc. (animals and birds included in the *Physiologus*), and the Sparrow (a bird which features in the *Aviarium* of Hugh of Folieto) (fos. 25ᵛ–26), but also the Bear, the Camel, the Dog, Fish and the Spider (fo. 26ᵛ). He literally showers the names of the various animals onto his pages, which gives to his text a particular richness and expressiveness. The Swallow is here next to the Leech, the Partridge next to the Mirmicoleon (fo. 23ᵛ).

William de Montibus' approach is based on a variety of attempts to group the material in different ways, so that each work was issued in a number of editions in slightly varying forms. The same method, which later will be typical of book production in universities, was used in the production of the sister-manuscripts of the Leningrad and Morgan bestiaries—another indication that these manuscripts were produced in the environment of a cathedral school and influenced by the methods of scholastic teaching.

That William de Montibus made enthusiastic use of material from the bestiary is beyond doubt. But only a careful study of his work could clarify the extent to which he was himself involved in the work of compiling bestiaries or encouraged their production. Philip's gift was made before the arrival of William in Lincoln as a master, probably on the invitation of St Hugh.[84] The only evidence of a meeting between the two that I was able to trace in the Lincoln records goes back to 1196–8, when they both, together with other Lincoln church dignitaries, witnessed a charter concerning the rights of the Order of Sempringham.[85] We do not know the exact nature of William's contacts with the Augustinians in Lincolnshire, but the fact that he corrected a prologue to the anonymous Life of St Gilbert of Sempringham[86] testifies to his close relationship with the

Augustinians, and particularly the Gilbertines. Thus, a consideration of the kind of environment which might promote the diffusion and production of bestiaries brings us once more to that of a cathedral school and Augustinian teachings, and above all to Lincoln Cathedral.

An intriguing question remains concerning the revival in England of a repertory of animal representations which clearly echoes the animal iconography of late antiquity, particularly in the illumination of bestiary manuscripts, probably related to the Lincoln and York areas.[87] The means by which they were transmitted are unknown, but the possibilities for speculation are numerous: the known expansion of contacts between England and the Mediterranean world during this period; the Crusades; dynastic, commercial, and various cultural links. There are numerous examples of cultural contacts between Englishmen and Rome, south Italy and Sicily, of journeys by English clerics and scholars to the courts of King Roger and of William I and William II of Sicily, of the presence of Italian clerics and scholars in England.[88] An example of this was Robert of Cricklade, an Augustinian canon at Oxford, who made several journeys to Rome and to Sicily and made a compilation of Pliny's Natural History for Henry II.[89] Another is Galterus Anglicus, Henry II's chaplain and tutor to William II of Sicily, who compiled a version of Aesop's Fables.[90] Or Simon of Apulia, chaplain to Geoffrey Plantagenet, master-scholar and dean of York Cathedral under Geoffrey, who was involved in the affairs of the Chapters of York and Lincoln.[91] These cultural relationships are particularly close during the period of the marriage of Henry II's third daughter, Joanna, with William II of Sicily (1177).

Her half-brother Geoffrey Plantagenet is himself a particularly important figure in this connection. By education and perhaps through his own baptism,[92] Geoffrey seems to have been closely connected with the Augustinians. He was educated in Tours, and was there between 1175 and 1178, when Bernardus Silvestris was probably still alive[93] and the glory of that famous teacher was at its zenith. His studies of the liberal arts in Tours in the atmosphere of Bernardus' teaching could have inspired him with a particular interest in allegorical interpretations of nature. It was undoubtedly under the influence of his recent studies in Tours that Geoffrey, still a very young man, when bishop-elect of Lincoln, began to attract a cultured élite to Lincoln Cathedral.[94] Could the use of extracts from Bernardus Silvestris in the Morgan bestiary be considered an indirect witness to the relationship of Lincoln scholars with Tours due to Geoffrey, or would this be mere speculation? Geoffrey himself travelled much to Italy in the 1170s and 1190s.[95]

Walter of Coutances, who succeeded Geoffrey as bishop of Lincoln briefly for one year, but who had been a canon in Lincoln before that, also travelled to Sicily and Rome, and accompanied Richard I to Sicily in the 1190s.[96]

Relations with the north of Spain should also be considered. We know that the presence of a bestiary cycle is attested in the monumental painting of the church of Boi in Cataluña in the eleventh century.[97] The English pilgrimage to Santiago de Compostela[98] and the development of the pilgrimage to the English shrine of St James in Reading Abbey[99] constitute important witnesses to Anglo-Spanish cultural links in this period. These relations became especially significant in the development of artistic contacts after the marriage of Henry II's second daughter, Eleanor, with Alfonso VIII of Castile (1170). The presence in north Spain of an outstanding English artist who created the cycle of Sigena paintings in Aragon[100] is a particularly eloquent example of these contacts. As is known, this cycle has several elements of representations which can be found in English bestiaries of *c.* 1200. The majestic animals on the fresco fragments from Arlanza in Castile, *c.* 1200 (Barcelona, Museo de Cataluña; New York, The Cloisters),[101] are further important witnesses to the presence of the bestiary cycle in north Spain. It is not clear, however, whether one can venture to suggest that this cycle goes back to models which were among the sources of English bestiaries, or whether, as is usually suggested, it should be seen as a testimony to the use of an English illuminated bestiary as a model in Castilian artistic circles.[102]

The twelfth-century catalogue of the Lincoln chapter library does not list a bestiary.[103] The manuscript of Isidore's Etymologies (MS 177), preserved in the library from the twelfth century,[104] and decorated with simple blue and red initials, is probably of local origin.

The copy of the Hamo catalogue, dated *c.* 1200, mentions a *Liber Scintillarum cum Solino de mirabilibus mundi in uno volumine* which has not survived, one of the manuscripts which might be a possible source of the material borrowed from Solinus in the bestiary.[105] It is worth noting that this manuscript was donated to the chapter library by Roger of Almeria, precentor of the cathedral in the middle of the twelfth century, a member of a Lincoln family, probably of Spanish origin.[106] His role as precentor made him responsible not only for musical arrangements and the cathedral choir, but also for the texts used in the cathedral school.[107] Roger's probable Spanish connections should be borne in mind when considering the international contacts of English cultured circles.

The Morgan and Leningrad bestiaries, decorated with miniatures painted in thick gouache, with the use of strong colour contrasts and abundant gold, apparently have little in common with the modest decoration of manuscripts preserved in the Lincoln chapter library. Decorated with ornamental and figured letters, the latter are no doubt of local origin and belong to the pictorial evolution of the Anglo-Norman decorated letter in the north of England. A particular softness in the pictorial treatment, the thick layers of paint and the very bright contrasts of pure, dense colours are, however, characteristic of this local pictorial work. The use of chromatic contrasts, among which a *viride hispanicum* (a deep, dense green), a very bright, pure cinnabar, a bright, clear emerald-green, a pale sky-blue and a clear ochre are particularly favoured, could be compared with the palette of both bestiary manuscripts. Some twelfth-century manuscripts possess decorated letters which reveal some acquaintance with the iconography of the *Physiologus* and bestiaries.[108]

It is known that Lincoln was an important centre of book production at the end of the twelfth century,[109] but the actual circumstances of its development are obscure.

The Morgan and Leningrad bestiaries can be associated with the pictorial trends which developed in north-east England in the second half of the twelfth century, on the basis of various stylistic and iconographical sources, including those of Canterbury, Winchester, St Albans and Bury St Edmunds, as well as those imported from the Continent. Some particular features of the pictorial work and of the stylization of forms, as well as the use of a particular typology of forms and details, permit us to distinguish this pictorial group and to attempt to characterize the artistic atmosphere of north-east England.[110] In particular, the evolution of a specifically painterly approach in the manuscript illumination, and the use of a distinctly unclassical type of human face, can be associated with this area. This suggests the existence of several workshops in this region which specialized in the production of illuminated manuscripts for various communities as well as for individual clients among the area's cultivated élite. These workshops spanned at least two or three generations of illuminators, using a large but defined repertory of models.[111] This artistic milieu produced a number of very important illuminated manuscripts during the forty years from *c.* 1170 to 1210. It may be argued that these include the Copenhagen Psalter (Copenhagen, Royal Library MS Thott. 143 2°)[112] and undoubtedly the Gough Psalter (Oxford, Bodleian Library MS Gough Liturg. 2),[113] which displays several technical and stylistic features occurring in both bestiaries. An important stage in this artistic evolution is the St Louis Psalter in the Leiden University Library (MS 76 A),[114] owned, probably, by Geoffrey Plantagenet in the 1190s when he was Archbishop of York.[115] On the one hand, the miniatures and decorated letters of this manuscript possess numerous details, animal representations and even whole compositions reminiscent of the illuminations of the Leningrad and Morgan bestiaries. On the other, the repertory of forms and the types of figures, vestments and various details in the Leiden Psalter have several points in common with the repertory of forms used in two of the most luxuriant English bestiaries of the 'second family'—Oxford, Bodleian Library MS Ashmole 1511[116] and Aberdeen, University Library MS 24[117]—representing the culminating point in the evolution of English illuminated bestiaries. These affinities enable us to suggest that they were produced in the same workshop or in closely related workshops, probably working for Geoffrey's entourage (pls. XXXIX, XL).[118]

Thus, Geoffrey's entourage again comes to the fore in relation to the production of luxuriantly decorated illuminated bestiaries.

The inclusion in the Ashmole and Aberdeen bestiaries of the *Aviarium*, the treatise on the allegorical meaning of birds by Hugh of Folieto,[119] a particularly popular Augustinian author of the twelfth century, brings us once more to the idea of the bestiary's special value as an aid to moral and spiritual teaching in Augustinian circles.

It is important to note the appearance in the Ashmole and Aberdeen bestiaries of iconographical and compositional schemes of Creation scenes which differ in many details from earlier English, northern French or Mosan iconographical tradition. On the one hand, these scenes are obviously related to Byzantine and Byzantinizing art in Italy—to Venice, southern Italy, and particularly to Sicily (Palermo and Monreale) (pls. XXXVII*b*, XXXVIII).[120] On the other, the iconography of the first Creation scenes has a striking resemblance to that of the drawings in the south German manuscript of St Ambrose's *Hexaemeron* in the Munich State Library (Clm. 14399) (pls. XXXVI, XXXVII*a*),[121] in part reproducing Italian Byzantinizing examples and in part going back to Ottonian schemes.[122] Can the use of identical models in English bestiaries of *c.* 1200[123] and in a German manuscript of the 1160s be put down to pure coincidence, due to the wide diffusion of Italian Byzantinizing models through Europe in the second half of the twelfth century, south Germany and England being important routes in this diffusion? It would be important to note, in this connection, the presence in bestiary illuminations dating to *c.* 1200 of certain iconographical schemes of the representation of animals which can be found in the *Hortus deliciarum* of Herrade of Landsberg.[124]

The appearance, in English art towards the end of the twelfth century, of Byzantinizing examples identical to those produced in south Germany might have come about as a result of close links between patrons and artists of which we know nothing. It would not be inappropriate to bear in mind the close relationship of the royal family with German princes: Matilda, the eldest daughter of Henry II, was the wife of Henry the Lion; Richard I spent several months in 1192–3 in captivity in Durrenstein castle near Vienna—an event which also might have influenced cultural relations between the two countries and might have had a significant effect on the circulation of artistic models. After his release from captivity Richard formed an alliance with several German princes,[125] which intensified cultural contacts between English and German aristocratic circles.

Thus, on the one hand, the varied historical, literary and artistic evidence permits the suggestion that the increase in popularity and diffusion of bestiaries in England in the second half of the twelfth century might be connected with the flourishing teaching and pastoral activities of the secular and Augustinian canons and the masters of cathedral schools in the north midlands, particularly in the areas of Lincoln and York. Encouraged by the Church prelates and prompted by the wide-ranging interests of the cultivated classes, these activities led to the production, in workshops in which the foremost artists were assembled, of luxury editions of bestiaries, destined for individual representatives of this cultural milieu and as their gifts to religious houses. The scarcity of references to bestiaries in the surviving twelfth- and thirteenth-century monastic and cathedral library lists[126] is an indirect witness to the fact that many bestiaries produced at the end of the twelfth century, and in the thirteenth, were destined above all for individual patrons. The early development, in England in the twelfth century, of a whole class of literate men with enquiring minds,[127] but who were not necessarily scholars in the strictest sense, must have been an important reason for the large-scale production of illuminated bestiary manuscripts.

On the other hand, many threads link the development and destiny of the bestiary in England with the royal entourage, with whom the Church prelates and the masters of the cathedral schools were often in close contact. As we have seen, dynastic links were of primary importance in promoting artistic contacts and the circulation of artistic models between countries. These contacts found direct expression in several bestiary manuscripts.

We do not find direct evidence for the possession of bestiaries by members of the royal family in the twelfth or beginning of the thirteenth century. However, the interest of English kings in natural history is attested on several occasions. The dedication by Robert of Cricklade of his compilation of Pliny's Natural History to Henry II[128] no longer seems a mere formality when one remembers that among the young Henry's teachers was William de Conches, a philosopher inclined towards metaphysical speculation on nature.[129] King John owned a book of Pliny from Reading Abbey.[130] And the sources tell us about the use of scenes from the bestiary to decorate royal palaces. The famous bestiary stories of Dogs, borrowed from Solinus[131] and going back to Pliny,[132] were depicted on the walls of the Painted Chamber of Henry III.[133] As is pointed out by J. J. G. Alexander,[134] these scenes represented allegories of fidelity, especially appreciated by the king and thus belonging to the realms of royal iconography. The story of the Eagle, which decorated Henry II's King's Chamber in Winchester Castle, could have been based, as was suggested by G. Henderson, on the illustration of the story of the Pelican in late twelfth-century bestiaries.[135] This story must have represented allegorically the relationship of Henry II with his sons, and their rebellion. Did perhaps Richard I, his brother John and, in particular, their half-brother Geoffrey Plantagenet share their father's inclination towards animal allegory? The most luxuriant bestiaries—MS Ashmole 1511 and Aberdeen Library MS 24—were undoubtedly made for persons of very high rank. As we have seen, several details of their illuminations manifest a link with those of the Leiden Psalter, probably made for Geoffrey. Several iconographical features reveal broad artistic links with Italy, Sicily and south Germany (countries visited by Richard I and his court). The Aberdeen bestiary is attested to have been in the royal collection in the sixteenth century,[136] and it is not improbable that it was acquired much earlier. But here one must cease to speculate for fear of confusing historical possibility with mere historical fantasy.

NOTES

[1] M. R. James, *Catalogue...of the Library of J. Pierpont Morgan, Manuscripts* (1906), no. 107, 165 ff.; C. M. Kauffmann, *Survey*, iii: *Romanesque Manuscripts 1066–1190* (London, 1975), 126–7; Pierpont Morgan Library, *William Morris and the Art of the Book, Collected Essays* (New York/Oxford, 1976), 103; X. Muratova, 'Les manuscrits-frères: un aspect particulier de la production des bestiaires enluminés en Angleterre à la fin du XIIe et au début du XIIIe siècle', in *Actes du Colloque 'Artistes, artisans et production artistique au moyen âge', Rennes 1983* (Paris, in press).

[2] The handwriting of the inscription is probably not the same as the handwriting of the beginning of the text, but it is very close to it.

[3] It is the only document mentioning the name of the Worksop prior, known from other documents dating between 1188 and 1199 only as 'A...'. See D. Knowles, C. N. L. Brooke and V. C. M. London, *The Heads of Religious Houses, England and Wales, 940–1216* (Cambridge, 1972), 190.

[4] 20th September.

[5] A great deal of information concerning donations of books to the chapter library of Lincoln Cathedral in the twelfth century can be found in the ancient catalogues of the chapter library, published in *Giraldi Cambrensis Opera*, vii, ed. J. F. Dimock (London, 1877), 165–71, and in R. M. Woolley, *Catalogue of the Manuscripts of Lincoln Cathedral Chapter Library* (Oxford, 1927), pp. v–xv.

[6] cf. the text of observances in use at the Augustinian priory of St Giles and St Andrew at Barnwell at the end of the thirteenth century—'Maiores autem et preciosiores libros sine licentia prelati nulli persone cognite vel incognite debet accomodare': O. Lehmann-Brockhaus, *Lateinische Schriftquellen zur Kunst in England, Wales und Schottland vom Jahre 901 bis zum Jahre 1307*, iii (Munich, 1956), no. 6423, 354.

[7] Adjectives describing the aesthetic qualities of books are very rare in English medieval documents. From the various written sources mentioning books, compiled by Lehmann-Brockhaus, only three, all of the thirteenth century, contain remarks upon their beauty: 'liber elegantissimus' (*Gesta Abbatum monasterii S. Albani*, i, 233–4); 'libri pulcherrimi' (decorated by the monk Willelmus: 'In libris vero variis optimis et pulcherrimis eleganter decoravit', *Chronicon abbatie de Parco Lude*, 16); and 'libri pulcherrimi' which belonged to Crowland Abbey (*Historiae Croylandensis continuatio*, 477). Lehmann-Brockhaus, *op. cit.* (note 6), i, no. 1195, 323; iii, no. 2995, 235; no. 3892, 439; v, 233–4.

[8] cf. the excommunication of the Earl of Leicester by Alexander, bishop of Lincoln, for the misappropriation of a bishop's castle at Newark in the middle of the twelfth century. *The*

Registrum Antiquissimum of the Cathedral Church of Lincoln, Lincoln Record Society (hereafter *RAL*), i (Lincoln, 1931), 239–40.

[9] *RAL*, ii (Lincoln, 1933), 199–202.

[10] cf. 'Et in pleno capitulo excommunicare fecimus omnes illos qui eam infregerit...': *RAL*, iii (Lincoln, 1935), 19.

[11] A. Konstantinowa, *Ein englisches Bestiar des zwölften Jahrhunderts in der Staatsbibliothek zu Leningrad* (Berlin, 1929); N. Morgan, *Survey*, iv: *Early Gothic Manuscripts*, 1: *1190–1250* (London/Oxford, 1982); X. Muratova, *The Medieval Bestiary* (Moscow, 1984); *ead.*, *op. cit.* (note 1). In the facsimile publication of the Leningrad bestiary, prepared more than fifteen years ago, I preferred to give an approximate date for this manuscript of *c.*1180–90. It is dated to *c.* the 1190s in Morgan (*op. cit.*). Further study of the manuscript decoration, in particular its initials, as well as detailed comparison with other manuscripts and with the Morgan bestiary, convince me more and more of the earlier dating. I would now like to propose a date in the early 1180s.

[12] On the Augustinian Order in England and its educational activity, J. C. Dickinson, *The Origins of the Austin Canons and their Introduction into England* (London, 1950), esp. 97 ff., 186 ff.

[13] On the tenth-century Anglo-Saxon *Physiologus* (Exeter, Cathedral Library MS 3501), A. S. Cook, *The Old English Elene, Phoenix and Physiologus* (New Haven, 1919); G. Ph. Krapp and E. van Dobbie, *The Exeter Book* (London/New York, 1936); L. J. Lloyd and A. M. Erskine, *The Library of Exeter Cathedral* (Exeter, 1967; repr. 1974), 3–4. See also L. Frank, 'Die Physiologus-Literatur des englischen Mittelalters und die Tradition', thesis, Tübingen University, 1971; T. P. Campbell, 'Thematic unity in the Old English Physiologus', in *Archiv für das Studium der neueren Sprachen und Literatur*, ccxv (1978), 73–9. On the *Liber Bestiarum* in Peterborough Abbey in the tenth century, M. R. James, *Lists of Manuscripts formerly in Peterborough Abbey Library*, Trans. Bibl. Soc. suppl. v (London, 1926).

[14] Kauffmann, *op. cit.* (note 1), no. 36, 75–6.

[15] F. J. Carmody, *Physiologus latinus versio B* (Paris, 1939).

[16] O. Homburger and C. von Steiger, *Physiologus Bernensis* (Basel, 1964).

[17] A. Grabar, *Les Manuscrits grecs italiens enluminés de provenance italienne, IXe–XIe siècles* (Paris, 1972), 29; X. Muratova, 'L'arte longobarda e il *Physiologus*', in *Atti del 6° Congresso Internazionale di studi sull'alto medioevo* (*Milano, 1978*) (Spoleto, 1980), 547–58 (with bibliography).

[18] R. Stettiner, *Die illuminierten Prudentius-Handschriften* (Berlin, 1895–1905), 17 ff.

[19] X. Muratova, 'The Study of Medieval Bestiaries. Problems, Enigmas, Quests', paper read during the symposium 'The Bestiary in Art', London, Soc. Antiq. and Linnean Soc., 1976; see also *ead.*, *op. cit.* (note 11), 26.

[20] E. Walberg, *Le Bestiaire de Philippe de Thaün* (Lund/Paris, 1900), xvii ff.

[21] BL MS Cotton Nero A.V; Oxford, Merton College MS 249; Copenhagen, Royal Library MS 3466.

[22] X. Muratova, 'The decorated manuscripts of the bestiary of Philippe de Thaon (the MS 3466 from the Royal Library in Copenhagen and the MS 249 in the Merton College Library, Oxford) and the problem of the illustrations of the medieval poetical bestiary', in *Third International Beast Epic, Fable and Fabliau Colloquium, Münster, 1979, Proceedings* (Cologne/Vienna, 1981), 217–46.

[23] X. Muratova, 'Les cycles des bestiaires dans le décor sculpté des églises du XIIe s. dans le Yorkshire, et leur relation avec les manuscrits des bestiaires enluminés', in *Atti del V Colloquio della Società Internazionale per lo studio dell' epica animale, della favola e del fabliau, Torino-Saint-Vincent, 1983* (Turin, in press).

[24] St Michael in Barton-le-Street, the churches of Foston, Fishlake, and Stillingfleet, the doorway of St Margaret of York, originally in St Nicholas Hospital in York. Note the relationship of this type of sculptural decoration with the analogous type of framing and of the insertion of animal figures in medallions in the illuminated bestiaries of the end of the twelfth century.

[25] J. Morson, 'The English Cistercians and the bestiary', in *Bull. John Rylands Library*, xxxix (1956).

[26] cf., for instance, the following passages from the sermons of St Aelred: *PL*, cxcv, cols. 223, 237, 238, 268, 292, 293, 415, 441, 447, 452, 467, 468, 477, 482, 483. Note that the ancient

catalogue of the Rievaulx Library, of the twelfth or beginning of the thirteenth century, mentions a 'liber sermonum et quedam excerpta de libris Justiniani et bestiarium in uno volumine': Morson, *op. cit.* (note 25), 170.

[27] cf. the following passages from the commentaries of Gilbert: *PL*, clxxxiv, cols. 69, 71, 73, 119, 123, 129, 142, 152, 294. On Gilbert of Holland, see Knowles *et al.*, *op. cit.* (note 3), 144.

[28] The earliest known manuscript of the bestiary of Philip de Thaon belonged in the twelfth century to the Cistercian house of Holmcultram (BL MS Cotton Nero A.V.). See Morson, *op. cit.* (note 25), 168; C. R. Cheney, 'English Cistercian libraries', in C. R. Cheney, *Medieval Texts and Studies* (Oxford, 1973), 340.

[29] According to the classification proposed and elaborated by M. R. James, *The Bestiary* (Oxford, 1928), and F. McCulloch, *Medieval Latin and French Bestiaries* (North Carolina, 1960), 33–4. On the sources, the contents and the cycles of the illustrations in the bestiaries of the 'transitional group' and of the 'second family' (which is still richer and more diversified than the bestiaries of the transitional group), McCulloch, *op. cit.*, 33–8; X. Muratova, 'Étude du manuscrit', in *Bestiarium. Fac-similé du manuscrit du Bestiaire Ashmole 1511, conservé à la Bodleian Library d'Oxford* (Paris, 1984), 44–55. The complete text of this study will be published as the commentaries to the same facsimile by the Akademische Druck- und Verlagsanstalt in Graz. Cf. also *ead.* in *Actes du VIᵉ Colloque de la Soc. Int. Renardienne, Spa, 1985* (in press).

[30] See discussion of the problem of the possible existence of the illuminated manuscripts of the *Etymologiae* by Isidore of Seville and bibliography in E. Panofsky, 'Herkules Agricola: a further complication in the problem of the illustrated Rabanus manuscripts', in *Essays in the History of Art Presented to R. Wittkower* (London, 1967), 20 ff.

[31] See L. Cogliati Arano, 'Il manoscritto C. 246 inf. della Biblioteca Ambrosiana, Solino', in *La miniatura italiana in età romanica e gotica* (Florence, 1979), 239 ff.

[32] On the survival of the tradition of zoological illustration from antiquity, K. Weitzmann, *Illustrations in Roll and Codex* (Princeton, 1970), 138–9; Z. Kadar, *Survivals of Greek Zoological Illuminations in Byzantine Manuscripts* (Budapest, 1978).

[33] The study of the illustrations to the texts on animals in Montecassino Library MS 132 has made possible the discovery of a number of representational schemes which can be found later in English illuminated bestiaries: X. Muratova, 'Problèmes de l'origine et des sources des cycles d'illustrations des manuscrits des bestiaires', in *Epopée animale, Fable, Fabliau. Actes du IVᵉ Colloque de la Société Internationale Renardienne, Evreux, 1981* (Paris, 1984), 395–7. It is a question not only of the traditional profile representations of animals, birds and serpents, but also of the representation of particular poses: e.g. a cat curled up in a ball and licking itself, which figures among the other animals on p. 189 of Montecassino Library MS 132, can be found among the illustrations of the Leningrad bestiary (fo. 5), in the decorated letters of the Leiden Psalter (Leiden University Library MS 76 A, fo. 120) and in Oxford, Bodleian Library MS Ashmole 1511 (fos. 34(35)ᵛ) and Aberdeen University Library MS 24 (fo. 23ᵛ) (see pl. XL).

[34] Some echoes of this pictorial tradition can be found in the *Hortus deliciarum* of Herrade of Landsberg (*c.* 1180), in the representation of the Creation of animals: R. Green, M. Evans, C. Bischoff and M. Curschmann, *Hortus deliciarum* (London/Leiden, 1979), fo. 8ʳ.

[35] After a famous book by C. Haskins, *The Renaissance of the Twelfth Century* (Cambridge, Mass., 1927), this subject hs been treated many times and now has a very extensive literature. The most recently published major collection of essays on this subject is *Renaissance and Renewal of the Twelfth Century*, ed. R. L. Benson and G. Constable (Cambridge, Mass., 1982) (with bibliography).

[36] Kauffmann, *op. cit.* (note 1), 117 ff.; Morgan, *op. cit.* (note 11), 26–7. The stylistic features of the illuminations of the Leningrad bestiary recall the style of certain late twelfth-century manuscripts associated with northern England (Oxford, Bodleian Library MS Gough Liturg. 2) and, in particular, with Durham (Durham Cathedral Library MSS A.II.9 and A.II.19 and later manuscripts such as BL MS Add. 39943). The style of the main artist of the Leningrad bestiary is more painterly and softer than the rather precise and linear style of the artist of the Morgan bestiary. The principal artist of the Leningrad manuscript has insisted on the strong contrast of the dark green colour with the pure red one; the palette of the master of the Morgan bestiary, which also includes the same green and red colours, is more variegated.

[37] Muratova, *op. cit.* (note 1).

[38] *PL*, clxxii, col. 122.

[39] *PL*, lxxxii, cols. 448–50, 397–419, 606–20; cols. 495–8; 503–5, 509–10.

[40] Bernardus Silvestris, *Cosmographia*, ed. P. Dronke (Leiden, 1978), 109–10.

[41] The first known case of textual additions from Isidore of Seville and St Ambrose to the text of the *Physiologus* is the Bern, City Library MS 318 of the ninth century, enriched with a passage on the Horse borrowed from the *Etymologiae* (fo. 22ᵛ) and with the passage on the Cock taken from the *Hexaemeron* of St Ambrose (fos. 21ᵛ–22ʳ).

[42] A. F. Leach, *The Schools of Medieval England* (London, 1915); H. H. Glunz, *History of the Vulgate in England from Alcuinus to Roger Bacon* (Cambridge, 1933); R. W. Hunt, 'English learning in the late twelfth century', in *Trans. Royal Historical Society*, xix (1936), 19–42; B. Smalley, *The Study of the Bible in the Middle Ages* (Oxford, 1941); K. Edwards, *English Secular Cathedrals in the Middle Ages* (Manchester, 1968).

[43] M. Manitius, *Geschichte der lateinischen Literatur des Mittelalters*, iii (Munich, 1931), 207, 371, 635, 786–7; P. Dronke, introduction to Bernardus Silvestris, *op. cit.* (note 40), 12–13.

[44] Alexander Nequam cites two lines from the *Cosmographia*, iii, 223–4: *Alexandri Neckam De Naturis Rerum*, ed. T. Wright (London, 1863), 252.

[45] cf. the use of verses iii, 217–18 of Bernardus Silvestris as an *epimythion* to a fairy-tale in the collection of tales by an anonymous imitator of Avianus: L. Hervieux, *Les Fabulistes latins*, iii (Paris, 1894), 162–3, 335; H. Walter, *Proverbia sententiaeque latinitatis medii aevi, Carmina medii aevi posterioris latina*, ii, 2 (Göttingen, 1964) (who did not know that the verses were by Bernardus Silvestris).

[46] R. W. Hunt, *The Schools and the Cloister. The Life and the Writings of Alexander Nequam* (Oxford, 1984), 73–5. It is important to note the originality of Alexander's reworking of the bestiary material.

[47] X. Muratova, *op. cit.* (note 1); *ead.*, 'More on workshops of the English illumination of the late 12th century and on the production of luxury bestiaries', in *The Caladrius. Essays on the Bestiary and Related Lore in Memory of Florence McCulloch* (Toronto, in press).

[48] D. Greenway, 'Canons whose prebends cannot be identified', in *John Le Neve, Fasti Ecclesiae Anglicanae, 1066–1300*, iii: *Lincoln* (London, 1977), 134.

[49] *Ibid.*

[50] D. Knowles and R. Neville Hadcock, *Medieval Religious Houses. England and Wales* (London, 1971), 180.

[51] *RAL*, ii, 216–17; iii, 251, 265.

[52] R. Stoll, *L'Art roman en Grande Bretagne* (Paris, 1966), 346.

[53] L. Landon. *The Itinerary of King Richard I* (London, 1935). Could Richard I have seen the manuscript there?

[54] Mentioned in Lincoln documents between 1196 and 1203. *RAL*, ix, no. 2652; K. Major, *The Minster Yard* (Lincoln, 1974), 15.

[55] On books willed by many Lincoln canons of the twelfth century to the chapter library, see note 5 above. See also J. de Ghellinck, 'En marges des catalogues des bibliothèques médiévales,' in *Miscellanea Francesco Ehrle* (Roman, 1924), 358.

[56] cf. *RAL*, iv, no. 1383, 222; viii, no. 2192; ix, no. 2494. He first appears as canon in Lincoln charters *c.* 1196–8. *RAL*, ii, 637.

[57] *The Great Roll of the Pipe for the Second Year of the Reign of King John. Michaelmas 1200, Pipe Roll 24*, ed. D. Stenton (London, 1934), 68: *ibid.* for 1201 (London, 1936), 6; *ibid.* for 1202 (London, 1937), 221; *ibid.* for 1203 (London, 1938), 108.

[58] *RAL*, ii, no. 637; ix, no. 2652; x, no. 2763.

[59] Of 187 members of the Lincoln Chapter under St Hugh seventy-nine were masters: J. Baldwin, 'Masters at Paris, 1179–1215', in *Renaissance and Renewal*, *op. cit.* (note 35), 155.

[60] H. Rashdall, *The Universities of Europe in the Middle Ages*, rev. edn. (Oxford, 1936), i, 278 ff.; iii, 472 ff.; Leach, *op. cit.* (note 42), 108, 156–7; Edwards, *op. cit.* (note 42), 187 ff.; N. Orme, *English Schools in the Middle Ages* (London, 1973), 167–79; D. Owen, *Church and Secular Life in Medieval Lincolnshire* (Lincoln, 1981), 38 ff.

[61] Rashdall, *op. cit.* (note 60), iii, 12, 34, 40.

[62] *Ibid.*, 295.

[63] *De vita Galfridi Archiepiscopi Eboracensis*, in *Giraldi Cambrensis Opera*, iv, ed. J. S. Brewer (London, 1873), 363.

[64] *Vita S. Remigii*, in *Giraldi Cambrensis Opera*, vii, ed. J. F. Dimock (London, 1877), 38.

[65] Gerald of Wales says about the cultural patronage of Geoffrey: 'Nobiles quoque personas literatosque viros, in ecclesia sua plerosque plantavit' (*Vita S. Remigii, op. cit.* (note 64), 37) and about that of St Hugh: 'Item personas egregias, literatura et honestate praeclaras, per regni amplitudinem quasi studio quodam ad hoc electas, fideles ecclesiae suae columnas erexit' (*ibid.*, 41). Cf. *Magna Vita Sancti Hugonis*, ed. D. Douie and H. Farmer (London, 1961), i, 110.

[66] *PL*, ccvii, col. 185.

[67] cf. Baldwin, *op. cit.* (note 59), 156–7. 46 per cent of the Chapter of York at the end of the twelfth and beginning of the thirteenth century were masters: *ibid.*, 155. On the use of masters in the service of the court: J. Baldwin, '*Studium et regnum*: the penetration of university personnel into French and English administration at the turn of the twelfth and thirteenth centuries', in *L'Enseignement en Islam et en Occident au moyen âge. Colloque international de La Napoule*, i (Paris, 1977) (*Revue des études islamiques*, xliv, (1976)).

[68] Baldwin, *op. cit.* (note 59), 149 ff., 157 ff.

[69] The close relations of the Lincoln Chapter with the Gilbertine houses of Lincolnshire is attested in numerous contemporary documents and charters: *RAL*, ii, 24 ff.

[70] Each Lincoln canon was obliged to preach a certain number of sermons in a year: Edwards, *op. cit.* (note 42), 217; Owen, *op. cit.* (note 60), 38.

[71] *Giraldi Cambrensis Topographia Hibernica et Expugnatio Hibernica*, ed. J. F. Dimock (London, 1867), preface, xlix–li; *Gerald of Wales, The History and Topography of Ireland*, ed. J. J. O'Meara (Harmondsworth, 1951; 1982), introduction, 15.

[72] *Giraldi Cambrensis Opera*, i, *De rebus a se gestis*, ed. J. S. Brewer (London, 1861), lvi, 93.

[73] On the history of the various editions of the *Topographia Hibernica*: J. J. O'Meara, *op. cit.* (note 71), 1–15.

[74] R. W. Hunt gives the autumn of 1187 as the *terminus post quem* for the writing of *De Naturis Rerum*, and the beginning of 1204 as the *terminus ante quem*: Hunt, *op. cit.* (note 46), 26. See also Leach, *op. cit.* (note 42), 117.

[75] Hunt, *op. cit.* (note 46), 33–5, 38–42; *id.*, 'The disputation of Peter of Cornwall against Symon the Jew', in *Studies in Medieval History Presented to F. M. Powicke* (Oxford, 1948), 143–56.

[76] For example, BL MS Roy. 12. F. XIII belonged to Rochester Priory, at the beginning of the thirteenth century.

[77] *Magna Vita Sancti Hugonis Episcopi Lincolniensis*, ed. J. F. Dimock, NMT (London, 1864), 115–21.

[78] *Giraldi Cambrensis Opera*, i, *ibid.* (note 72); Alexander Nequam, *De laudibus divinae sapientiae*, in *Alexandri Neckam De Naturis Rerum, op. cit.* (note 44), 460; J. Leland, *Commentarii de Scriptoribus Britannicis*, i (Oxford, 1709), *cap.* cciv, 273.

[79] *RAL*, ii, 26.

[80] *RAL*, i, 252 (1203–5); ii, 27 (1192–1200), 32 (1191–5); iii, 40 (1198–1203), 106 (*c.* 1200), 333 (1203–6), 400 (1196–1203); iv, 6 (1192–1205), 32 (1196–1203), 33 (1196–1203), 129 (1196–1203), 204 (*c.* 1200), 206 (1196–1203), 209 (late twelfth century), 217 (1196–1202), 261 (*c.* 1200) and so on.

[81] Rashdall, *op. cit.* (note 60), i, 282 ff.; Edwards, *op. cit.* (note 42), 216; Owen, *op. cit.* (note 60), 38.

[82] *DNB*, lxi, 364; Hunt, *op. cit.* (note 42), 21–2; H. McKinnon, 'William de Montibus, a medieval teacher', in *Essays in Medieval History presented to Bertie Wilkinson* (Toronto, 1969), 32–45. We await the publication of a monograph on William de Montibus by J. W. Goering (Toronto, in preparation). I thank Dr Margaret Gibson for this information.

[83] cf. the text on fo. 21 of Bibliothèque Mazarine MS 774 and the end of the passage on the Horse (*Etym.* xii.1. 46–60, in particular, 58) included in bestiaries.

[84] Leland, *op. cit.* (note 78); *Magna Vita Sancti Hugonis, op. cit.* (note 65), 110–24, on St Hugh's choice of Lincoln canons.

[85] *RAL*, ii, 330.

[86] BL MS Cotton Cleo. B.I.,fo. 34 (35)ᵛ.

[87] This point must be clarified. Among the illustrations of English bestiaries of the second half of the twelfth century, accompanying the new textual additions from Isidore of Seville, Solinus and St Ambrose, we find numerous representations whose iconography recalls without any doubt antique sources (e.g. Fish, the Tiger). But these sets of illustrations also include fantastic images which seem less familiar to antique zoological tradition (for example, the Crocodile, for which a tradition of naturalistic representation existed in late antique art; but it is represented in the bestiaries of the twelfth and of the first half of the thirteenth century as a fantastic monster. Only in Oxford, Bodleian Library MS 764 (second half of the thirteenth century) does it reappear for the first time under its more naturalistic aspect).

The major role of the antique tradition of animal representation in the art of Roman Britain should be taken into account when considering the means by which this repertory was transmitted, though the paucity of material remains does not allow us to trace this tradition through into English medieval art (see J. M. C. Toynbee, *Art in Britain under the Romans* (Oxford, 1964); D. J. Smith 'Orpheus mosaics in Britain', in *Mosaique. Recueil d'hommages à Henri Stern* (Paris, 1983), 315–28; M. Henig, 'Graeco-Roman art and Romano-British imagination', *JBAA*, cxxxviii (1985), 1–22). The new repertory of animal representations appearing in English bestiaries and deriving from antique sources has too little in common with the animal iconography of Romano-British mosaic pavements or with palaeochristian and Mediterranean iconography transmitted through Anglo-Saxon illumination. The sudden appearance of such a repertory in England in the second half of the twelfth century testifies rather to the fresh introduction of a whole series of exemplars going back to the classical world.

[88] C. H. Haskins, 'England and Sicily in the 12th century', in *English Historical Review*, xxvi (1911), 433–47, 641–65; E. Jamison, 'Alliance of England and Sicily in the second half of the 12th century', *JWCI*, vi (1943), 20 ff.; F. Saxl and R. Wittkower, *British Art and the Mediterranean* (Oxford, 1948), nos. 24–7; E. Kitzinger, 'Norman Sicily as a source of Byzantine influence on western art in the twelfth century', in *Byzantine Art: an European Art, Lectures* (Athens, 1966), 127–47; E. Kitzinger, *I mosaici di Monreale* (Palermo, 1960), 19; O. Demus, *Byzantine Art and the West* (London, 1970), 121–61.

[89] Leland, *op. cit.* (note 78), cap. ccxiii, 234–5; E. Rück, 'Das Exzerpt der *Naturalis Historia* des Plinius von Robert von Cricklade', in *Sitzungsberichte der Bayerischen Akademie der Wissenschaft*, 1902, 195–285; id., *Die Geographie und Ethnographie der* Naturalis Historia *des Plinius im Auszüge des Robert von Cricklade* (Munich, 1903); id., *Die Anthropologie des* Naturalis Historia *des Plinius im Auszüge des Robert von Cricklade* (Neuburg, 1905). The Pliny manuscript compiled by Robert of Cricklade for Henry II (probably Eton College, MS 134) has decorated initials but no illuminations. M. R. James, *A Descriptive Catologue of the Manuscripts in the Library of Eton College* (Cambridge, 1895), 63; P. Danz Stirnemann, 'Bibliothèques princières et la naissance de la production privée au XIIᵉ siècle', in *Actes du colloque 'Artistes, artisans et production artistique au moyen âge', Rennes, 1983* (Paris, in press); *Texts and Transmission. A Survey of the Latin Classics*, ed. L. D. Reynolds (Oxford, 1983), 307 ff; R. M. Thomson, *Manuscripts from St Albans Abbey*, i (Woodbridge, 1985), 126.

[90] Manitius, *op. cit.* (note 43), 771–3.

[91] *Giraldi Cambrensis Opera*, iv, *op. cit.* (note 63), 383; *RAL*, iii, 325–6, 319, 320; Edwards, *op. cit.* (note 42), 190.

[92] Geoffrey's half-sister, Matilda, was baptized at Holy Trinity, Aldgate. The discussion of Geoffrey's Augustinian connections: P. Danz Stirnemann, 'The Copenhagen Psalter', Ph.D. thesis, Columbia University, 1976, 177–8 of the manuscript. I am very grateful to P. Danz Stirnemann, who permitted me to consult her manuscript.

[93] Dronke, introduction to Bernardus Silvestris, *op. cit.* (note 40), 2.

[94] See note 65 above.

[95] *DNB*, xxi, 139 ff.; M. Lovatt, 'The Career and Administration of Archbishop Geoffrey of York', Ph.D. thesis, University of Cambridge, 1974–75.

[96] *DNB*, xii, 315 ff.

[97] O. Demus, *Romanische Wandmalerei* (Munich, 1968), 156–7. J. Ainaud de Lasarte, *Arte romanica. Guia. Museo de Arte de Cataluña* (Barcelona, 1973), 54–8.

[98] C. M. Storrs, 'Jacobean Pilgrims from England from the Early Twelfth to the Late Fifteenth Century', Ph.D. thesis, University of London, 1964.

[99] J. B. Hurry, 'The shrine of St James at Reading Abbey', in *The Antiquary*, li (1915), 382 ff.

[100] O. Pächt, 'A cycle of English frescoes in Spain', in *Burl. Mag.* ciii (1961), 169 ff.; Demus, *op. cit.* (note 97), 168–70; W. Oakeshott, *Sigena. Romanesque Artists in Spain and the Artists of the Winchester Bible* (London, 1972). Note, however, that the representation of barnacle geese can already be found in eleventh-century Catalonian illumination: Roda Bible, Paris, BN MS lat. 6, I, fo. 7^v.

[101] Demus, *op. cit.* (note 97), 169–70; Ainaud de Lasarte, *op. cit.* (note 97), 193–4.

[102] Demus, *ibid.*; F. Avril, 'Les arts de la couleur', in F. Avril, X. Barral i Altet and D. Gaborit-Chopin, *Les Royaumes d'Occident* (Paris, 1983), 251.

[103] See note 5 above.

[104] MS 29 of the Hamo catalogue. The text of the Twelfth Book of the Etymologies has been cut out of this manuscript.

[105] The presence of the manuscript of Solinus in the Lincoln chapter library is rather important in this connection. The work of Solinus was known in England at least from the tenth century on, but references to manuscripts of Solinus in English medieval libraries are much rarer than to the works of Isidore of Seville. Cf. introduction by Th. Mommsen to *C. J. Solini Collectanea Rerum Memorabilium* (Berlin, 1895), xxix–lii, who lists eleven manuscripts of the eleventh to twelfth centuries in English libraries; and N. R. Ker, *Medieval Libraries of Great Britain. A List of Surviving Books* (London, 1964), 83, who mentions only one manuscript of the twelfth century (Bodleian Library MS Auct. F.3.7), from Exeter. Cf. also J. D. A. Ogilvy, *Books known to the English, 597–1066* (Cambridge, Mass., 1967), 245; Reynolds (ed.) *op. cit.* (note 89), 391–3.

[106] *RAL*, i, 262–3; iii, 263. The mid twelfth-century records mention also a certain Gilbert of Almeria (*RAL*, i, 84–5) and Richard of Almeria, who was also a precentor of Lincoln Cathedral (*RAL*, iii, 156).

[107] *RAL*, i, 262; Edwards, *op. cit.* (note 42), 161–8 (of the edition of 1949).

[108] MS 155, St Augustine in Psalms (Hamo catalogue, MS 25), MS 174, Gloss on the Psalms (Hamo Catalogue, MS 90), MS 199, Honorius of Autun, *Gemma animae, Speculum Ecclesiae*.

[109] Edwards, *op. cit.* (note 42), 218.

[110] Morgan, *op. cit.* (note 11), 26–7.

[111] Muratova, *op. cit.* (note 47).

[112] Kauffmann, *op. cit.* (note 1), no. 96; P. Danz Stirnemann, *op. cit.* (note 89).

[113] Kauffmann, *op. cit.* (note 1), no. 97.

[114] Morgan, *op. cit.* (note 11), no. 14, 60–2; X. Muratova, *ibid.*

[115] The obituary of Geoffrey's father Henry II (d. 1189) is added in the calender by a hand which differs from that of the manuscript and is, possibly, slightly later. Geoffrey became Archbishop of York in 1189 but was consecrated by the Pope only in 1191.

[116] Morgan, *op. cit.* (note 11), no. 19, 65–6; Muratova, *op. cit.* (note 29); *ead.*, *op. cit.* (note 47).

[117] Morgan, *op. cit.* (note 11), no. 17, 63–4; Muratova, *op. cit.* (note 47).

[118] *Ibid.*

[119] *PL*, clxxvii, cols. 13–56. On the work by Hugh of Folieto, F. Ohly, 'Probleme der mittelalterlichen Bedeutungsforschung und das Taubenbild des Hugo de Folieto', in F. Ohly, *Schriften zur mittelalterlichen Bedeutungsforschung* (Darmstadt, 1977), 32–92 (with bibliography); W. Clark, 'The illustrated medieval Aviary and the lay-brotherhood', *Gesta*, xxi (1982), 68–74.

[120] Muratova, *op. cit.* (note 29), 32 ff.

[121] E. Klemm, *Die romanische Handschriften der Bayerischen Staatsbibliothek*, i (Wiesbaden, 1980), no. 34, 32–4; J. Zahlten, *Creatio Mundi* (Stuttgart, 1979), 75.

[122] Klemm, *ibid.*; Muratova, *op. cit.* (note 29), 37 ff.

[123] I incline now to the slightly earlier dating of MSS Ashmole 1511 and Aberdeen 24. See Muratova, *op. cit.* (note 29); *ead.*, *op. cit.* (note 47).

[124] It is particularly important to note that several animals represented in the scene of the Creation of animals (see note 34 above), as, for example, a cat with a mouse, can be found represented in a similar manner iconographically in the illuminations of MS Ashmole 1511 (fos. 6^v, 9^r) and of Aberdeen University Library MS 24 (fos. 2^v, 5^r). These representations are interesting testimonies to a broad international circulation of models at the end of the twelfth century.

[125] A. L. Poole, 'Richard the First's alliances with the German princes in 1194', in *Studies in*

Medieval History Presented to F. M. Powicke (Oxford, 1948), 90–9.

[126] The Peterborough Abbey library is an exception to this rule. Its *Matricularium* of the fourteenth century mentions four treatises on the nature of animals, and a treatise on the nature of birds: James, *op. cit.* (note 13). These manucripts do not survive, or have not been identified. The style of the illuminators who were working on Bodleian Library MS Ashmole 1511, finds distinctive echoes in the style of Peterborough manuscripts of 1210–20, but the illuminations of MS Ashmole 1511 itself have more points in common with the art of the Lincoln and York area. Muratova, *op. cit.* (note 29), 41–55.

[127] See notes 59 and 67 above.

[128] See note 89 above.

[129] *DNB*, lxi, 355. On the intellectual atmosphere at Henry II's court; E. Türk, *Nugae Curialium. Le Règne d'Henri II Plantagenêt et l'éthique politique* (Geneva, 1977).

[130] *Rotuli Litterarum Clausarum*, ed. T. D. Hardy, i (London, 1833), 108 b, cited in Reynolds (ed.), *op. cit.* (note 89), 314.

[131] *C. J. Solini Collectanea, op. cit.* (note 105), 15.8–10.

[132] Pliny the Elder, *Hist. Nat.*, VIII. lxi (40), 142–5.

[133] T. Borenius, 'The cycle of images in the palaces and castles of Henry III', *JWCI*, vi (1943), 46; D. J. A. Ross, 'A lost painting in Henry III's palace at Westminster', *JWCI*, xvi (1953), 160.

[134] J. J. G. Alexander, 'Sigmund or the King of Garamantes?', in *Collected Essays in Honour of G. Zarnecki* (London, in preparation). I am very grateful to Dr Alexander for kindly sending me the text of his article before its publication.

[135] G. Henderson, 'Giraldus Cambrensis' account of a painting at Winchester', *Arch. J.* cxviii (1961), 175–9.

[136] M. R. James established that the manuscript belonged to the Old Royal Library: no. 518 of the Inventory of 1542, M. R. James, *A Catalogue of the Medieval Manuscripts in the University Library of Aberdeen* (Cambridge, 1932), pp. xi–xii, 19.

Intellectuality and Splendour: Thomas Becket as a Patron of the Arts

Ursula Nilgen

Patronage of the arts is not what people generally associate with the name of Thomas Becket. This may partly be due to biased views still current about the great archbishop which do not allow room for such worldly or intellectual inclinations. The very rich and detailed written sources on Becket could provide a different view; but focused as they are on his struggle with Henry II, they have in fact done more to conceal than to reveal the evidence for such a comparatively minor matter, their hero's interest in, or patronage of, the arts. The few scattered remarks are drowned in the flood of information about the conflict.[1] To evaluate these scraps of information properly, we must consider them beside those works of art and literature which are still preserved and can be connected with Becket, and to get the 'flavour' of this combined material, we must look at it in the context of Becket's life.

All the 'Lives' agree that Thomas had a special taste for the beautiful things of the world, be it luxurious dress, choice food, or the splendour and display of his household and entourage. This style of life is generally associated with the eight years when Becket was Chancellor of England.[2] But these tastes can already be discerned before he reached the peak of his secular career, and they by no means ended with his election to the archbishopric of Canterbury, although some of his biographers try to make us think so. The magnificence of the archbishop's household and table was notorious; and the amusing story describing the care with which Thomas chose his simple, but still beautiful, new regular canon's habit—yielding to the reproaches of his monks, who were scandalized by his custom of entering the choir in fashionable court dress—speaks for itself.[3] Even after six years of exile and hardship, when Thomas returned from France, convinced that he was in imminent danger of his life, he ordered a shipload of French wine to be sent after him. We know this because the royal coastguards

145

seized the ship, and only after Becket's sharp protest was the wine eventually sent to Canterbury.[4]

Even more revealing is the detailed report given by the French biographer Garnier of Pont-Ste-Maxence about the plundering of the archbishop's palace after the murder. Among the precious objects which fell into the murderer's hands, he mentions Becket's 'good blade, worth the price of a city, and a ring with a very choice sapphire set in it ..., and a great piece of very rich crimson samite; his books were taken and all his writings, and the gold chalice the saint used at mass ..., vestments, clothes, ... spoons, cups, goblets of silver and of refined gold ...; also all his jewels that he kept so carefully and would not show to everyone ....'[5] The sword and the jewels were obviously cherished relics from his years as Chancellor, which had been his happiest years, although spent in sin, as the archbishop himself occasionally admitted in letters to the Pope or cardinals.[6] He did hard and secret penance for the sins of that happy time, but he never denied his own past. One only wonders how Thomas managed to save these delightful and costly vanities over the years of exile and privation. They must have been very dear to him.

Only the shadow of one such costly object in Becket's possession is preserved (pl. XLI*b*). It is the impression of his privy seal attached to a charter in the Public Record Office. In the charter the archbishop confirms the grant of the church of Bexley in Kent, with other privileges, to the Augustinian priory of Holy Trinity at Aldgate, London. It must probably be dated to Becket's very first years as archbishop, about 1162–3.[7] On the obverse the wax, which once must have shown the impression of the archiepiscopal seal, is completely defaced. The reverse, authenticated with the privy seal or *secretum*, however, still shows the impression of an antique intaglio of a standing naked god, probably Mercury, and on the flat rim in which the gem was set the legend in bold letters: + SIGILLVM TOME LVND(onienis). The impression is not in perfect condition. It shows the naked figure standing in a Polyclitean *contrapposto*, with his left leg set back behind his right one, his left arm resting on a column and his right hand propped on his hip and carrying the *kerykeion*. Round the head turned in profile to the right one can make out the rim of the winged hat, the *petasos*. The intaglio is slightly oval and measures 18 mm. in height by 15 mm. in width.

The inscription calls the owner 'Thomas of London', without any official title. The only possible interpretation of this is that Thomas had this private seal made *before* he was promoted to the archdeaconry of Canterbury in 1154 and *before* he became Chancellor of England in 1154–5 and Archbishop of Canterbury in 1162.[8] One may compare the seal of Rainald of Dassel, Chancellor of the Empire from 1156 to 1159,[9] later Archbishop of Cologne, and in several respects a counterpart (on the the opposite political side) to Thomas Becket: there a (probably medieval) intaglio of a griffin is surrounded by the inscription REINALDVS ROMANOR(um) IMP(er)AT(oris) CANCEL(larius). Rainald also continued to use this seal when he became Archbishop of Cologne and Archchancellor for Italy. He had it made when he was promoted to his first leading secular office, and he clearly indicated his title on it. Thomas would surely have done so, too. The lack of any title on his seal means that he did not yet have a title when he had the precious gem set for his private use. He was still a clerk in lowest orders, perhaps already one of the first in Archbishop Theobald's entourage, well equipped with prebends and benefices, but nothing more.[10] The pretentious private seal sheds a sudden light on Becket's taste for beautiful and costly *objets d'art*, even in the earliest years of his career. It goes well with Garnier's remark about the jewels which he would not show to everyone. There may have been more antique gems among these.[11] Moreover, the choice of an antique intaglio with a figure of Mercury for his privy seal tells us something about Becket as an intellectual. It was among the most educated of the high clergy that these antique stones came into fashion during the twelfth century. The pagan representations were often interpreted in a Christian or in a magical sense.[12] Thomas may have chosen his Mercury deliberately, as a sort of magical guarantee of irresistible wisdom and grace in speech and appearance—gifts which in fact were his in plenty, as all the written sources agree. A thirteenth-century treatise concerning the images on precious stones attributes exactly these virtues to an intaglio portraying Mercury.[13] And for John of Salisbury, the outstanding humanist of the twelfth century, a good friend of Thomas, and his colleague at Archbishop Theobald's curia, Mercury is the often-cited symbol of eloquence and wisdom, a sort of patron of the emerging class of intellectuals who no longer came from the cloister but from the schools, especially from those in northern France.[14] Thomas had studied in Paris and elsewhere. He had been called back by family affairs before receiving a degree, but he obviously thought of himself as an intellectual, standing under Mercury's magic protection. It was very fashionable among the intelligentsia of the twelfth century to toy with all sorts of pagan superstition, and in this Thomas was no exception.[15] But for a simple cleric from mere bourgeois background—as Thomas was—to use such a pretentious and costly private seal was surely *not* common practice.

That Thomas possessed and loved precious art objects is attested by some other random remarks occurring in medieval chronicles and inventories. John Flete, in his History of Westminster Abbey, written in the mid fifteenth century, describes the solemn translation of St Edward the Confessor on 13th October 1163. There 'Saint Thomas, Archbishop of Canterbury, presented to St Edward an ivory image of the blessed Virgin, a very beautiful piece for which he had a special love'.[16] Although this source is rather late, the details given seem to rely on old information. A fourteenth-century inventory of the vestry of Christ Church Cathedral records another costly art object, St Thomas's psalter, as having a silver-gilt cover with gems and with an ivory Christ in Majesty surrounded by the four Evangelists.[17] Both these precious pieces are mentioned as possessions of Archbishop Becket, but the ivory Madonna, at least, which he liked so much may already have been his when he was Chancellor of England.

It is in another field that Thomas Becket's patronage first comes really to the fore: that of scholarly literature. It is common knowledge that two of the most famous and outstanding books written in the twelfth century, John of Salisbury's *Policraticus* and *Metalogicon*, as well as his long poem *Entheticus de dogmate philosophorum*, were dedicated to the Chancellor Thomas Becket.[18] The relevance of these dedications is sometimes unduly played down by modern historians, as a mere formality securing some sort of protection and financial support from an influential patron. But the evidence in the books themselves tells quite a different story. The prologue to Book VII of the *Policraticus* is especially revealing.[19] John, addressing the Chancellor, reminds him of the story which gave rise to his book. John had spent twelve years at the schools of northern France, especially in Paris. In 1148 he had entered the service of Archbishop Theobald of Canterbury, in spite of his mainly scholarly inclinations.[20] Now, after more than ten years in the job of secretary and confidential clerk to the archbishop, he felt uneasy about his mis-spent life, to such an extent that he planned to leave the curia of Canterbury. Thomas, to whom he had 'laid bare the anxieties of his heart', had held him back. He had persuaded his friend to stay in his job (which included a high measure of political responsibility for the Church in England),[21] but to make good the tedium of his life by writing, or, as Thomas styled it, by 'lamenting to the Muses fortune's cast'. Now, in a long, brilliantly formulated passage constantly oscillating between gravity and jest, John piles up the reasons which should prevent him from following Becket's counsel: his personal incapacity, the difficulty of satisfying both courtiers and philosophers, the hostile tongues of his colleagues and enviers, and all the adversities of his job, including lack of time and money. The last is, of course, the point of the whole *mise en scène*: 'And so, if you wish me to write, grant me . . . freedom of time, and spare me annoyance of domestic necessities'. Finally, with God's help, John shows himself willing to follow Becket's exhortations, and he will dedicate the 'gift of a jejune heart and arid tongue' to his friend, who, in effective contrast to John's own misery, is addressed as 'vir nostri aetatis elegantissimus', swimming in all the delights and riches of the world.

What we learn from this, and from several other passages in John of Salisbury's books,[22] is that it was Thomas who pushed his friend to write. Up to that date, the later 1150s, John had written nothing more than letters—masterpieces, of course, which he himself was going to publish later—but nothing more comprehensive. Moreover, after having finished his voluminous works dedicated to Becket, John would not publish any more major books; his *Historia Pontificalis* was to remain a fragment.[23] Thomas, with his sense for outstanding quality probably knew what was to be expected from his friend, if only he could be persuaded to write.

In addition, the topic of the *Policraticus*—a critique of the frivolities of court life, contrasted with a truly philosophical attitude and with a responsibly working machine of government—seems to have been conceived at Becket's instigation. At least this is what John hints at now and then in an *obiter dictum*. Moreover, several chapters of the *Policraticus* obviously reflect old disputes between John and Thomas about such philosophical questions as, for instance, predestination and free will. The whole argument of the book hinges on 'quod me et te urit', 'what burns me and thee alike'.[24]

The *Metalogicon* at first sight appears to be less closely concerned with the Chancellor's interests than the *Policraticus*. Nevertheless, it seems also to have been conceived and written at Becket's request. John himself again stresses the point that it was Thomas who pushed his friend to formulate his scholarly opinion on the *Trivium* and the most appropriate way to study philosophy. John's views had been challenged by a group of adversaries, the Cornificians, as he calls them. Now Thomas wished to investigate the dispute and asked John to formulate his ideas.[25]

Perhaps we may allow for some flattering exaggeration in these repeated hints at Becket's role as the instigator of John of Salisbury's principal works. But the hints are too many and too detailed in their information to be simply swept aside. I think we have to accept the inner evidence of John's writings, which makes it quite clear that it was Thomas the Chancellor who, with his demanding impetus, pressed his friend to formulate his wealth of ideas in comprehensive discourses and so pushed John into his own, as it were. This is much more than simple protective patronage. It reveals Becket's capacity to stimulate extraordinary achievements and testifies to his strong interest in high-level intellectual enterprise *and* in brilliance of literary form. What he promoted was the highest quality available in both.

In June 1162, Becket was consecrated Archbishop of Canterbury. Two years later he had to flee to France in the face of a threatened condemnation for treason. Two years is a short time for a new archbishop to carry out conspicuous enterprises in the arts. We hear of plans to have a hospital for the poor built just outside Canterbury, but nothing came of them.[26] Nevertheless, in spite of the short period of peaceful government given to Becket, he left his mark at Canterbury Cathedral in one of the finest wall-paintings preserved from medieval times: the St Paul with the Viper in the apse of St Anselm's Chapel (pl. XLI*a*). This masterpiece of English late Romanesque painting is all that remains of a painted cycle which must once have covered the walls of the whole chapel. It has been dated on stylistic evidence to the third quarter of the twelfth century. As I have shown elsewhere,[27] there is reason to connect the decoration of the chapel, which was then consecrated to Sts Peter and Paul, with the translation of the remains of Archbishop Anselm to this place, and with Becket's personal endeavour to have his great predecessor canonized. The date of the solemn *translatio* can be reconstructed from rather complex evidence as, most probably, 7th April 1163. Thomas was the most interested promoter of the elevation of a man whom he venerated as a theologian of outstanding intellectual capacity *and* as an unyielding fighter for the freedom of the Church. We must assume that he himself determined what the decoration of the chapel should look like, and that he himself paid for it.

This assumption is corroborated by an analysis of the iconography and meaning of the preserved wall-painting. To summarize the conclusion of the complicated argument: the painting, which has a prominent place in the apse although it represents a minor event in St Paul's life, was chosen because of certain connotations relating to Becket's career and spiritual situation as he saw it. Medieval exegesis interpreted St Paul's adventure with the viper on the isle of Malta, after his escape from shipwreck, as signifying the transition to a virtuous life of those rescued from spiritual and moral shipwreck, and the repulsion of the evil spirit who tries to prevent the spiritual teacher from fulfilling his duties. Confronted with Becket's personal situation in 1162–3 we can well imagine that Thomas experienced strong personal associations with the scene. He felt that he himself had just barely escaped spiritual shipwreck, and that he had to rebuff any temptation to neglect his spiritual duties by compromising with secular power. Both these thoughts are repeatedly expressed in Becket's letters.[28]

Given this strong personal involvement, we can assume that Thomas also selected the artist (or workshop) who was to put his ideas into suitable form. His choice fell on one of the most outstanding masters of the late Romanesque 'clinging curvilinear damp-fold style' which made its first full appearance about 1135 in the great Bible from Bury St Edmunds.[29] However, St Paul with the Viper represents a definitely later stage of that stylistic variant. It can be linked most closely with some book illuminations of high quality from both sides of the Channel, that is, the Copenhagen Psalter, generally dated about 1170, and the fifth volume of the Sawalo Bible from St-Amand in northern France, now in Valenciennes, which cannot be dated precisely but may be a little earlier.[30] The artists of the wall-painting and of the two books must have had at least some sort of workshop relationship with each other. They belong to that small group of first-class international painters, itinerant professionals, who executed important commissions on both sides of the Channel. It was again the best which Becket chose. It was the best in a stylistic mode which, because of its elegant sweep and mannered beauty, could be termed 'late Romanesque Courtly Style'. The *formal* values of the wall-painting had nothing to do with conversion and change yet. Courtly and elegant as ever, they proclaimed Becket's unaltered taste for splendour.

Yet, hard times were still to come. During the years of his exile in France from November 1164 to November 1170, Becket had no regular income and with his co-exiles had to rely on financial support from the King of France and several friends, French as well as English. One would not expect a man living in such circumstances of insecurity and financial shortage to patronize the arts. Becket reacted quite differently, however. He found a refuge in the Cistercian monastery of Pontigny by arrangement of the Pope, who had enjoined on him a life of penance and retreat, and complete abstinence from any political activity for the time being.[31] Thomas obeyed—although inactivity must have been nearly intolerable for a man like him. Debarred from politics, he moved into scholarship and its management. He kept his many unemployed clerks and co-exiles busy copying rare and important texts, for which exemplars could be found in the French libraries. These books Becket brought with him to England in December 1170, and bequeathed them, together with the rest of his important library, to Christ Church, Canterbury.[32]

Some ten or twelve volumes from Becket's collection have been identified in English libraries. Most interesting among these are six volumes from a glossed bible which originally consisted of more than twenty volumes.[33] As Dr de Hamel has shown, these volumes, which were made during Becket's exile, between 1165 and 1170, are the earliest datable copies to survive of a then brand new edition of the Gloss characterized by a new and rationalized layout, the 'alternate line system' (pl. XLII). This new edition had been prepared for publication by the pupils of Peter the Lombard, the famous teacher of the Holy Page in Paris, who died in 1160, leaving his *Magna Glossatura* on St Paul's Epistles in an unfinished state. The revised edition of the glossed bible became *the* fundamental textbook for scholars of the Holy Page. It spread through Europe with extraordinary speed during the 1170s, a true bestseller.[34] Thomas was among the first to scent out the book to which the future belonged. In spite of his limited financial resources he managed to have a set of more than twenty big volumes copied, and he even managed to have them illuminated, including a portrait of himself (pl. XLIII).

The decoration of Becket's glossed bible has nothing in common with the

PLATE XLI

a. St Paul with the Viper: St Anselm's Chapel, Canterbury Cathedral

b. Impression of Thomas Becket's private seal. PRO, London

Photographs: a, RCHM (England); b, PRO

b

PLATE XLII

*Photograph: by courtesy of the Master and
Fellows of Trinity College, Cambridge*

Cambridge, Trinity College MS B.5.5, fo. 79

PLATE XLIII

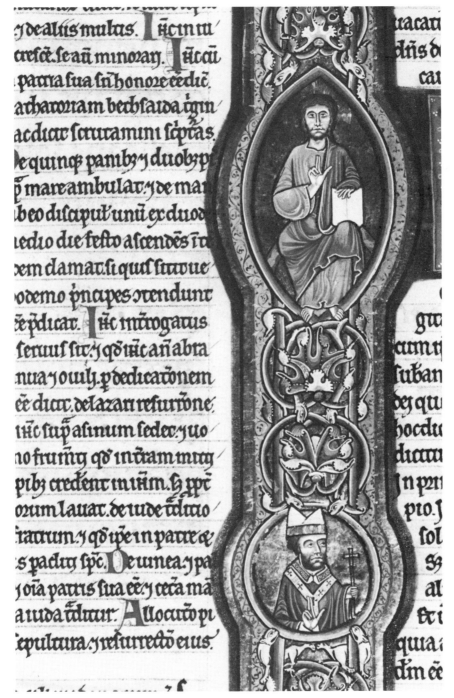

Photograph: Bildarchiv Marburg, by courtesy of the
Master and Fellows of Trinity College, Cambridge

Cambridge, Trinity College MS B.5.5, fo. 130ᵛ (detail)

wall-painting at Canterbury. It is limited to initials with rich ornamental fillings and some figural motifs. The glory of these books is the controlled symmetry and beauty of their script and the rational clarity of their page layout, with the bible text in double-size letters set on every second line of the ruling within the gloss (pl. XLII). The decoration is restrained in order not to divert attention from these more abstract aesthetic features. A large initial accentuates the beginning of each of the biblical books. The letters are constructed of thin bars set against a coloured background foil and filled with and interwoven by tendrils with metallic-looking, thin, elastic concentric scrolls ending in large orchid-like blossoms. Hordes of little white lion-cubs swarm through the tendrils. Their fiercely aggressive attitude has a humorous aspect, as do the grotesque heads in the scrolls. There is a deliberate contrast between the precision and elasticity of the tendrils, on the one hand, and the wantonness of the blossoms reaching with their leaves through the scrolls and the snapping ferocity of the lions on the other. Figural elements are interspersed here and there (pl. XLIII): medallions with busts of saints, clerics or evangelist symbols, the writing evangelist in the dress of a secular cleric, fighting and wrestling groups.[35] But all this is firmly integrated into the dominating structure of the letter.

A closer look at the figural elements discloses a stylistic attitude completely different from that displayed by the Canterbury St Paul: nothing is left of the curvilinear elegance and sweetness. The figures are restrained and realistic in their proportions, attitudes and dress. The drapery falls in smooth and natural folds over the body, forming trough-shaped shadow areas, a first dawning of the so-called *Muldenfaltenstil* which was brought to its peak later by Nicholas of Verdun. It is a more sober art style, well suited to its secondary role to the letter—and to letters. Splendour is still there, but controlled and made subordinate to reason.

The style of the decoration in Becket's books has its roots in northern French and some English book-painting.[36] Known among art historians as the 'Channel Style,' it was to spread, together with the new glossed bible, throughout Europe and to live on well into the thirteenth century.[37] Thomas scented out the coming art as well as the coming texts. Compared with the 'late Romanesque Courtly Style', there is a flavour of disillusion about this new art, but it is a disillusion leading to a new clarity. Becket may have perceived this as corresponding better to his own state of mind at this period. He had his portrait included in the initial to St John's Gospel, directly below the enthroned Christ and the Princes of the Apostles, the guarantors of the freedom of the Church (pl. XLIII). It is the most direct means of indicating both his cause and his personal initiative as the patron of this new scholarly book. Becket's portrait is the only authentic contemporary one to survive. It indicates the essentials, but without showing individual traits.[38]

One other commission of Becket's should be mentioned, although it was only carried through after his death. During the exile, Thomas charged Master Herbert of Bosham, his confidential secretary and teacher in the Holy Page, to prepare something unheard of in these times: a true critical edition of Peter Lombard's *Magna Glossatura* on the Psalter and St Paul's Epistles. The editors of the Lombard's Gloss, which was part of the new glossed bible, obviously had done little to correct misquotations in their master's text. Herbert of Bosham's critical edition, however, presents the unchanged text of Peter Lombard's *Magna Glossatura* surrounded by a complicated critical apparatus indicating and correcting errors. The undertaking, explained in detail in Herbert's prologues, obviously went beyond the scholarly ethos of his time. The four big volumes, which Herbert had made at the expense of Archbishop William of Sens and later gave to Christ Church, Canterbury, were never copied.[39]

This review of Becket's life and search for evidence which could indicate his relationship to, and patronage of, the arts has proved revealing in more than one sense. Thomas emerges as a very individual patron, with an unfailing instinct for quality. His strong taste for beauty and splendour in the arts is counterbalanced by a piercing interest in new philosophical questions and scholarship—sometimes so new that they were not followed up during his epoch. Himself no scholar, but an intellectual, a leader and politician, he provided the living space and the conditions under which new ideas could be pursued. Becket's patronage was of a different hue to that of famous colleagues such as Henry of Winchester. His appetite was also for the splendour of the arts, but with a strong inclination towards intellectual values. He strove to sponsor beauty and reason combined—those same qualities for which Mercury stood as guarantor.

NOTES

[1] *Materials for the History of Thomas Becket, Archbishop of Canterbury*, ed. J. C. Robertson (vols. i–vi) and J. B. Sheppard (vol. vii), Rolls Series, 67 (London, 1875–85) (hereafter *MTB*); *Thómas Saga Erkibyskups*, ed. E. Magnússon, 2 vols., Rolls Series, 65 (London, 1875–83). For the scattered material on art patronage, see O. Lehmann-Brockhaus, *Lateinische Schriftquellen zur Kunst in England, Wales und Schottland vom Jahre 901 bis zum Jahre 1307*, 5 vols. (Munich, 1955–60), index.

[2] *MTB*, i, 5–6; ii, 363–5; iii, 18–35 (esp. 20–3, 29–33); 173–7, 180–1; iv, 12–4, 84. Lehmann-Brockhaus, *op. cit.*, iii, nos. 6032–5.

[3] *MTB*, ii, 308, 368; iii, 37, 192–8 (esp. 196–8), 226–36; iv 20–1, 89. Lehmann-Brockhaus, *op. cit.* (note 1), iii, nos. 6039, 6041. For the story about the change of dress, see esp. *La Vie de Saint Thomas le Martyr par Guernes de Pont-Sainte-Maxence*, ed. E. Walberg (Lund, 1922), 20–1; Garnier's Becket, translated from the twelfth-century *Vie Saint Thomas le Martyr de Cantorbire of Garnier of Pont-Sainte-Maxence*, by J. Shirley (London/Chichester, 1975), 15–6. Garnier gives a more convincing report of the incident than the more 'pious' versions in *MTB* ii, 368, or iv, 21.

[4] *MTB*, i, 117; ii, 7; iii, 124; iv, 73.

[5] Walberg, *op. cit.* (note 3), 191; Shirley, *op. cit.* (note 3), 150; cf. Lehmann-Brockhaus, *op. cit.* (note 1), iii, no. 6052.

[6] e.g. *MTB*, v, (29) 48; vii, (617, 643) 187, 243.

[7] Published in *Arch. J.* xxvi (1869), 84–9.

[8] For the details of Becket's life and the dates of his career, see D. Knowles, 'Archbishop Thomas Becket: a character study', in *id., The Historian and Character, and other Essays* (Cambridge, 1963), 98–128; *id., Thomas Becket* (London, 1970); see also R. Winston, *Thomas Becket* (London, 1967).

[9] *Die Zeit der Staufer*, exhibition catalogue (Stuttgart, 1977), no. 159, Abb. 89.

[10] For Becket's early career, see esp. L. B. Radford, *Thomas of London before his Consecration* (Cambridge, 1894). For Archbishop Theobald's curia, see A. Saltman, *Theobald, Archbishop of Canterbury*, University of London Historical Studies, ii (London, 1956).

[11] Some of these jewels, among them a green intaglio and two others, obviously survived the pillage or were given back later; cf. the list of the 'jocalia s. Thome' in the inventory of the

vestry of Christ Church, Canterbury, recorded in 1315–21, in Lehmann-Brockhaus, *op. cit.* (note 1), i, no. 938.

[12] G. Demay, *Des pierres gravées employées dans les sceaux du moyen âge* (Paris, 1877); J. Adhémar, *Influences antiques dans l'art du moyen âge français* (London, 1939), 106–8, 249–50; M. Henig, 'Archbishop Hubert Walter's gems', *JBAA*, cxxxvi (1983), 56–61 (kindly brought to my attention by Margaret Gibson).

[13] *De sculpturis lapidum*, in London, BL MS Harley 80, published in *Archaeologia*, xxx (1844), 449: '9. Est et alius lapis in quo habetur Mercurius, habens alas in dextra, et in sinistra manu virgam serpente involutam: qui hunc habuerit tantum abundabit sapientia atque gratia ut nemo sibi resistere possit. Gratus erit Deo et omni populo, et perpetua gaudebit sanitate.'

[14] R. E. Pepin, 'The "Entheticus" of John of Salisbury: a critical text', in *Traditio*, xxxi (1975), 127–93, esp. 142 ff.; *Ioannis Saresberiensis . . . Policratici . . . libri VIII*, ed. C.C.I. Webb, 2 vols. (Oxford, 1909), see index; *Ioannis Saresberiensis . . . Metalogicon libri IV*, ed. C. C. I. Webb (Oxford, 1929), see index; *The Letters of John of Salisbury*, i: *The Early Letters (1153–61)*, ed. W. J. Millor, H. E. Butler and C. N. L. Brooke (London etc., 1955), xLVIII f., 183–4; ii: *The Later Letters (1163–80)*, ed. W. J. Millor and C. N. L. Brooke (Oxford, 1979), 392–5.

[15] For Becket's inclination towards astrology and magic, see *Policraticus* book 2 (Webb, *op. cit.* (note 14), i, 65–169), with a heated discussion of these topics, including sharp reproaches against Thomas, and John's letter no. 301 to Archbishop Thomas, as late as summer 1170 (*Letters*, ii, 708–11); see also L. Thorndyke, *A History of Magic and Experimental Science During the First Thirteen Centuries of Our Era*, ii (London, 1923),155–70.

[16] 'S. Thomas Cantuariensis archiepiscopus obtulit s. Edwardo imaginem b.virginis eburneam, pulchram nimis et sibi specialissimam' (Lehmann–Brockhaus, *op. cit.* (note 1), ii, no. 2515).

[17] 'Item textus cum psalterio s.Thome argento deaurato coopertus gemmis, ornatus in circumferentia cum magestate [*sic*] eburnea tenente librum in medio et 4 evangelistis sculptis' (Lehmann-Brockhaus, *op. cit.* (note 1), i, no. 940). I do not include the wooden casket from the Carrand Collection in the Bargello, Florence. The association of its nineteenth-century copy in Paris with Thomas Becket seems to be a modern legend. The style of the human figures on the casket definitely indicates a date after Becket's death in 1170. For a different view, see G. Zarnecki, 'A Romanesque casket from Canterbury in Florence', *Canterbury Cathedral Chronicle*, lxiv (1969), 37–43; reprinted in *id.*, *Studies in Romanesque Sculpture* (London, 1979), article no. xix.

[18] C. C. J. Webb, *John of Salisbury* (London, 1932; repr. 1971), *passim*; H. Liebeschütz, *Mediaeval Humanism in the Life and Writings of John of Salisbury*, Studies of the Warburg Institute, 17 (London, 1950), 15–6, 20–1; M. Kerner, *Johannes von Salisbury und die logische Struktur seines Policraticus* (Wiesbaden, 1977), 96–9, 109–11 (with comprehensive bibliography). For the editions, see note 14.

[19] Webb, *op. cit.* (note 14) ii, 90–2.

[20] *Letters*, i, xiv–xix.

[21] *Letters*, i, xxiv, xxix f.; see John's own remarks in the prologue to book 1 and at the end of *Metalogicon* (Webb, *op. cit.* (note 14), book 3, 218–19).

[22] *Entheticus . . .*, v. 1291 (Pepin, *op. cit.* (note 14) 177): 'Qui iubet, ut scribas, solet idem scripta fovere . . .'. *Policraticus: Enthet. in Policr.*, prologues to books 1, 2, 7, 8, and book 8, 25 (Webb, *op. cit.* (note 14), i, 13–7, 65; ii, 90–2, 226–7, 418); esp. book 6, 30 (*ibid.*, ii, 88–9): 'urgear . . . auctoritate superioris amici ad hoc stilum . . . impellentis; . . . in verbis tuis calcaribus urgebuntur ut in publicum prodeant'; also book 7, 25 (Webb, ii, 225): 'Utor ergo libertate Decembri, et iussis tuis obtemperans, quod me et te urit . . . fidenter arguo . . . .'

[23] *Ioannis Saresberiensis Historia Pontificalis = John of Salisbury's Memoirs of the Papal Court*, ed. M. Chibnall (London, 1956), xix, xxiv–xxx, xlvi–xlix.

[24] See book 7, 25, quoted above in note 22. For Becket's interest in the topic of the *Policraticus*, see the other quotations in note 22, esp. Webb, i, 65; ii, 88–9, 418. For the dispute about predestination, see book 2, 19–26 (*ibid.*, i, 107–43).

[25] *Metalogicon*, prologue to book 4 (Webb, *op. cit.* (note 14), 165): '. . . quoniam temeritas emuli [=Cornificii] non quiescit, et tu, cui mos gerendus est, opinionis mee sententiam queris, que pro tempore licuit, succincta brevitate percurram . . . Quia tamen visum est tibi meum et Cornificii examinare conflictum, . . .'; cf. also prologues to books 1 and 2 (*ibid.*, 3–4, 60).

[26] Lehmann-Brockhaus, *op. cit.* (note 1), i, no. 379.

[27] U. Nilgen, 'Thomas Becket as a patron of the arts. The wall painting of St Anselm's Chapel at Canterbury Cathedral', *Art History*, iii (1980), 357–74.

[28] Sce esp. Becket's vehement words written to Gilbert Foliot, Bishop of London, in July 1166, repelling, as it were, the temptation (*MTB*, v, (224) 516): 'Absit a me ista dementia, avertat a me Deus dementiam istam, ut aliquatenus persuadear aliquibus tergiversationibus inire commercium de Christi corpore, unde ego Judae venditori, et dominus meus [= Henricus rex] Judaeis assimiletur emptoribus Christi.'

Raymonde Foreville recently attempted to refute my arguments concerning Becket's patronage of the wall-painting in St Anselm's Chapel; but, with all respect for the distinguished French Becket specialist, I cannot accept her arguments and hypotheses as convincing. A more detailed reply must be reserved for another place (R. Foreville, 'Regard neuf sur le culte de Saint Anselme à Canterbury au XIIᵉ siècle', *Actes du Colloque International du CNRS*, Études Anselmiennes IVᵉ session (1982), 'Les mutations socio-culturelles au tournant des XIᵉ–XIIᵉ siècles' (Paris 1984), 299–316).

[29] Cambridge, Corpus Christi College MS 2; C. M. Kauffmann, *Survey*, iii: *Romanesque Manuscripts 1066–1190* (London, 1975), no. 56, with bibliography. For the definition of the variants of 'damp-fold style', see E. B. Garrison, *Studies in the History of Mediaeval Italian Painting*, iii (Florence, 1958), 200–10.

[30] Copenhagen, Royal Library. Thott. 143,2°; Kauffmann, *op. cit.* (note 29), no. 96. Valenciennes, Bibliothèque Municipale MS 5; N. Garborini, *Der Miniator Sawalo und seine Stellung innerhalb der Buchmalerei des Klosters Saint-Amand* (Cologne, 1978), 67–70, 194–8, Abb. 46–9; W. Cahn, *Romanesque Bible Illumination* (Fribourg, 1982), no. 115.

[31] *MTB*, ii, 344–5; iii 357–8; v, (95) 179–80; see Winston, *op. cit.* (note 8), 213; Knowles, 1963, 114–15 and 1970, 106, 108: *op. cit.* (note 8).

[32] *MTB*, iii, 77, 358–9, 379; i, 86–7; see the 'Libri sancti Thome' in the early fourteenth-century catalogue of the library of Christ Church, Canterbury, in M. R. James, *The Ancient Libraries of Canterbury and Dover* (Cambridge, 1903), 82–5.

[33] These six volumes are: Pentateuch in Oxford, Bodleian Library MS Auct. E.inf.7 (T.S.R. Boase, *English Art 1100–1216*, 2nd edn. (Oxford, 1968), 185–7, pl. 67b; O. Pächt and J. J. G. Alexander, *Illuminated Manuscripts in the Bodleian Library Oxford*, iii: *British, Irish and Icelandic Schools* (Oxford, 1973), no. 200, pl. 20). Gospels in Cambridge, Trinity College B.5.5 (U. Nilgen, *English Romanesque Art 1066–1200*, exhibition review in *Kunstchronik*, xxxvii (1984), 202–15, Abb. 3a). Twelve minor prophets, Jeremiah, Joshua/Judges/Ruth/Chronicles, Kings, in Cambridge, Trinity College B.3.11, B.3.30, B.3.12, B.4.30 (Boase, *op. cit.* pl. 67a; C. R. Dodwell, *The Canterbury School of Illumination 1066–1200* (Cambridge, 1954), 107, 111, pl. 65a, c). For the identifications, see James, *op. cit.* (note 32), 510; N. R. Ker, *Medieval Libraries of Great Britain*, 2nd edn. (London 1964), 32, 38, 238: Boase, *op. cit.*, 185 n.4; Dodwell, *op. cit.*, 107; see now esp. C. de Hamel (note 34 below).

[34] C. F. R. de Hamel, *Glossed Books of the Bible and the Origins of the Paris Booktrade* (Woodbridge, 1984), 38–45, also 7–9, 12, 22–7, and *passim*, pls. 13, 14b, 18c, e.

[35] Good examples of text pages, *ibid.*, pl. 13; of decorative initials, *ibid.*, pl. 18c; Dodwell, *op. cit.* (note 33), pl. 65c; Pächt and Alexander, *op. cit.* (note 33), pl. 20, no. 200. Figurative initials occur almost only in Becket's glossed Gospels in Cambridge, Trinity College B.5.5, fos. 3ᵛ, 51, 51ᵛ, 78, 79, 130ᵛ; see Nilgen, *op. cit.* (note 33), Abb. 3a, and pls. XLII—XLIII in this paper.

[36] De Hamel, *op. cit.* (note 34), 43–54, rightly rejects the localization to Canterbury or Pontigny (Dodwell, *op. cit.* (note 33), 108) or Sens and pleads for Paris instead. The roots of this decorative repertoire known as 'Channel style' (see following note), however, have not been traced so far. In northern France they can be traced back at least to a manuscript of St Augustine's *Expositio in epistolas Pauli*, from Corbie, in Paris, BN lat. 11575–6, dated by colophon to 1164 (*Manuscrits à peintures du VIIᵉ au XIIᵉ siècle*, exhibition catalogue (Paris, 1954), no. 140; L. Ayres, 'A miniature from Jumièges and trends in manuscript illumination around 1200', in *Intuition und Kunstwissenschaft, Festschrift für Hanns Swarzenski* (Berlin, 1973), 115–39, esp. 122, Abb. 11). The decorative elements and character occur already in the mid twelfth century on the other side of the Channel, in some initials of the Lambeth Bible, London, Lambeth Palace MS 3 (Kauffmann, *op. cit.* (note 29), no. 70), esp. on fos. 57 and 182.

[37] For the 'Channel style' see Boase, *op cit.* (note 33), 183, 186; W. Cahn, 'St Albans and the Channel Style in England', in *The Year 1200: a Symposium* (New York, 1975), 187–211; de Hamel, *op. cit.* (note 34), 44–54.

[38] De Hamel, *op. cit.* (note 34), 54; T. Borenius, *St Thomas Becket in Art* (London, 1932), 12–13. The few preserved examples of Becket's archiepiscopal seal seem to be doubtful: see *Arch. J.* xxvi (1869), 88–9; *Burl. Mag.* xxiii (1913), 263, fig. 4; F. Saxl and H. Swarzenski, *English Sculpture of the Twelfth Century* (London, 1954), pl. ivd.

[39] The four volumes are: *Psalterium glossatum* I and II in Cambridge, Trinity College B.5.4, and Oxford, Bodleian Library Auct. E.inf.6, and *Epistolae Pauli glossatae* I and II in Cambridge, Trinity College B.5.6 and 7. See James, *op. cit.* (note 32), 85; Boase, *op. cit.* (note 33), 185–8, pl. 67c; Dodwell, *op. cit.* (note 33), 104–9; R. Schilling, 'The "Decretum Gratiani" formerly in the C. W. Dyson Perrins Collection', *JBAA*, 3rd ser., xxvi (1963), 27–39, pl. 24/2; Pächt and Alexander, *op. cit.* (note 33), pl. 20, no. 201a–c; Kauffmann, *op. cit.* (note 29), 27, fig. 15; de Hamel, *op. cit.* (note 34), 42–4, 53–4, 57–60, and *passim* (see index). Herbert's prologues are printed in H. H. Glunz, *History of the Vulgate in England from Alcuin to Roger Bacon* (Cambridge, 1933), 341–50.

Henry of Blois as a Patron of Sculpture

George Zarnecki, F.S.A.

From his birth in *c.*1098, Henry of Blois was destined for high office. He was the son of Stephen, Count of Blois, one of the wealthiest men in France, and Adela, the daughter of William the Conqueror. King Henry I of England was his uncle and King Stephen his brother. On the death of his father, who lost his life in battle in the Holy Land in 1102, the county passed to Henry's older brother Theobald, while Adela retired to the Cluniac nunnery of Marcigny in Burgundy. It was no doubt her wish that Henry should be educated in nearby Cluny and it was there that, in due course, he became a monk. Thus he spent his early and impressionable years in the mother-house of a vast monastic order during a time of intense artistic activity connected with the completion of the new abbey church, known to architectural historians as Cluny III. Henry's life-long devotion to Cluny and his wide artistic interests must have been engendered by these early experiences. It is very likely that Henry's stay at Cluny had the approval of King Henry I, an admirer and benefactor of Cluny, who clearly had great hopes for the future of his young nephew and showered high and profitable offices on him—the abbacy of Glastonbury (1126) and the bishopric of Winchester (1129)—and subsequently, barely forty years old, Henry of Blois became papal legate in England (1139–43). It is small wonder that a contemporary writer thought of Henry as a man 'with fortune smiling favourably on his wishes'.[1]

Dom David Knowles described Henry of Blois thus: 'The commander who erected half a dozen fortresses in his diocese and burnt out his episcopal city, together with a great monastery and nunnery, was also the man who rebuilt Glastonbury on a grand scale, who re-established Cluny, who founded the hospital of St Cross and who decorated his cathedral with the most precious and varied works of art, from the fonts which still remain to illuminations and enamels and masterpieces of the goldsmith's art which have almost entirely disappeared.'[2]

Considering the importance of this princely figure who played such a significant role in English political and ecclesiastical history, it is surprising how little has been published about his art patronage. In this short paper I shall be able to do no more than give a brief outline of Henry's taste in sculpture or, more accurately, in the stone used for sculpture. This subject was first explored by Josephine Turquet in a Courtauld Institute M.A. dissertation in 1974, to which I am greatly indebted.[3]

The font in Winchester Cathedral mentioned by Knowles in the passage quoted is well known. It is made of black Tournai stone and was imported, ready-made, from Belgium.[4] On stylistic grounds, it has been dated to *c.*1150,[5] and since Henry was bishop of Winchester from 1129 for forty-two years, it is assumed, with every justification, that it was he who acquired it. Of the eight Tournai fonts surviving in England, four are in Hampshire and, as Francis Bond astutely remarked in 1908, the three of these fonts which are outside Winchester are in churches which were, during the twelfth century, in the gift of the bishop and thus were, no doubt, the result of Henry's generosity.[6]

Throughout his life Henry could indulge in expensive gifts,[7] for he was the wealthiest churchman in England. Glastonbury, of which he was abbot from 1126 till his death in 1171, was the richest monastic house in England, and Winchester, of which he was bishop in plurality, was the richest bishopric after Canterbury.[8]

Tournai fonts are not of a particularly high quality, that at Winchester being one of the best, and it must have been the material rather than the artistry which appealed to Henry. When polished and waxed, Tournai stone assumed a jet-black appearance and it probably reminded him of some Roman sculptures in coloured marble which he admired and collected. We know of this passion from the chance information in *Historia Pontificalis* that, when he was in Rome between 1149 and 1151, he scandalized the Curia by buying pagan statues for his palace in Winchester.[9]

It is very likely that the acquisition of at least four fonts by such an important person as Henry of Blois started the fashion in England for Tournai products, such as fonts, tombstones, columns and capitals. Henry travelled a great deal and so he had ample opportunity to see works in black Tournai stone, probably in Tournai itself. That he was in close touch with the artistic production in the territories which are now Belgium is evident from the fact that he commissioned a Mosan artist to execute a work from which two enamelled plaques now in the British Museum survive, one containing a portrait of Henry.[10]

In 1138, Henry embarked on building, close to Winchester Cathedral, the castle known as Wolvesey Palace.[11] During his excavation of this building in 1965, Martin Biddle found a section of a carved door-jamb which, as he at once realized, matched in design another section of the same jamb which was already in the Winchester City Museum (pl. XLIV*a*).[12] In the same museum there is another fragment which is the lowest part of the second jamb (pl. XLVII*a*) and in Wolvesey Palace there is yet another fragment from this doorway.[13] Their decoration consists of medallions with figural subjects, such as mermaids and harpies. Intertwining with the medallions are branches of foliage which terminate in a great variety of leaves, including pod-leaves, 'island' leaves and leaves with berries. These leaves are very close to those used on the walrus-ivory arm of a stool in the Museo Nazionale in Florence, which John Beckwith attributed to Winchester and dated *c.*1150. Such leaves also occur profusely in the so-called

Psalter of Henry of Blois of a similar date.[14] Nevertheless, both Turquet and Biddle have dated these jamb fragments to *c.*1135 and *c.*1140 respectively.[15] My own belief is that they are a little later and date to between 1140 and 1150. The reason for this is given in my catalogue entry for these fragments when they were shown in the *English Romanesque Art 1066–1200* exhibition: 'Although the motifs of these door jambs can be paralleled in English manuscripts and ivories, the general character of the decoration brings to mind the colonnettes of St-Denis Abbey',[16] a view not shared by one reviewer of the exhibition, Willibald Sauerländer.[17] However, I still maintain that the crisp, almost metallic handling of the foliage design on these jambs is inspired by works executed shortly before, and shortly after 1140 for Abbot Suger at St-Denis. These works include not only the colonnettes from the west façade (pl. XLIV*b*), but also the borders of the ambulatory windows and the Apostles (the so-called Crosby) relief.[18]

The façade of St-Denis Abbey was consecrated on 14th July 1140,[19] and on 30th September of that year Henry crossed to France[20] and stayed there for two months to confer on English affairs in his role as papal legate in England with King Louis VII and with many ecclesiastical leaders. He must certainly have visited Abbot Suger at St-Denis on that occasion. It is not surprising, therefore, to find in his own palace, which was being built at that very time, the influence of the decoration used at St-Denis. Not only do the door jambs owe a debt to the style employed to decorate the colonnettes at St-Denis, but the beautiful fragment of a head found by Biddle in the palace excavations (pl. XLV*a*) seems to derive from the column-figures of Suger's façade.

In the catalogue entry of the *English Romanesque Art* exhibition I described the head as follows: 'The top of the head is uncarved, presumably because the sculpture was placed high up and that part of it was out of sight. The fragment includes only the upper part of the nose, the left eye and hair, which is parted in the centre but with a few tufts forming a fringe. Perched on the hair is a small figure with its hands holding the hair as if to prevent it from falling into the eye. The little figure is round-headed with puffy cheeks and delicate features. It wears a conical cap with a beaded band. At first sight, the figure appears to be nude, the ribs clearly visible under the skin, but a damp-fold is carved on the legs, as if to imply a thin, tightly fitting dress.'[21]

Both Biddle and Turquet compared the little figure to the work of the Master of the Leaping Figures in the Winchester Bible and consequently dated the fragment to *c.*1140–60 (Biddle) and the 1150s or 1160s (Turquet).[22] My dating of the head to between 1140 and 1150 was based on the similarity of the fragment to the column-figures of St-Denis executed between 1137 and 1140. Reviewing the exhibition, Professor Sauerländer writes: 'The amusing head from Winchester (no. 148) is quite convincingly compared with the earliest parts of the Winchester Bible. This is an excellent local explanation and one wonders why this piece had to be further ennobled by an unconvincing reference to St-Denis?'[23] Professor Sauerländer views English Romanesque sculpture as very original and independent. 'It was only with the reign of Henry II—after 1150–60—that the situation became more internationalized'.[24] This statement should not pass unchallenged, for English sculpture, and indeed English art in all media, did not exist in isolation. For instance, Sauerländer does not accept that there are any links between English and Italian sculpture and he 'found difficult to endorse' the suggestion in the catalogue that the South Cerney wooden crucifix fragments have a German connection.[25] Yet he endorses their similarity to the St Albans Psalter, about which Otto Pächt stated a quarter of a century ago that it contains strong Ottonian ingredients.[26]

Of the twenty column-figures of the three portals of St-Denis, only four heads survive, three in American museums and one in a private collection in Paris.[27] This last was first published by Léon Pressouyre in 1976.[28] This head (pl. XLVb) combines a gentle, smooth modelling of the face and hair with the bold treatment of the bulging eyes, and is somewhat similar in style to the Winchester fragment. Pressouyre convincingly evokes metalwork as the chief source for the St-Denis heads and all the other sculpture of the façade.[29] The modelling of the Winchester head is, in my judgement, sufficiently close to all the four heads from St-Denis, but especially to that in Paris, to warrant the belief that this relationship was due to Henry of Blois. The Winchester fragment measures 155 mm., so when complete it must have been just over 300 mm. high, which is exactly the same as the St-Denis heads, a detail not without some significance. In the catalogue entry for this piece, I mentioned the possibility that the head was originally part of a column-figure. I now think that the evidence for this is inconclusive.

Amongst the episcopal victims of the Civil War, the most famous were Bishop Roger of Salisbury and his two nephews, Nigel of Ely and Alexander of Lincoln. In 1139 they were arrested and their castles seized by King Stephen. Their early release was due to the intervention of Henry of Blois, who took strong objection to his brother's unjustifiable action. Roger died a few months later, his rebuilding of Old Sarum Cathedral almost finished.[30] Nigel's building activities at Ely were still in progress, but the three carved doorways of this cathedral date to before these dramatic events and reflect the powerful influence of Lombard sculpture.[31] On the other hand, Bishop Alexander 'the Magnificent' was about to embark on the embellishment of the façade of his cathedral at Lincoln by the insertion of three elaborate doorways which included acanthus capitals, richly carved colonnettes and a pair of column-figures, all of which imitate Suger's work at St-Denis.[32] It may, of course, be pure coincidence that Alexander, like Henry of Blois before him, sought sculptural inspiration from St-Denis, but when it is remembered that he also acquired a large Tournai font for Lincoln, the suspicion that he was emulating Henry becomes irresistible.

Although Henry was an absentee abbot of Glastonbury, the monks there had nothing but praise for his care and generosity, and no wonder, since he was an excellent administrator, rebuilt all the monastic buildings and lavished precious gifts on their church.[33] These buildings perished in the devastating fire of 1184 and only a few fragments of sculpture from the cloister have been recovered in excavations.[34] In addition, a portion of a twin capital from the cloister is in Salisbury Museum (pl. XLVc). All these sculptures are carved in dark-grey limestone from the Somerset-Gloucestershire area. This stone, when polished, is like marble and is remarkably similar in appearance to Tournai limestone, so much so that the Salisbury capital has masqueraded for many years as Tournai stone.[35] In the use of local stone at Glastonbury as a substitute for Tournai stone, which had to be imported and was presumably expensive, Henry's practical sense and good management are at once evident.

PLATE XLIV

Photograph: Courtauld Institute of Art

b. Section of a colonnette from the façade of St-Denis Abbey. Musée du Louvre

a. One of the four door-jamb fragments from Wolvesey Palace. Winchester City Museum and Winchester Research Unit WP.WS. 203

PLATE XLV

Photograph: Léon Pressouyre

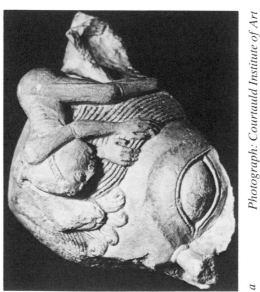

Photograph: Courtauld Institute of Art

a. Fragment of a head from Wolvesey Palace. Winchester Research Unit WP. WS. 609

b. Head of a queen from the central doorway of St-Denis Abbey. Paris, collection of M. Jean Osouf

c. Twin capital from the cloister of Glastonbury Abbey. Salisbury and Wiltshire Museum

PLATE XLVI

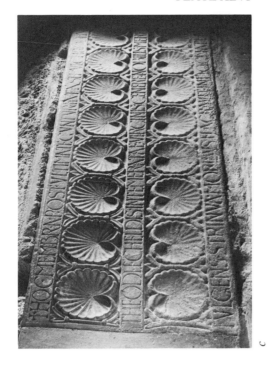

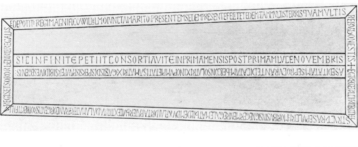

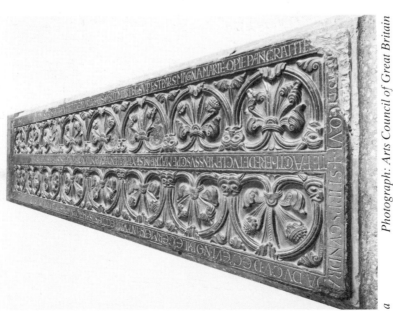

a. Gundrada's tombstone. St John the Baptist, Southover, Lewes; originally in Lewes Priory

b. Queen Matilda's tombstone in La Trinité, Caen: etching by John Sell Cotman (from the *Architectural Antiquities of Normandy*, i (1822), pl. 33)

c. Sarcophagus of Abbess Theodechilde in Jouarre Abbey

Photograph: Arts Council of Great Britain

PLATE XLVII

c

b

a

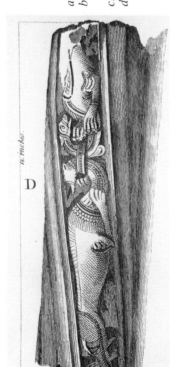

d

Photograph: Crown copyright

a. Fragment of a door jamb from Wolvesey Palace. Winchester City Museum
b. Fragment from a lavabo, originally in Lewes Priory. Anne of Cleves Museum, Lewes
c. Capital from Faversham Abbey. The Maison Dieu, Ospringe
d. Lost shaft from Hyde Abbey, Winchester (from *Archaeologia*, xiii (1800), pl. XXIII)

There is an undoubted stylistic relationship between the Glastonbury sculpture and the fragments from Wolvesey Palace and thus, ultimately, with St-Denis, but there is also yet another connection which leads to Tournai stone and Bishop Henry.

It is well documented that Henry was educated at Cluny and throughout his life considered himself a Cluniac.[36] He introduced certain Cluniac observances to Glastonbury and was represented at Glastonbury by a Cluniac monk from Lewes, Robert, who later became Bishop of Bath. It is, therefore, hardly surprising that Henry took an interest in the affairs of Lewes Priory, which was the mother-house of the English Cluniacs.

Lewes was founded by William de Warenne, Earl of Surrey and his wife Gundrada (or Gundreda), in the 1070s,[37] and they were both buried in the chapter house. However, in the second quarter of the twelfth century, the priory church and the chapter house were rebuilt and the bodies of the founders reburied in the new chapter house before the consecration in 1147.[38] The tombstone of Gundrada still exists (pl. XLVI*a*). It is made of Tournai stone, but was carved in England in a style which is so close to the Glastonbury cloister fragments that it must have been executed by the same sculptor.[39] There is a probability that Henry of Blois was not only instrumental in choosing the material for this tomb, but also provided the sculptor, who had been trained at Winchester and who later worked at Glastonbury.

There were other Tournai sculptures at Lewes Priory, such as capitals, colonnettes, and bases, which were imported ready-made.[40] But a fragment from the lavabo shows clearly that this also, like the tombs of the founders, was carved in England (pl. XLVII*b*).[41] The foliage on this fragment is unmistakably a Winchester design (see pl. XLVII*a*) and reinforces the likelihood of Henry's involvement in the rebuilding of Lewes. Not surprisingly, Henry and his protégé Robert, Bishop of Bath, both attended the consecration ceremony at Lewes in 1147.[42] Professor R. H. C. Davis identified Robert as the author of the *Gesta Stephani*.[43] It may be of some relevance to learn that Bishop Robert was, according to John of Worcester, *Flandrensis genere sed natus in partibus Angliae*,[44] so perhaps he played some part in bringing to the notice of Henry of Blois the Flemish stone resembling marble.

According to old tradition, Gundrada was the daughter of William the Conqueror and Queen Matilda, and if so she would have been Henry's aunt. But modern historians will have none of this; she was apparently Flemish.[45] Be this as it may, it is nevertheless intriguing to find that the strange arrangement of the inscription which frames the Gundrada slab and then runs lengthwise down its middle, repeats a similar layout of the inscription on the tomb of Queen Matilda in La Trinité at Caen (pl. XLVI*b*). Matilda was the foundress of La Trinité and was buried in the choir of the church in 1083.[46] Her tombstone, so handsomely etched by J. S. Cotman,[47] has no decoration, but only a long inscription. The slab is a coffin-lid, wider at one end, and was intended to be in a horizontal position accessible from all sides, for in order to read the inscription it is necessary to walk around the slab, exactly as in the case of the Gundrada tombstone.

The placing of the inscription on the Matilda tombstone seems to be a distant echo of the arrangement on the front and back of the celebrated sarcophagus of Abbess Theodechilde at Jouarre (pl. XLVI*c*), dating from the late seventh century.[48] The two rows of shells on that sarcophagus provide a rather striking parallel for the palmettes on the Gundrada slab.

Matilda was the daughter of Baldwin V, count of Flanders, and it is perhaps no accident that her tombstone is made of Tournai stone and is in fact the earliest surviving tombstone in this material.[49] Henry of Blois undoubtedly knew the tomb of his grandmother. After all, his own mother Adela, having died a Cluniac nun at Marcigny-sur-Loire on 8th March 1138, was buried in La Trinité at Caen, 'Norman to the last'.[50] Unfortunately, her tomb has not survived, otherwise it would probably have provided a further link with Henry's work in England. He very likely had a hand in commissioning it.[51]

If the purchase of the Tournai font by Alexander, Bishop of Lincoln, was in emulation of Henry, then the Tournai tombstone of Alexander in Lincoln Cathedral was also an imitation of Henry's patronage at Lewes and possibly at Caen.[52]

By the middle of the century, the fashion for highly polished sculpture received a further boost from the use of carved Purbeck capitals at Faversham (pl. XLVII*c*),[53] of which, sadly, only one example survives, which has been dated to *c.* 1150. Faversham was a Cluniac foundation of Stephen and it is a matter of speculation to what extent, in his role as an art patron, he was advised by his brother.

The use of Purbeck certainly points to Henry. This material, not in use since Roman times, became increasingly popular in the twelfth century. It was extensively employed in Henry's Wolvesey Palace and I am grateful to Martin Biddle for telling me that, in his revised dating, the first use of Purbeck in the palace was between 1141 and 1154, thus pre-dating Faversham.

Biddle's new dating of the first use of Purbeck in Wolvesey Palace agrees with another work in Winchester, which involved carved colonnettes, one of which was illustrated in 1798, but which are all now lost (pl. XLVII*d*).[54] They came from Hyde Abbey, destroyed by Henry of Blois in 1141 in that act of savage revenge which he was to regret for the rest of his life. He tried to repair the damage to his reputation by restoring some of the destroyed objects, and the Purbeck colonnettes could well have formed part of the tomb of Alfred, as restored after 1141.

Tournai stone continued to be used for some time, for instance for the colonnettes in the cloister of Rochester Cathedral (about 1150), and the chancel arch of Iffley Church (about 1170).[55] Such columns must have been regarded as the nearest thing to classical marble. But it is significant that where classical material was available, it was preferred to Tournai stone, for example, the onyx columns from Roman ruins extensively employed at Christ Church, Canterbury, in the 1150s.[56]

The future, however, belonged to Purbeck marble. According to Prior and Gardner: 'Nearly every English church of importance that was built from 1170 to 1350 made use of the polished pillars, the capitals, bases and string-courses' of Purbeck marble.[57]

The man who was so influential in starting the fashion for this material was buried in his cathedral in 1171. The Purbeck tomb, which is generally considered as that of William Rufus, is more likely to be his own.[58] The silver chalice found in it rules out a secular burial and the small ivory head was probably the terminal of Henry's crosier.[59] The plain cover without any ornament or inscription was probably commissioned by Henry himself. Such a simple tomb would have been most appropriate for one who a few years before his death gave away all his possessions and devoted himself to prayer and acts of penitence. Even his most severe critic, St Bernard, had he lived, would have approved of this change from lavish patronage to such austerity.[60]

NOTES

[1] *Gesta Stephani*, ed. and transl. by K. R. Potter, with new introduction and notes by R. H. C. Davis, OMT (1976), 8–9.

[2] Dom D. Knowles, *The Monastic Order in England* (Cambridge, 1940; 2nd edn. 1963), 289.

[3] J. C. Turquet, 'Henry of Blois, Patron of Sculpture', M.A. dissertation, Courtauld Institute of Art, 1974.

[4] C. H. Eden, *Black Tournai Fonts in England* (London, 1909), 12–16 and 4 pls.

[5] E. Schwarzbaum, 'Three Tournai tombslabs in England', *Gesta*, xx–xxi (1981), 95.

[6] F. Bond, *Fonts and Font Covers* (London, New York, and Toronto, 1908), 204–5. Bond, as well as Eden (see note 4), lists seven Tournai fonts in England: Winchester, East Meon, St Michael's in Southampton, St Mary Bourne in Hampshire, Lincoln, Thornton Curtis in Lincolnshire and St Peter's, Ipswich, in Suffolk. To this number should be added a mutilated bowl in the Ipswich Museum: see G. C. Dunning, 'The distribution of black Tournai fonts', *Antiq. J.* xxiv (1944), 66.

[7] For Henry's gifts, see references in Turquet, *op. cit.* (note 3), 45 n. 5. Also O. Lehmann-Brockhaus, *Lateinische Schriftquellen zur Kunst in England, Wales und Schottland vom Jahre 901 bis zum Jahre 1307* (Munich, 1955), i, no. 1878 (for Glastonbury) and ii (1956), nos. 4745, 4748, 4764–4767 (for Winchester). See also E. Bishop, 'Gifts of Bishop Henry of Blois, Abbot of Glastonbury, to Winchester Cathedral', *Liturgica Historica*, 392–401. For gifts to Cluny, see L. Voss, *Heinrich von Blois* (Berlin, 1932), 118.

[8] Knowles, *op. cit.* (note 2), 287 and 702.

[9] *Historia Pontificalis*, ed. M. Chibnall, NMT (1956), 79 and 91–94, and Lehmann-Brockhaus *op. cit.* (note 7), ii, no. 4760. Nothing survives of this unique collection. Jean Adhémar, in his *Influences antiques dans l'art du moyen âge français* (London, 1939), 97, writes: 'Henri de Blois, évêque de Winchester (1129–1171), autre amateur d'antiques, fit charger à Ostie un navire entier de marbres et de pierres recueillis dans les ruines de la Rome Impériale, et ramena heureusement ce précieux butin jusqu'à son évêché anglais. A sa mort, on l'enterra sous un bloc de marbre romain sur lequel on grava le vers suivant: "Hic portat lapides quas portavit ab Urbe" '. Adhémar's reference is to E. Rodocanachi, *Les Monuments de Rome après la chute de l'Empire* (Paris, 1914), 25, who, however, attributes this story to Robert de Ware, Abbot of Westminster. He should have given the abbot's correct name, Richard de Ware, who died in 1283. The story is taken from John Flete's *The History of Westminster Abbey*, ed. J. Armitage Robinson (Cambridge, 1909), 115. I am very grateful to the late Mr Nicholas MacMichael, and Professor C. R. Dodwell, for their help in tracing this reference.

[10] Discussed most recently by Neil Stratford, *Catalogue*, nos. 277a and b.

[11] 'Hoc anno [1138] fecit Henricus episcopus aedificare domum quasi palatium cum turri fortissima in Wintonia', *Annales monasterii de Wintonia*, ed. H. R. Luard, *Annales monastici*, 2 (London, 1865), 51. Also Lehmann-Brockhaus, *op. cit.* (note 7), ii, no. 42752. From his other castles and palaces no sculpture has survived. At Farnham (M. W. Thompson, 'Recent excavations in the keep of Farnham Castle, Surrey', *Med. Arch.* iv (1960), 81–94) there are wooden capitals of a scallop form, which could be part of the original building of *c.* 1140. Recent excavations at Witney revealed no sculpture (B. Durham, *Witney Palace: Excavations at Mount House, Witney in 1984*, Oxford Archaeological Unit (n.d.). I am grateful to Mrs Glen Popper, Mr A. R. Dufty and Mrs Freda Anderson for information about Farnham and to Dr Margaret Gibson and Mr T. G. Hassall, Director of the OAU, about Witney).

[12] For the excavations see M. Biddle, 'Wolvesey: the *domus quasi palatium* of Henry of Blois in Winchester', *Château Gaillard*, European Castle Studies, ed. A. J. Taylor (1966), 28–36; also *Antiq. J.* xlvi (1966), 327.

[13] Turquet, *op. cit.* (note 3), 19, pls. 30–31.

[14] These similarities were first noted by Turquet, *op. cit.* (note 3), 19–20. It is generally accepted that the Winchester Psalter was made for Henry of Blois (F. Wormald, *The Winchester Psalter* (London, 1973), 125). The inclusion of the two miniatures copied from a Byzantine or Italo-Byzantine model in this psalter, perhaps an icon as Francis Wormald suggested (*op. cit.*, 90), supports, in my view, the possibility that this model was amongst the gifts which Henry received from his nephew William Fitzherbert, the deposed archbishop of York, when, on returning from Sicily, he was given refuge at Winchester. The elegant Virgin and Child relief in York Minster, which we were fortunate to have in the exhibition (*Catalogue*, no. 153), is, I believe, the result of copying a similar model given by William to his cathedral when he was reinstated in 1153 (G. Zarnecki, *Later English Romanesque Sculpture, 1140–1210* (London, 1953), 29–31).

   The reliefs from the Durham screen which Fritz Saxl and Hanns Swarzenski (*English Sculptures of the Twelfth Century* (London, 1954), 66) so convincingly compared to the Winchester Psalter, and which represent another aspect of Byzantine influence in England, are also, to some extent, linked to Henry of Blois, since they were clearly commissioned by Hugh du Puiset, who was Henry's nephew and was Archdeacon of Winchester before becoming the Bishop of Durham in 1153.

[15] Turquet, *op. cit.* (note 3), 20 and *Antiq. J.* xlvi (1966), 327.

[16] *Catalogue*, 147.

[17] *Burl. Mag.* August, 1984, 515.

[18] The most recent discussion of the colonnettes is found in *The Royal Abbey of Saint-Denis in the Time of Abbot Suger (1122–1151)*, the catalogue of the exhibition held in the Metropolitan Museum of Art, New York, 1981, no. 2A. For a full analysis of the borders of the relevant stained glass windows at St-Denis see L. Grodecki, *Les Vitraux de Saint-Denis*, i (Paris, 1976), 126–31. The borders (nos. 14 and 15) exhibited in New York are particularly significant, since they share with the Winchester jambs the characteristic form of leaves in which the concave surfaces are 'shaded' in an identical manner by criss-cross lines. This is a method frequently used in surface enrichment in metalwork: see, for instance, The Pierpont Morgan Library, *The Stavelot Triptych*, pls. 1–7. For the most recent views on the Crosby relief see the Metropolitan Museum catalogue (above), no. 6, where it is suggested that it was originally intended for Suger's own tomb and that it dates to about 1150–1, a view questioned by Neil Stratford, in his review of the exhibition (*Burl. Mag.*, August 1981, 509), who believes the relief to be later. However, the similarity of decorative motifs on this relief to the colonnettes from the façade make such a big difference in their dates unlikely and I prefer a date in the early 1140s for the Crosby relief.

[19] E. Panofsky, *Abbot Suger on the Abbey Church of St-Denis and its Art Treasures*, 2nd edn. by G. Panofsky-Soergel (Princeton, 1979), 100. The consecration of the choir took place on 11th June 1944: *op. cit.*, 112.

[20] Voss, *op. cit.* (note 7), 26.

[21] *Catalogue*, 148.

[22] M. Biddle, *Winchester, Saxon and Norman Art*, exhibition catalogue, Winchester Cathedral Treasury (1973), no. 94, and Turquet, *op. cit.* (note 3), 22.

[23] *Burl. Mag.*, August 1984, 515.

[24] *Ibid.*, 512.

[25] *Ibid.*, 515.

[26] O. Pächt, C. R. Dodwell and F. Wormald, *The St Albans Psalter (Albani Psalter)* (London, 1960), 125.

[27] The four heads are conveniently reproduced and briefly described in the *Saint-Denis* catalogue (*op. cit.*, note 18), no. 3.

[28] L. Pressouyre, 'Une tête de reine du portail central de Saint-Denis', *Gesta*, xv (1976), 151–60.

[29] *Ibid.*, 156. For an interesting connection between sculpture and metalwork, see D. Kahn, 'Recent discoveries of Romanesque sculpture at St Albans', *Studies in Medieval Sculpture*, ed. F. H. Thompson, Soc. Antiq. London Occ. Paper (n.s.) iii (1983), 87.

[30] R. A. Stalley, 'A twelfth-century patron of architecture: a study of the buildings erected by

Roger Bishop of Salisbury', *JBAA*, 3rd ser. xxxiv (1971), 71.

[31] G. Zarnecki, *The Early Sculpture of Ely Cathedral* (London, 1958), 28 ff. The Italian models for Ely are further discussed by J. Meredith in an unpublished thesis, 'The Impact of Italy on the Romanesque Architectural Sculpture of England', presented to Yale University, 1980, 62 ff.

[32] G. Zarnecki, *Romanesque Sculpture at Lincoln Cathedral*, Lincoln Minster Pamphlets, 2nd ser. no. 2, 2nd edn. (1970), 13 ff.

[33] Knowles, *op. cit.* (note 2), 290 with refs.

[34] References to the excavations of Glastonbury Abbey can be found in Turquet, *op. cit.* (note 3), 8 and 47, n. 8.

[35] Zarnecki, *op. cit.* (note 14), 17–18; T. S. R. Boase, *English Art, 1100–1216* (Oxford, 1953), 122.

[36] Voss, *op. cit.* (note 7), 108 ff.

[37] Knowles, *op. cit.* (note 2), 151 and Lehmann-Brockhaus, *op. cit.* (note 7), ii, no. 2309; R. B. Lockett, 'A catalogue of Romanesque sculpture from the Cluniac houses in England', *JBAA*, 3rd ser. xxxiv (1971), 51. In a recent paper, 'The Tournai marble sculptures of Lewes Priory', *Sussex Arch. Coll.* cxxii (1984), 99–100, F. Anderson calls the link between Henry of Blois and Lewes unsubstantiated and dates the tombslab to the last quarter of the twelfth century. She accepts the stylistic similarity between the tomb slab and the capitals from Glastonbury apparently without realizing that the Glastonbury fragments came from the buildings erected by Bishop Henry.

[38] Lehmann-Brockhaus, *op. cit.* (note 7), ii, no. 2314.

[39] For the inscription, discussion and references, see *Catalogue*, 45.

[40] The rich collection of sculpture from Lewes Priory in the Anne of Cleves Museum, Lewes, and scattered in the town and elsewhere is at last being carefully catalogued by Mrs Freda Anderson.

[41] Turquet, *op. cit.* (note 3), 10. There is some, however distant, connection between the lavabos at Lewes and Glastonbury and that of the Cluniac priory at Much Wenlock: see *Catalogue*, 169. The Purbeck marble fountain from the Palace of Westminster (B. Davison, 'A carved fragment of Purbeck marble from a late twelfth-century fountain in the Palace of Westminster', *Antiq. J.* lv (1975), 399, pl. LXXXIII) is a later version of this type of structure.

[42] Lehmann-Brockhaus, *op. cit.* (note 7), ii, no. 2314.

[43] *Gesta Stephani* (see note 1), xxxiv ff.

[44] *The Chronicle of John of Worcester, 1118–40*, ed. J. R. H. Weaver (Oxford, 1908), 38.

[45] Sir Charles Clay, *Early Yorkshire Charters*, viii (1949), 40–6 and esp. 44.

[46] M. Baylé, *La Trinité de Caen, sa place dans l'histoire de l'architecture et du décor romans* (Paris, 1979), 15.

[47] J. S. Cotman, *Architectural Antiquities of Normandy*, i (London, 1822), pl. 33*. Cotman visited Normandy in 1817, 1818 and 1820 and stayed in Caen on all three occasions. The original from which the etching was made is in Norwich: see M. Rajnai, *John Sell Cotman, Drawings of Normandy in Norwich Castle Museum* (1975), 57.

[48] J. Hubert, *L'Art pré-roman* (Paris, 1938), 156 ff., pls. xxxvia and xxxviia.

[49] J.-C. Ghislain, 'Dalles funéraires romanes tournaisiennes, en Belgique', *Art & Fact*, no. 2 (Liège, 1983), 54. According to the author, amongst the earliest Tournai tombslabs were those of the counts of Flanders in the Abbey of St-Pierre-au-Mont-Blandin in Gent, dating to the first years of the eleventh century, but destroyed in 1566.

[50] R. H. C. Davis, *King Stephen, 1135–1154* (London, 1980), 5 and n. 11.

[51] Baylé, *op. cit.* (note 46), 14–15, discusses the identity of Adela *filia regis*, whose tomb is listed in *Gallia Christiana*, xi, col. 434, and suggests that it dates from either 1078 or 1081. She has very kindly supplied me with a photograph of a drawing by La Bataille-Auvray in the Mancel MS 80, fo. 22, in the Musée des Beaux-Arts at Caen. The drawing shows a plain slab through the centre of which, lengthwise, runs an inscription ADELIA FILIA REGIS. It is most unlikely that this was the tomb of 1138.

[52] For Alexander's tomb, see Zarnecki, *op. cit.* (note 32), 20–1. Dr Elizabeth Bradford-Smith (Schwarzbaum, *op. cit.* (note 5)) has recently argued that Alexander ordered not only his own tomb but that of his dead uncle Roger of Salisbury and of his cousin Nigel, Bishop of Ely, who, because he sided with the Empress Matilda and suffered reprisals from King Stephen,

was in no position to pay for his own. This is difficult to accept. In 1145 Nigel made his peace with the king and as he witnessed at least six charters for Stephen after that date, it has been argued that he was restored to some official position in the royal administration (Davis, *op. cit.* (note 50), 91 n. 37). He was certainly not so impoverished as to require Alexander to pay for his tomb.

[53] For Faversham, see D. Kahn 'Romanesque Architectural Sculpture in Kent', Ph.D. thesis, Courtauld Institute of Art, University of London, 1982, 54–7 and *Catalogue*, 146.

[54] *Archaeologia*, xiii (1800), pl. xxiii d and Society of Antiquaries, Prints and Drawings (Early Medieval), fo. 5. Neil Stratford compares this shaft to the beautiful flask now in St-Maurice d'Agaune, *Catalogue*, 296.

[55] J. Bony, 'Origines des piles gothiques anglaises à fûts en délit', *Gedenkschrift Ernst Gall* (Munich-Berlin, 1965), 107–8.

[56] Kahn, *op. cit.* (note 53), 12 and 75.

[57] E. S. Prior and A. Gardner, *Medieval Figure-Sculpture in England* (Cambridge, 1912), 568.

[58] The Revd J. G. Joyce, 'On the opening and removal of a tomb in Winchester Cathedral, reputed to be that of King William Rufus', *Archaeologia*, xlii (1869), 309 ff. For further references see Turquet, *op. cit.* (note 3), 29 ff. See also F. Barlow, *William Rufus* (London, 1983), 430–1.

[59] The silver chalice is mentioned in Joyce, *op. cit.* (note 58), 314. The carved ivory head (*op. cit.*, 312, and pl. xvii) is dated both by J. Beckwith (*Ivory Carvings in Early Medieval England* (London, 1972), no. 54) and P. Lasko (*Catalogue*, 186) to the eleventh century. In my view it is from the second quarter of the twelfth century. It is sad to record that several of the textiles found in 1868 in the tomb are now missing. Of those reproduced by Joyce, *op. cit.*, pl. xvii, 1–7, only three are still kept in the cathedral treasury. I am very grateful to Canon Paul Britton for allowing me to examine the objects surviving from the tomb.

[60] This paper was read at the Symposium *Patronage of the Arts in England 1066–1200* at the Victoria and Albert Museum on 25th February 1984. It is printed here with only minor changes.

General Index

Aachen (W. Germany), basilica at, as model for Bishop's Chapel at Hereford, 87, 88, 92, 93, 94

Aaron of Lincoln, moneylender: St Albans Abbey in debt to, 110; Philip Apostolorum debtor of, 123

Aberdeen, *see* Manuscripts

Abingdon (Oxon.), design of buildings at, 92

Abou-El-Haj, Barbara, on the Life of St Edmund, cited, 62, 67

Absalon of Lund, archbishop, nielloed ring of, 30

Adela (Aelis), Queen, bestiary dedicated to, 121

Adela, d. of William I, m. of Henry of Blois, 159, 168

Aelis, *see* Adela

Aelred, St, of Rievaulx, use of *Physiologus* in teaching of, 121, 132

Ål (Norway), acrobatic lion motif in church at, 10, 15

Alcuin, prior at St Albans, and seals, 51

Alexander, bishop of Lincoln, and Henry of Blois, 162, 168

Alexander, J. J. G., on bestiary scenes, cited, 136

Alfonso VIII, king of Castile, links with England of, 133

Alfred, King, tomb of, at Winchester, 168

Alne (N. Yorks.), bestiary cycle at Church of St Mary, 121

Alsleben (W. Germany), font from, 17, 22

Ambrose, St, texts derived from, in bestiaries, 121

Anchetil, prior of Radford, 118

Anglo-Danish style, at St Mary's Church, Campsall, 9

Anglona, Lucania (Italy), beak-heads in cathedral at, 23

Anglo-Saxon motifs: at Canterbury, 9; at Ely, 10

Anglo-Scandinavian motifs, at Ely, 10

Anketil, goldsmith at St Albans, 51

Anselm, St, Thomas Becket and translation of, 149

Antiquaries, opinions of, on Ely Infirmary, 77–86

Antiquaries, Society of: cast of 1st great seal of Richard I at, 51, 54, 58; drawings of Bishop's Chapel, Hereford, commissioned by, 88, 89; engraving of seal matrix of Lincoln Cathedral chapter at, 38, 53; seminar at, v, 2, 25; Stothard's engravings of Bayeux Tapestry of, 2, 24, 25

Aquitaine (France), art of, influenced by Italy, 22, 23; *see also* Cultural links

Aragon (Spain), paintings depicting bestiary scenes at, 133–4

Architecture: 'The Bishop's Chapel at Hereford: the Roles of Patron and Craftsman', by Richard Gem, 87–96, cited, 3; 'The "Old Conventual Church" at Ely: a False Trail in Romanesque Studies?', by Thomas Cocke, 77–86, cited, 2; *see also* Sculpture

Arlanza, Castile (Spain), frescoes depicting bestiary scenes at, 134

Arnold I, archbishop, chapel of St Gothard at Mainz built by, 88

Arts Council of Great Britain, 'English Romanesque Art' exhibition mounted by, v, 5

Arundel, Earl of, and St Albans, 110

173